BUSINESS
—— *for* ——
TRANSFORMATION

Mike & Father,

God bless you in your B4T adventure.

Patrick Z.

BUSINESS
— *for* —
TRANSFORMATION

GETTING STARTED

PATRICK LAI

WILLIAM CAREY
LIBRARY

Published by William Carey Library
1605 E. Elizabeth St.
Pasadena, CA 91104 | www.missionbooks.org

Melissa Hicks, editor
Brad Koenig, copyeditor
Hugh Pindur, graphic design
Rose Lee-Norman, indexer

William Carey Library is a ministry of
Frontier Ventures
Pasadena, CA 91104 | www.frontierventures.org

Printed in the United States of America
19 18 17 16 15   5 4 3 2 1 BP1000

Library of Congress Cataloging-in-Publication Data

Lai, Patrick.
  Business for transformation : getting started / by Patrick Lai.
    pages cm
  Includes bibliographical references and index.
    ISBN 978-0-87808-542-2 -- ISBN 0-87808-542-4 1. Part-time missionaries. 2. Missions--Finance. 3. Business--Religious aspects--Christianity. I. Title.
  BV2063.L248 2015
  266.0068--dc23
                        2015003671

CONTENTS

FOREWORD

Something is changing in the world of missions, and it is happening all over the world. This change is not being directed by one person or organization. The evidence is mounting that Heaven's Kingdom is behind the change, influencing men and women to think and act differently in the realms of business and mission.

It is clear that Jesus is reclaiming His role in the workplace, especially in parts of the world where He is not invited. As He does this, we are seeing His influence explode into the lives of individuals and in a few cases communities. We are finding the eternal goals of business (eternal profit) to be complimentary with the goals of missions. We are discovering that He wants us to integrate both our walk with Him and our business life in ways we never imagined before. This book demonstrates that kind of integrated life; doing business while constantly listening to the voice of God.

As Christian workers in countries unfriendly to Jesus were drawn into doing business, they began to discover each other and a network formed between them. No one knows this network better than Patrick. In researching his first book Patrick surveyed over four-hundred field workers who were exploring this new way of effectively expressing what God's love looks like in the working world. Patrick has experienced and heard many stories of both successes and failures. He has talked to hundreds of people as they tried again and again to reuse old paradigms to manage what God was doing, only to find new paradigms were required, but hard to find. Fifteen years later, Patrick and his wife, May, are still coaching and mentoring B4T workers in over twenty countries. During their thirty-one years overseas, Patrick has started thirteen businesses in three Muslim countries, so he's not only studied the subject he's done it. In addition, he not only knows business, he also is sold out for Jesus. His life is a model of the integration of business and missions among unreached peoples. The simple fact is that no one today knows more about what has happened, and is happening, in the collision of missions and business than Patrick.

As I began my journey twenty eight years ago, there were no books to help us understand tentmaking, BAM and B4T. Thanks to Patrick and others, that is changing. This book is for anyone considering entering a country where Jesus is not welcome and starting a business for the blessing of the people there. Whether people come through an organization or come on their own, they will be greatly helped by what Patrick shares here.

In the business world people collect what are referred to as "best practices." These are observations about how the best and most successful businesses conduct their operations. In this book, you will find dozens of "best practices." The value of learning from one another's mistakes is that you can leap frog into successful situations without paying the price of making the same mistakes. The price I have paid by not knowing "best practices" could be counted in wasted years and hundreds of thousands of dollars. This book is a great value to anyone who doesn't want to waste that kind of time and money.

It has been said that the only thing that matters in the end is what has been executed. All the best plans and theories really mean nothing, unless they are executed. In order to know what and how to execute, you need specifics. Patrick provides many specifics for a new start up, and for anyone who wants to take a fresh look at their BAM/B4T business operation. I recommend everyone interested in this change within the mission world, to read this book.

Bill Job
Meixia International

ACKNOWLEDGMENTS

This book has been in progress since I wrote the last page of *Tentmaking* in 2004. It has taken ten years to come to fruition. In that time there have been hundreds of workers from the OPEN Network who shared their stories with us, both successes and failures. There have been hundreds of thousands of miles traveled as my wife and I coach and mentor dozens who are doing business for transformation. We even sold our main B4T business, started a new business, and bought into another one during this time. Not to mention the term "B4T" (business for transformation) was birthed. God is teaching us a lot.

First, I wish to acknowledge and thank Jesus for the wonderful life He has given us. This book and all that we are and do is dedicated to Him.

Second, I wish to acknowledge the other half of "us," my wife, May. She has been alongside me in almost all of my travels; endured living out of a suitcase the last seven years, sickness, depression, weariness, missing our children; and sacrificed in many other ways, giving 100 percent toward fulfilling God's assignment for us—to *do missions better. Doing missions better* includes seeing BAM/B4T become a viable strategy for reaching the unreached. She has talked with hundreds of field workers and businesspeople and answered even more emails while working alongside me. She is the engine that keeps things moving forward. She puts wheels to my ideas. She has fretted over bills, prayed for staff, and done all of the bookkeeping for our businesses, keeping an eye on how the businesses are run, freeing me to work with people. She does 70 percent of the work and gets less than half the credit. Thank you, May.

First Chronicles 12:38 speaks of *"fighting men who volunteered and served in the ranks."* They were not seeking leadership or glory, nor were they in the army for themselves. While working with many leaders, field workers, and mission agencies, I have met many kinds of people with many kinds of gifting. Yet few have been as selfless and faithful as the team God has assembled around us. Most do not wish to be named here, but to those unnamed soldiers: thank you!

Holli did the bulk of the editing, with help from Lauren, Laurie and Melissa, who also did the majority of proofreading. Various others edited a chapter or two. Tiffany Nicole, whose husband, Curran, was the main editor of my first book, also chipped in. Thank you to each of you!

Finally, without the input of hundreds of OPEN workers, this book would never have come to pass. It is their stories and lessons learned in doing B4T with God that are the basis of this entire book. These unnamed workers are making B4T happen to the glory of Jesus. Thousands have come to Christ through them. Thousands of jobs have been created, and lives have been touched in numerous other ways in Jesus' name. You men and women are my heroes.

Each one has contributed with the desire to do BAM/B4T better. May the Master use this book to help thousands better transform lives and communities for His glory.

In Acts 18:1–3 we read,

Paul left Athens and went to Corinth. There he met a Jew named Aquila, a native of Pontus, who had recently come from Italy with his wife Priscilla, because Claudius had ordered all Jews to leave Rome. Paul went to see them, and because he was a tentmaker as they were, he stayed and worked with them.

*"The Lord God took the man and put him in the
Garden of Eden to work it and take care of it."*

—GENESIS 2:15

*"Whatever you do, work at it with all your heart,
as working for the Lord, not for human masters."*

—COLOSSIANS 3:23

*"Enter through the narrow gate. For wide is the
gate and broad is the road that leads to destruction,
and many enter through it. But small is the gate
and narrow the road that leads to life, and only a
few find it."*

—MATTHEW 7:13-14

*"I have been crucified with Christ and I no longer
live, but Christ lives in me. The life I now live in the
body, I live by faith in the Son of God, who loved
me and gave himself for me."*

—GALATIANS 2:20

*"For what we preach is not ourselves, but Jesus
Christ as Lord, and ourselves as your servants for
Jesus' sake."*

—2 CORINTHIANS 4:5

"Starting into B4T is learning to walk by faith, not by memory."

—PATRICK LAI

Chapter 1

WELCOME TO THE WORLD
OF B4T!

Welcome to the *B4T world*. The business for transformation world cannot be seen, but it can be felt; it cannot be touched, but it can make you sweat or give you chills. It originates from God's Spirit, so it is overpoweringly strong, yet it leaves your knees feeling weak. It draws scores of people to yourself, yet you feel alone. It is a place full of exploding energy, overflowing with wonderful (some say crazy) ideas. When starting out, you feel an overwhelming frustration intermixed with wild excitement. The B4T world is not a place to fear or flee from. Your feelings are normal. That's right, *normal*. No need to call a shrink. The Master Builder has called you into this world, and He will sustain and guide you.

There are schools where you can study the B4T world, but you cannot master it. Once you enter the B4T world, instead of encouragement, friends are likely to tell you, "That will never work," and ask, "How are you going to make money from that?" Your spouse will probably become a critic too, fearing he or she is going to lose all you own, or that you have gone totally insane. It is the "No one believes in what I am doing except for me" zone. Nonetheless, listen to God's voice. Do not succumb to the naysayers. Stand firm; stay the course. Leave the old wineskins for the old wine. Step forward and keep moving. Today is the day you identify who you are. The answer to many of your questions, and the steps you need to take, may be found in this book. As you chart a course that will lead you into your B4T life and work, utilize this book as a tool to enhance your ability to glorify Jesus in a place where few have done so before. You will find the answers if you take the time and keep your courage centered on Him.

Jesus said, "*Truly, I tell you, unless you change and become like little children, you will never enter the kingdom of heaven.*"[1] I don't know who said, "*Dream like a child, decide as an adult,*" but it fits the B4T

---

[1] Matthew 18:3

world. The B4Ter needs to be free to dream like a child. As you set out into the world of B4T, look at the world through a child's eyes and see the possibilities. Just as a child does shamelessly and frequently, do not hesitate to ask for help. Never delay, never fear for even one second to humbly admit, *"I don't know how to do this."* Like a child, *do* ask for help. Then decide as an adult. Take the data, ideas, and information you are given in this book, and with Jesus' Spirit, prayerfully use your intuition, experience, and knowledge to decide on the next action steps. Tapping into the possibilities and taking action energizes you to move forward and accomplish your goals.

What is the first thing you can do today to make your B4T business become a reality? What is the next step after that? This is important for maintaining the balance between your dream and your reality, especially when the rest of the world isn't wholly supportive. Pray. Keep close to the Master Builder. Never let the dreamer inside you become too quiet, and always remember when to let the adult take over. The adult seeks advice and wisdom on how to get from here to there.

You will find like-minded peers and elders in the OPEN Network. Connect with them via their website: *www.OPENNetworkers.net*. If you are overseas already, you can find coaches and mentors there. They can provide you with interns and apprentices, too. If you are preparing to go overseas or are a church leader involved in sending new workers, then contact *www.NEXUSB4T.com*. NexusB4T will connect you with people who can assist you with the ideas you read about in this book. And if you are looking to do an internship or apprentice somewhere, they can also help with that.

Utilize the tools in this book. B4T softens the soil for His seed. It will also soften your own heart. But it will require work. Be diligent to continually strive to expand your knowledge by cross-referencing answers with the resources around you. Pray. Interact with other B4Ters in your field; learn from them and then avoid their mistakes. Keep the possibilities alive and your B4T life and work moving forward. Pray.

The Master has enabled my wife and me to live and work in the B4T world for over twenty years. During this time, we have started fourteen businesses—six of which have failed, and four just limped along for years till being closed. By grace, we have learned much through our failures, and hopefully you can learn from them too. This book is an accumulation of experiences and stories, successes and failures, of the nearly seven hundred members of the OPEN Network, plus our own. This book is written especially to the young men and women who are striving to start businesses where there are few to no churches, so that the glory of Jesus may be proclaimed among all people.

Living in the B4T world is not your choice—the Master sent you here. (If He has not sent you here, then put this book down immediately and run!) You already realize doing B4T is not about what you can get, but rather what you can give. You are beginning to live your life from true intent—that burning feeling He has placed in your heart. B4T is very hard work, but there is nothing more powerful and nothing more exciting than doing business and reaching people with the Master. There will be challenges. There will be moments of exhaustion. There will be times of feeling completely overwhelmed with everything presently going on and everything that has yet to be achieved. Whenever that moment arrives, you will know because your stomach does a sideways flip and your brain tank goes to empty. But never fear, we have been there too. *It is okay.* At such times, give a like-minded brother or sister a call. Pray. And remember, "*Blessed is the one who perseveres under trial, having stood the test, that person will receive the crown of life that the Lord has promised to those who love Him.*"[2]

Not only that, but "*we also glory in our sufferings, because we know that suffering produces perseverance; perseverance, character; and character, hope. And hope does not put us to shame, because God's love has been poured out into our hearts through the Holy Spirit who has been given to us.*"[3]

Remember God has not called you into B4T for the sake of the lost, but for His sake. He is much more concerned about the worker than He is with the work. The assignment of doing B4T is a heart-changing assignment—it changes our own hearts, as well as others.

Becoming a B4Ter is a journey of a thousand little steps. You will need desire, dreams, recognition of opportunities, seriousness about the opportunity, responsibility, an expectation of loneliness and fear and second guessing, serious study of the situation, a business plan, adequate capital, advice from experienced people, the drive to follow through, a positive attitude, and a will to empower others. Laying out these steps is easy and is what you will learn as you continue to read this book; following through—that is the hard part.

Persevere. Stay present and focused on the one step you can take right here, right now. A business is a natural crossroads where God's and Satan's worlds collide. The temptations, turmoil, troubles, and time invested

---

[2] James 1:12
[3] Romans 5:3—5

3

will test even the strongest person. God will use your B4T experience to teach you more about yourself than you ever imagined was inside you. The question is: are you ready to see yourself for who you are? Caleb, in India, told me, *"I thought I was a mature Christian. I had been a pastor and discipled men, but running a business here has forced me to face issues about myself I am not sure I want to face, yet I know God brought me here to face them."* B4T is not just God's tool for reaching the unreached; it is also His tool for reaching, renewing, and revealing a reality about yourself. Transformation does not begin with transforming the lives of the unreached—it begins with transforming ourselves.

Jesus and Jobs—Priority #1

Sali is a Muslim man who lives in Dakar, Senegal. I was in Dakar for a week doing some consulting work with a nongovernmental organization (NGO). The NGO director put me up in a guest house in the European/ Western part of the city. While looking for a taxi, Sali was the only driver in a long queue of taxis parked near the guest house who spoke English. Everyone else spoke French or Wolof, the native language. Consequently, I rode with Sali every day, and as we drove we became better acquainted with one another.

I learned that Sali grew up in a poor village in the eastern part of the country and came to Dakar to find a better life. After putting himself through the university, he met his wife and they had two daughters. While his wife worked, he earned a master's degree in business arts (MBA). Surprised, I asked Sali why he was driving a taxi if he had an MBA. He replied, *"Sir, there are no jobs and I have two little girls. They both like to eat, so to keep them fed, I drive a taxi."*

The very next day, I was with the director of the NGO and we summoned Sali to take us to a restaurant. During a lull in the conversation, I said to Sali, *"My friend here has a charity organization, an NGO that works in your country with your people. They provide clean water and medicine. They set up clinics and schools. They provide food for refugees out east, where you come from. As a businessperson, I want to invest in one of these projects. Sali, you know what your people need. Which project would you say is the greatest need of your people? You choose and I'll give to that project."*

Sali paused, made eye contact with me in the rearview mirror, and then said, *"Don't waste your money on any of them."*

Surprised I queried, *"Well Sali, then what do you think I should invest in? Building homes?"*

"No."

"Well, what do you think the NGO should be doing? Should they go home?"

"No," Sali answered, "They should be creating jobs."

"Why jobs?"

Sali replied, "You asked me what we need. What we need are jobs. If the NGO creates jobs for us, then we can decide if we need water or medicine or education. If they create jobs, then we can be in control of what we need, rather than having you imperialist Americans telling us what we need."

Stop and contemplate Sali's words. Who is going to be more receptive to the gospel? I have had similar conversations with perhaps a dozen nationals in a dozen different countries. What is the greatest physical need of people? Spiritually they need Jesus, but physically what is their deepest need? Food, water, education—or respect? I would argue that respect is a greater need. When you give a person respect, she in turn respects you. A job is the most fundamental nonspiritual need of a human being. With a job comes food, water, medicine, and education. With a job comes an identity, value, and an acceptance in the community.

If we come to a city and tell the people what their needs are, then provide the goods to meet the needs of those people, does that give respect? Nobody likes to be a charity case. What if we instead went in to serve the people by creating opportunities for them, so they can provide for their families and determine for themselves what their needs are?

We have seen time after time in many different countries that Muslims are persecuted when they come to faith, but if the new believer is the primary breadwinner for that family or a community of families, they are not persecuted. Like a steady income, adding a tangible value to a family trumps religious zeal four out of five times. In addition, there is a very different attitude towards someone who is feeding their own family versus an outsider who is doing the same.

I have come to the conclusion that after receiving Christ, the greatest need of a human being is a job. Yes, there are starving people who do not have food and water and therefore lack the strength to work, but that number is steadily shrinking. If you have ever been unemployed, you understand the value of having a job. A job provides more than money: it provides dignity and gives a person a role and value in their family and the community. A job provides an identity, giving people a way to explain to friends and others what they contribute to the world. A job provides self-esteem and honor, especially from others who work jobs that are deemed to be of lower status.

Jesus' Model

Think about how Jesus worked and operated while on earth. When He was approached by John the Baptist's disciples in Matthew 11:3–4, they asked Him, *"Are You the one?"* He didn't say, *"I was born of a virgin. That's kind of special isn't it?"* Nor did He say, *"Look at the great messages I preach in the synagogues and out in the hills to the people—don't my words prove who I am?"* He said nothing of the sort. Rather, He said to them, *"Tell John what you have seen Me do."*

Jesus downplays words and puts the emphasis on doing. Why? Because if a person does not understand something, then the quickest way to bring about understanding is not to explain with words, but to show by doing with actions. Jesus understood a person's basic need. He realized that *seeing is believing.*

Often we try to tell Muslims what to believe, but they have never seen it. They have no reference point for our words. *"God loves us." "God forgives us." "God extends grace to us."* These are all foreign concepts. They translate our words about Jesus from their frame of reference, and it does not make sense.

Business creates reference points for verbal proclamation. People are amazed when they see how we deal with corrupt government officials. They are shocked when they see the ways we deal with employees who cheat us or customers who lie to us. They are stunned when they receive bonuses and experience the ways we reward good work. They have no precedent to comprehend how we pray in staff meetings or how we invite Jesus in as our CEO. They are watching. They see our faith first. They experience love, forgiveness, and grace. Experiencing God in these ways creates points of reference for later opportunities to verbally explain who Jesus is, which nearly always comes if we are patient. We tell B4T workers, *"Don't talk. Don't tell. Show them the good news first."* Ultimately, non-believers see so much that they are overwhelmed, and as a result they finally ask, *"Why? Tell me, why? I want to know more."*

When is it easier to sell an item to someone? When they come into your shop looking to buy a product, or when you go street-to-street, door-to-door-to-door trying to sell your goods? Obviously it's easier to sell goods to those who come looking for it. This is what we are learning and seeing as we do business with Muslims, Hindus, and Buddhists. People see the product (a relationship with Jesus), and then they want it. It takes some time. It doesn't happen the first year. It doesn't happen the third year. It sometimes does not even happen the fifth year. However, it *will* happen. They are watching, and if one works his job full of the Holy Spirit, sooner or later the people will come and ask why.

Out of the B4Ters who have seen more than three churches planted between 2011 and 2014, every single one of them has been doing business for at least seven years. One worker had been working almost fifteen years and had seen only two people baptized. Finally, this year he planted eleven communities of believers with at least six new believers in each community. People need more than words, they need to *see* the Gospel lived out before them. They need to experience it really works in real life. People are watching, and they want to see how your life matches your faith.

All Business Is Not the Same

My professor at the University of Oregon taught three basic business rules:
1. Better before cheaper: Compete on your strengths, not just on price.
2. Revenue before cost: Prioritize increasing revenue over reducing costs.
3. There are no other rules: To change anything you must follow Rules 1 and 2.

A lot of information exists on how to start a business, win at business, work fewer hours, make more money, and on and on. All of these books, articles, and blogs have some value, but doing business is not the same everywhere. Yes, business basics are the same everywhere, but once someone has become bicultural—meaning the businessperson literally has become two people thinking and acting differently depending upon where he is—he understands that nothing is the same from culture to culture. On the surface things may look the same, but if he has learned another language well and adopted a way of life different from the one he was raised with, he knows that looks can be deceiving. A local Muslim and an American Christian may both observe the same situation, but what a local perceives of that situation and what the Westerner perceives often is totally different.

While 80 percent of business done in the West and the East is the same, the unfamiliar 20 percent will bankrupt the B4T worker—both financially and spiritually. Yet we should not let this fear of the unknown slow us down. Many of us are afraid to pursue the dreams God has given us because we do not know how to begin, how to set new goals, or how to do the kinds of thinking and planning that assure the best chance of success. B4T is new and unfamiliar territory.

About This Book

When starting any business, many questions exist that every person needs to ask, research, validate, and answer. This book will ask the most pertinent questions in relation to doing B4T and provide examples of how other B4T workers have answered them. It is a tool to help you get started on the B4T path with God. However, each individual will need to prayerfully research the answer for his or her particular situation, validate the research before God and man, and then select the answer or the direction to proceed.

This book is built on my first book, *Tentmaking: The Life and Work of Business as Missions.* If you have not discovered that book yet, I would suggest you do so soon. This book stresses the business issues involved in starting a B4T business, while *Tentmaking* stresses the non-business issues in doing B4T. If you are starting out on the B4T adventure, both books should be read.

In this book, there are many practical stories and quotes given by real people who are presently serving in the uttermost parts of the earth. When possible I took notes, but some workers did not want me to write anything down. Consequently, my memory of events may differ occasionally from that of others. The best I can do is to write the events as I recall them. For obvious reasons, most of the names have been changed, along with many of the locations. Where last names are given, they are real names, used with the person's permission. Names of real locations are sometimes used simply for the sake of interest. Bottom line: this book attempts to be practical in laying out the issues involved in starting a B4T business.

"Tentmaking" is the historical and biblical term that refers to integrating business with evangelism, discipleship, and church planting. It originates from Paul's work with Aquila. So the term "tent" can be substituted with the modern-day word "business" as related to doing B4T or BAM. I have used the term "tent" in the chapter titles of this book in reference to Paul and his team to both remember and honor our roots and as a play on words as we get started in building our B4T business.

Before reading further, you may wish to read appendix B, "Terminology." This will help you to better understand the terms used in this book.

May this book be a tool by which the Holy Spirit guides you, for Him to use you to *open the eyes of the blind,* including friends like Sali.

DISCUSSION QUESTIONS

1.   What excites you about doing B4T?
2.   Describe how God is leading you toward doing B4T?
3.   Would you agree that having a job is a person's greatest nonspiritual need?

"In business you are constantly meeting people, because business is about people."

—CRAIG

Chapter 2

UNDERSTANDING BUSINESS FOR TRANSFORMATION

Two coaches came to visit me two weeks apart. One was a businessman from my home church, the other a senior leader in my mission agency. The businessman said to me, "I am so glad to see your business prospering, I was afraid when we last talked that all you were doing was ministry and the business was a cover." The mission leader said, "I am so glad to see your ministry taking off, I was afraid when we last talked that all you were doing was business and ministry was a sideline."

- A worker in Central Asia

The fact that business is central to any city and most communities is enough to demand that Christians be involved in the marketplace. The fact that business provides benefits to Christian workers in terms of visas, community acceptance, personal relationships, identity, and income is enough to warrant its use as a mission strategy. The challenge is to be aware of the differences between the two systems and to practice the same ethics in integrating both systems. It is a process of putting business into mission and then putting mission into the business. Jon, a worker in Central Asia who shared the above story, has integrated his life, work, and outreach to the point that his life is seamless to everyone around him, even his own coaches. *This is a solid example of Business for Transformation (B4T).*

Business for transformation—whether building a business, school, or coffee shop, while doing ministry—is nothing less than running a marathon. It is not a sprint. I often hear of workers who raised thousands of dollars but failed because the business wasn't built to last. Building a company that makes a difference in reaching the lost takes time and depth of mission. This book touches on a number of factors that, if not built into your business plan, will result in failure. There is a great opportunity to reach people via the workplace, if you focus on the fundamentals. This book is designed to lay out those fundamentals.

God develops each of us over our lifetime. He is not slow in keeping His promises. He knows where we are to be headed and how to keep us pointed there. This book is a tool for Him to guide you, encourage you, and give you fresh ideas about doing business for transformation. God's development plan for us is a function of the events, people, and good and bad experiences He has taken us through. Yet how we process His working in our lives will often determine our effectiveness for Him. Usually we need a road map to point out the way God wants to take us. Each person's journey with God is unique, but a map serves to direct and clarify what God is doing both in and through us. A map helps us understand the training and experiences He has brought us through and opens our eyes to what we might expect up ahead. This book should help to integrate your experiences and ideas in order to be more effective in reaching the unreached. B4T begins with God and His working in and through us.

B4T is not a financial strategy. Rather, it is a strategy of the people of God using their gifts *from* God for the glory *of* God among the unreached. Paul clarifies in Colossians 3:23, "*Whatever you do, work at it with all your heart, as working for the Lord, not for human masters.*" B4Ters strive to live an integrated, seamless life; everything we do is ministry. We believe all the good that we do in our lives and work is meant to be a reflection of God's character being revealed through us. Our drive to be productive and to work is intimately tied to His created purpose for us to imitate and glorify God.

B4T is not intended to compromise or water down the primacy and priority of our apostolic calling to establish a community of believers in Jesus. The "eternal" is at the forefront of life and work. Whatever we do, we work at it with all our heart, as working for the Master and not men. B4Ters are not seeking greater security or wishing to avoid persecution. By being in business, we ensure that any offense to our listeners is rooted in the gospel alone and not in labels such as "missionary" or "Christian" or affiliation with organizations that "target" the unreached. B4Ters communicate their faith with a diaphanous identity, speaking words that are *"seasoned with grace and salt."* The cross Jesus has assigned us to carry includes loving others and laying down our life so that those beyond the hearing of the good news may have an opportunity to know the Way, the Truth, and the Life. B4Ters seek to freely share their faith and identity with a clear conscience. They proactively and preemptively struggle to meet twenty-first-century needs with twenty-first-century tools, while ensuring our apostolic calling is rooted in God's word and is linked with like-minded workers. B4Ters understand that life, work, and ministry are interconnected—a holistic, integrated whole.

Christian workers are too often concerned with the appearance they think they have in the community, rather than the actual way the locals perceive them. The emphasis is on the mission workers' thinking and perspective on themselves. Instead, mission workers should invest time seeking to understand how the locals truly perceive them. The difference is in our focus: is it on the locals or on ourselves? For example, during the years I had a platform (false or cover business), I felt my identity was secure. Because of my platform, I felt I knew who I was in the eyes of the community. However, not until many years later was it revealed to me that who I thought I was and who my neighbors thought I was were two different things. My neighbors saw me at home every day; they knew I was not really working. In their eyes, I must have had some other reason for living in their backward community. My assumed identity (how I perceived myself) and my given identity (how the locals perceived me) were quite different. They did not base their thinking on what I said but what they saw me doing. Only after establishing my business with fourteen employees was it revealed that they thought I had worked for the CIA!

Change comes slowly to missions. Gallup points out that the church tends to be late adapters to cultural change. I would include mission organizations too. Paul Hillhouse, who served in India for many years, told me:

> This is a broad statement, but the church and missions may have missed their day in India. No one foresaw in 1990 that the economy would open up and create all the small businesses it has. This was a huge opportunity that we missed. If the church had recognized the role business would play in developing an emerging middle class and building a consumer orientated economy, if the church had developed a way to reach these people and use business as a tool for the kingdom, the church could have released the values that impact lives for the kingdom. The church missed a huge opportunity for credibility amongst the upper classes, and so the gospel still sits in lower class castes. We should have set up B4T back then; we could have changed communities. Instead, we took them out of their networks and supported them and created a system that is not sustainable.

Church planting movements (CPMs)—the rapid reproduction of churches—needs a spark. Business can provide that spark. Every society needs to sustain itself. Every person needs a job. Many societies have been handicapped because the rich keep the poor impoverished. However, business enables people to create their own wealth and alleviate poverty; business motivates people in a way government initiatives never have. It empowers people in a way NGOs rarely can. When we create jobs, we not only help people to feed themselves, but we also give them an identity that enhances their self-esteem. Business can be the spark to change the world.

Another B4T worker writes:

> Having a business in which the culture receives its first witness to the Gospel provides some interesting holistic models. For example, our business demonstrates the Christian ethic of hard work and of doing one's fair share in the community. It has also provided a new basis in personal integrity and honesty in an ever-watching community. Done correctly, the ethical model of an expatriate-managed business can be a surprising avenue to witness. Common practices associated with bribery are given a second look, and moral statements can be lived out as we react to complex cultural situations.

B4T businesses create jobs, and thus provide salaries for families. Many of these jobs provide specialized training and, therefore, enhanced job potential. The business may provide an additional market for local firms, a valuable service to the community, or valuable export earnings. B4T workers model their faith, as well as engage in discussions about God and ethics. If the B4T business is run as a "social enterprise," then it may provide additional benefits to local communities. For example, OPEN Network businesses fund orphanages, provide scholarships for children whose parents cannot afford to send them to school, offer health-care services, provide alternative employment for oppressed women, and much more. Another practice of some B4T enterprises is to designate a share of the profits to the employees in a profit-sharing plan. The idea is that in time employees will own a significant proportion of the company. Employees may then decide to expand the business or start related businesses elsewhere. Each illustration underscores the concept of Christian holism in a commercial framework. The objective is to address and meet the core needs of the community.

Creative B4T models are springing up all over the Muslim, Hindu, and Buddhist world. There are few closed doors to doing business. The opportunities are as wide as a man's ingenuity, as deep as his character, and as high as his faith in God.

"I tried to be contextualized. I tried a very contextualized C-5 approach. I tried to be a holy man—even calling myself a Muslim follower of Jesus— but realized over the years that true insiders work a job!"—A B4T worker in Indonesia

First Things First

Business for transformation enables us to share the gospel in tangible, practical ways. In one sense, we are the hands and feet of Jesus living and working in the marketplace.

Some people may believe that they don't have the talent, the skill, or the courage to create and implement the innovations that are needed to succeed at B4T. Though possibly true, it is probably not. Consider Caleb, a Bible college graduate and a pastor from rural Canada with no business background at all. Today he has one of the top B4T businesses in the world. Or Jon, another excellent B4Ter, who has a blue-collar education with no formal schooling beyond high school. However, by God's grace and Jon's personal efforts, his business is transforming a whole country. Or Chris, who has an MBA. His business is doing well, and he has also planted numerous churches.

On the other hand, we know of people with MBAs who have failed in their business and seminary graduates who have not introduced one person to Jesus. B4T is not about our abilities or even us; it is about God and giving our abilities to Him to make what He wants, both in us and through us.

So what is the key to success? God's grace alone? Clearly there isn't only one answer. Yet we can tell you there is no such thing as a "B4T business in a box." In the OPEN Network we have seen English language schools succeed in places where there was no apparent market, while other schools, located in cities of millions of people, failed. Restaurants and coffee shops that the critics said would never make it are thriving today and introducing Muslims to Jesus. Meanwhile, others using similar business plans have shut their doors. Some B4T businesses have no business plan at all, while others have Harvard Business School–quality business plans; some of each succeed while others fail. Some start with literally US$1 million in funding and others with pennies, and still we find successes and failures in both categories. So I am sorry to inform you, there is no magic formula.

Transformation Begins with Us

It is essential to acknowledge that God does not use strategies to reach the unreached, He uses *people*. One morning I had breakfast with David, who is like a son to me. He initially came to Asia to run one of my businesses and has since bought out the business with his local partner. He has tripled the sales and is a solid B4Ter. David and I meet every week. The discussion that day touched on rapidly multiplying churches and the ways God reaches the unreached. We compared the prophets and contemporary movements to Christ. We also reminded ourselves that God does not use strategies, He uses people. We concluded that God works in ways that only God understands, and He rarely works in the same way twice. Our duty is to trust and obey.

Therefore, though B4T is a *strategy* that can impact communities for Jesus, it all starts with God in us—*you and me*. God leads us overseas and into business not only for the sake of those who are perishing, but also for our sake. He is as much at work in us as He is in those around us. Transformation begins with God working in and through us to impact others for His glory. He will not work *through* us unless He is already working *in* us.

B4T workers recognize that business is the context in which most of our relational interaction takes place. Therefore, the work we do is part of our witness. Nonbelievers are observing the quality, integrity, and timeliness of our work. The workplace provides the setting to be a witness for Christ overtly through holistic lifestyle evangelism and verbal proclamation. Moreover, by stepping out of our traditional comfort zones and secular/spiritual separation, we allow God to transform us.

This transformation must continue until our last breath. In 2 Chronicles 14–16, we read the story of Asa. In the beginning we find that, *"Asa did what was good and right in the eyes of the Lord his God."* At the end we read, *"Asa was angry . . . oppressed some of the people . . . Though his disease was severe, even in his illness he did not seek help from the Lord, but only from the physicians."* The first fifteen years of his reign, Asa sought God before any major decision or battle; he won every war and was recognized as a good leader. Subsequently, God gave him twenty years of peace. In the ensuing wars and other problems, Asa sought out various men, including physicians, for help but he did not seek God.

It is tempting to trust *our* strategies and *our* tools, but we must resist this and keep our hearts and minds focused on Jesus.

Spiritual character and a relationship with Jesus are foundations that are deeper and more critical than any of the building blocks this book will address. Strategies are good. They are helpful in getting us moving in doing the things God has guided us to do. However, strategies—B4T included—are not the most critical thing. We must understand that if the carpenter is not qualified, equipped, and skilled with the core skills for the task, he will fail to do the job. Therefore, transformation begins first with us. If we have not been regenerated and renewed in His Spirit, then the tools this book offers will be of little use.

Excellence, surrender, and *transparency* are three points that will be repeated throughout this book.

Excellence is defined first by the person, then the product. The Scripture teaches us, "*And whatever you do, whether in word or deed, do it all in the name of the Lord Jesus, giving thanks to God the Father through Him.*"[4] It is a rare person who can create a product or service that glorifies God without centering their life and work on Jesus.

Surrender: if starting a business is attractive because of the money it will earn, the desire to use your education, or the hope for success and significance, then you need to surrender. If we value fame, titles, and material possessions, much of our lives will be spent fighting to achieve, protect, and keep them. A surrendered life is a denied life. It involves someone who has taken up his cross and is following Jesus. I, the individual, am dead; my rights to have financial security, success, or significance are gone. I may still have them in Him, but my rights to have them are gone.

Transparency means living and working in such a way that it is easy for others to see both the actions performed and the source from which they are performed. B4Ters should be capable of transmitting Light so that objects or images can be seen as if there were no intervening material.

God does not allow us to continue to reduce Him to a size and shape we can manage or control. He moves in our lives in ways that keep us uncomfortable, so as to destroy our assumptions and overwhelm our finiteness. Once we realize God is truly bigger than anything we can get our minds around, we can begin to relax and enjoy Him. Too often our careers, degrees, and desires determine where and how we will serve God. Many times I am asked, "Can God use an engineer or doctor (or whatever

---

4   Colossians 3:17

degree one has) overseas?" I wonder, when we ask such questions, does it reflect a faith in God, or a trusting in our own career and achievements? My reply to these questions is always, "God does not use degrees overseas, He uses obedient servants who are totally committed to His love and will, no matter what their degrees or backgrounds." Too often, like Asa, we think as long as God's plan for us is in agreement with our own desires, then of course we will obey Him. But how we respond when our personal goals and desires collide with His will—that is where we discover who the real Lord of our lives is.

Transformation begins with us. The workplace is not only a place for outreach, it is an instrument for our spiritual growth. Knowing and applying this is critical, as it allows one to discern how her life and work integrate together. In the workplace there will be failure and sin. These situations are often the best opportunities for modeling the gospel.

A B4T worker in the Middle East told me:

> My job involves pumping near-boiling water out of the ground, and once in a while the hoses carrying this water burst, and whoever is standing nearby gets doused with this very hot water. Almost every time that happens, the guy shouts and curses while trying to shake off the water. One day I was working near a hose when it burst. All eyes looked at me when I shouted, "Hallelujah!" That day, and for several days following, a number of my coworkers came to me when we were alone together and asked, "How could you do that?" This opened the door to share the Lord.

It is essential first and foremost to have a strong spiritual character to be able to discern the voice of the Holy Spirit and a desire to obey Him in all cases. God rarely works exactly the same way twice.

Another B4T worker said:

> My witness, my identity as a Christian, needs to be wrapped up in actions—radical actions. I need to overflow with love; I need to do things that are marked by a disarming humility, an uncanny excellence, and above all, an inexplicable love. I need to do things that cause people to question what they think they know, what they assume about Christians and human nature, the whole of this world and the nature of the spiritual one existing alongside it. I need to live in the power of the Holy Spirit so that

men look and say, "Wow, those deeds—that life—is only possible
by some higher power."

Though making money is essential for our business or jobs, sharing
our faith by word and action is equally important. B4Ters embrace Roland
Allen's point that

> It is of comparatively small importance how the missionary
> is maintained; it is of comparatively small importance how
> the finances of the Church are organized. What is of supreme
> importance is how these arrangements, whatever they may be,
> affect the minds of the people, and so promote or hinder the
> spread of the Gospel.[5]

We need to ask ourselves daily if we are seeking success, significance,
or Jesus.

When a person is born again, the new nature often is fighting the old
nature. It is not unusual to feel this inconsistency in our life and work as
well as our emotions and spirit. Clearly the Apostle Paul had a strong and
steady underlying consistency in his life.[6] Consequently, Paul could let his
external life change without internal distress because he was rooted and
grounded in God. If we are inconsistent spiritually, often it is because we
are more concerned about being consistent externally. Concerning the
external expression of things, Paul lived in the basement while his critics
lived upstairs. Understand that these two levels do not begin to touch each
other. Paul's consistency was found deep down in the fundamentals. The
great basis of his consistency was the agony of God in the redemption of
the world; namely, the cross of Christ.

If we understand that the ultimate bottom line of transformational
business is the greater glory of God, then we have to recognize that our
"market" is more than a product or service. It is the people and culture
we engage as coworkers, friends, neighbors—and it begins with His Holy
Spirit in us.

---

[5] Roland Allen, *Missionary Methods: St. Paul's or Ours?* (Grand Rapids, MI: World Dominion
Press, 1962), 49.

[6] See Romans 7:15,19

Transformation via the Workplace

God created us to work, so from a spiritual point of view work is what makes us what we are. Unless we work, our identity is merely theoretical; work enables us to externalize who we are. Identity is truly tied up with our expression of work. Our roles in our home, church, clubs, and so forth are each an expression of our personal character—a character given by God—and each role is part of what God designed us to be and do.

Work is thus an integral part of God's plan for maturing us and putting us in a position where we can serve others in order to bless His name. Work creates incredible opportunities to learn, witness, and grow. When our Muslim friends participate in God's maturing of us, they in turn are impacted. One day I asked my office manager Sue to do something. She paused, and then left my office without a word. About an hour later one of our department heads came in and asked, *"Did you tell Sue to do this?"* When I nodded yes, he said, *"Did you know this is illegal here?"* *"What!"* I exclaimed as I called Sue into my office. The ensuing conversation helped me to see that I had made a huge mistake and, in the process, offended Sue. When I stopped and asked her to forgive me, she was totally embarrassed—bosses in Asia do not ordinarily admit to making mistakes, let alone ask for forgiveness of employees. Less than a week later she came to me and asked if I could get her a Bible. Today, she and her family have all put their trust in Jesus.

Identity is not based upon what you say about yourself, but what you do. When I tell people I am a consultant, but they never see me consulting or going to an office, they know the truth. The root word of integrity is "integrate." When your relationship with Jesus is integrated into everything you do, that reflects maturity. An integrated life leads B4Ters to strive for transparency. Our life and work must be understandable to the people around us, beyond question. Matt, a good friend of mine, puts it this way: *"Any mission worker who has to do missions with a 'cover' is antiquated and out of date."* When we hide the truth about ourselves, we limit what we share with people. Mark Twain clarified the issue from a worldly perspective when he said, *"Always tell the truth, that way you don't have to remember what you said."*

Business for Transformation

Business for transformation workers strive to respect, value, encourage, disciple, nurture, and empower their employees and their families, as well as their suppliers, customers, and all others they interact with. Through training their people in the appropriate skills, B4Ters unleash the full potential of their coworkers. This usually happens when the business acts in a holistic manner and looks after not only training, but all aspects of the employees' environment: social, economic (including family issues), and spiritual. This is holistic ministry.

B4Ters do all this, not for the sake of being considered good employers or coworkers, but for the glory of God. Jesus' glory is the cornerstone for all our thinking and actions. B4Ters model kingdom values in the way they work or run a business and the way they relate to others in the community. When a Christian goes the second mile by giving people more than they expect, providing a quality product or service and having happy and fulfilled employees, all while making money, customers, suppliers, and others think, *"What can I do to become like her?"* The B4Ter's answer is that Jesus Christ is the Head of the business, since she works first and foremost for Him. The most effective witness any of us can have is living believably and doing our jobs with excellence. In a world full of deceit and corruption, this in itself is a powerful witness.

Often corruption in business is normative. B4Ters model a better way, and they can put pressure on society to adopt that better way. They show genuine concern for hunger, injustice, and suffering in the community. Plus, their business income enables them to take real action toward improving problems within the community. As both employees and business leaders, OPEN Networkers encourage other businesspeople to follow their example in fighting injustice and corruption, while helping the poor in contextually appropriate ways. In other words, business for transformation seeks to change the whole spiritual climate in the marketplace and the community.

Understanding B4T

David Befus, formerly of Latin America Mission and now leading a microfinance initiative in Colombia, says,

> If we simply make people healthier or more prosperous without telling them the ultimate source of human satisfaction, all we have

done is make them more comfortable for their journey to hell. The holistic approach can easily become the "halfistic" approach when the present physical suffering is more important than the potential eternal suffering that the people may experience. Henry Ford once said, "A business that only makes money is a poor kind of business."

Just as a "shell business" that does not possess a profit motive would not be doing B4T; a business that does not deliver on both the economic and spiritual bottom lines is not doing business for transformation either.

In the book *In His Steps*, Charles Sheldon asks his congregation to do nothing without first asking the question, *"What would Jesus do?"* Sheldon outlines six principles that Jesus would implement if He ran a business:

1. He would engage in the business first of all for the purpose of making money.
2. All money he made he would never regard as his own, but as trust funds to be used for the good of humanity.
3. His relations with all the persons in his employ would be the most loving and helpful. He could not help thinking of all of them in the light of souls to be saved. This thought would always be greater than his thought of making money in the business.
4. He would never do a single dishonest or questionable thing or try in any way to take advantage of anyone else in the same business.
5. The principle of unselfishness and helpfulness in the business would direct all its details.
6. Upon this principle, he would shape the entire plan of his relations to his employees, the people who were his customers, and the general business world with which he was connected.[7]

As we evaluate the goals and ultimately the effectiveness of B4T, these principles are a good starting place. Mats Tunehag, a prolific Business as Mission (BAM) advocate, talks of four bottom lines: prayer (spiritual), profit (economic), people (social), and planet (environmental). Jesus has clearly called us to be stewards of His creation, so working all four

---

[7] Charles Sheldon, *In His Steps* (Grand Rapids: MI. Zondervan, 1967).

bottom lines into our business plan brings out the best in a business and the kingdom.

Spiritually: Jesus clarifies, *"What good is it for someone to gain the whole world, yet forfeit their soul?"*[8] The purpose of missions is to bring people into relationship with Jesus. Sheldon reminds us, *"Jesus' relations with all the persons in his employ would be the most loving and helpful. He could not help thinking of all of them in the light of souls to be saved. This thought would always be greater than his thought of making money in the business."*[9] Though we sincerely wish to impact all four bottom lines, B4Ters begin with the spiritual. If no spiritual agenda exists, there is no need to be working cross-culturally. Our witness must be a mix of word and deed. Business is the "deed" and provides the opportunity to model the gospel. Then as our modeling creates opportunities, we need to be forthright in proclaiming the gospel with our words as well.

Economically: Sheldon's first principle that *"Jesus would engage in the business first of all for the purpose of making money"* is right in line with B4T. A business, by definition, is *"the act of commerce, buying, and selling."* A business must be profitable or it will cease to be a business. If we, acting as Jesus' hands and feet, are going to tell others that we are in business, then that business must be profitable. A not-for-profit business is a charity or an NGO (nongovernmental organization). We greatly appreciate charities and NGOs, but they are not businesses.

In B4T, the spiritual and economic bottom lines are nonnegotiable. Although it is common for a business to lose money in the start-up phase, if a business continues to lose money after two to three years, it is not wise to use a church's or anyone else's money to sustain it. As an illustration, if a B4T business is losing money but impacting the local community—seeing Muslims come to Jesus and churches planted—would you keep the business open and subsidize it with church money? A businessman would probably say, *"No, the business is not working,"* while a mission worker might say, *"Yes, it's reaching people."* On the other hand, if a B4T business is making money but having no impact on the local community God has told the team to reach—creating no jobs for nationals, no local services, *nothing*—would you keep that business open? The businessperson will likely say, *"Yes, it's making money,"* while the mission worker would most likely say, *"No, it's a distraction from the main thing."* In B4T, we would recommend closing both of these businesses. A B4T business

---

8 Mark 8:36
9 Ibid.

must be profitable *and* impacting the local community in Jesus' name. We do not separate work and ministry, because our work is interwoven with our ministry.

Socially: A B4Ter's presence and interaction in the community should lead to a sense of goodwill and grace between neighbors in the community. For example, OPEN Network businesses have built orphanages, taught English or reading skills to children and the poor, led anti litter campaigns, and scores of other activities to bless their communities.

Muhammad Yunus, the Nobel Prize winner and founder of The Yunus Centre in Bangladesh, coined the term "social business." Those doing B4T might also use this term to describe their businesses. The objectives of social businesses are very similar to the objectives for doing business for transformation. Using the term "social business" allows B4Ters to explain our work and ourselves in terms that are readily understandable to both the Muslim and secular worlds.

Yunus defines social business as a "cause-driven" business. Clearly this is befitting of B4T work as well. Yunus explains:

> In a social business, the investors/owners can gradually recoup the money invested, but cannot take any dividend beyond that point. The purpose of the investment is (normally) purely to achieve one or more social objectives through the operation of the company; no personal gain is desired by the investors. The company must cover all costs and make a profit . . . The impact of the business on people or environment rather than the amount of profit made in a given period measures the success of social business. Sustainability of the company indicates that it is running as a business.[10]

Yunus goes on to clarify:

> Social business is a new category of business. It widens the market by giving a new option to consumers. It does not intend to monopolize the market and take the existing option away. It adds to the competition. It brings a new dimension to the business world and a new feeling of social awareness among . . . business people. Social business is about making a complete sacrifice of financial rewards from business. It is about total delinking from

---

[10] Muhammad Yunus, Yunus Centre, http://www.muhammadyunus.org/Social-Business/social-business/ (page discontinued).

the old framework of business. It is not about accommodation of new objectives within the existing framework. Unless this total delinking from personal financial gain can be established, you'll never discover the power of real social business.[11]

Again Sheldon agrees: *"All money he made he would never regard as his own, but as trust funds to be used for the good of humanity."*[12] Many B4Ters' businesses have made a lot of money, yet many choose to live simply and invest their earnings in needy people or kingdom projects, including other B4T businesses.

Social enterprise involves the promotion and building of businesses that create wealth with the intention of benefiting not just the owner or his family, but a defined constituency, sector, or community (including the church). Notice that this definition has two elements: Wealth creation—i.e., it is going to operate in the market—the place where exchange of goods takes place. (Secondly) the profits generated are not for the enrichment of a few individual families, but for a community of worker-owners—in particular, the poor and marginalized sectors of society. In other words, it is not a "private" enterprise but a "social" enterprise.[13]

Though Yunus' emphasis is based on his own life experience and concern for the poor, he rightly stresses the social aspects of work.

Environmentally: Our businesses should enhance the sustainability of our environment. This may be done in a variety of ways, such as recycling paper, exploring the use of solar energy, recycling water, promoting environmental issues in the community, etc. This is a new but growing area of interest for B4Ters.

Business as Mission Terminology

Mission, like most disciplines of life and work, has its own language: mission-speak. Business as Mission (BAM) is a growing topic in the church and among mission agencies. As BAM has developed over the

---

[11] Ibid.

[12] Sheldon, *Steps*, 1967.

[13] Leslie M. Fox and S. Bruce Schearer, *Sustaining Civil Society: Strategies for Resource Mobilisation* (Washington, DC: CIVICUS, 1997).

past decade, it too has birthed its own vocabulary. To clarify, I wish to define three common and related terms so that we understand what we are talking about. (See appendix B for a more extensive glossary of terms.)

Tentmaker

For many years there was one word: "tentmaker" or "tentmaking." The term originates from Acts 18 where Paul is referred to as a tentmaker. Prior to 2004, "tentmaking" was the only term being used in evangelical circles to describe those integrating business and mission. However, it has evolved to mean the following. *Tentmaker: a believer who intentionally takes a job with a company in another culture, is fully supported by that job, and strives to witness cross-culturally.*

Note the differentiating factor for being a "tentmaker" is income. If you receive 100 percent of your income from your job and you are working abroad, then you are a tentmaker.

Business as Mission

In 2004 the Lausanne committee on business coined the term "Business as Mission" (BAM). The Lausanne Occasional Paper No. 59 gives a thorough discussion of BAM.[14]

BAM is defined as follows.

> Business as Mission (BAM): a term being used in Christian circles to describe the integration of ministry goals and business goals in making an impact for God's kingdom. As a strategy, BAM generally describes any for-profit business endeavor that seeks to reach people and communities for the glory of God and is not artificially supported by donor funds.

A brief definition of BAM by Brian Walck states:

> Business as Mission . . . has four core components. First, it involves the creation of a business entity, controlled by Great Commission minded owners and senior management who seek to glorify God with every aspect of their business operation. This eliminates *tentmaking*, which focuses on individual impact rather than the business impact. Second, it has profit (or at least sustainability) as

---

[14] Lausanne Committee for World Evangelization, "Business as Mission," Lausanne Occasional Paper No. 59, 2005, http://www.lausanne.org/docs/2004forum/LOP59_IG30.pdf.

a goal. This eliminates business "platforms" and other ministries and *NGOs* which cannot operate without donor funds. Third, it exists primarily to advance the gospel among less reached peoples of the world. This eliminates marketplace ministries that are typically not cross-cultural in emphasis. Fourth, it is socially responsible; it does not seek profit at any cost. Restricting our definition in this way is not to say that these excluded strategies are not desirable or effective.[15]

As defined and described, "BAM" is the generic term that includes all cross-cultural business being done in less reached or non-Christian areas.

Business for Transformation

"B4T" is a more recent term. We cannot attribute this term to any one individual, but it developed for use in the OPEN Network because of its emphasis on both business and church planting.[16] In OPEN, we define it as the following. *Business for Transformation (B4T): businesses strategically placed in unreached areas that are profitable and serving the local community, generally through transformation, and specifically through evangelism, discipleship, and church planting.*

The purpose of B4T is to show people around the kingdom. B4T workers do not see business as a "platform" or a "vehicle" for ministry. Rather, the business constitutes ministry in and through its daily activities. B4T businesses are authentic and sustainable, contributing to the welfare of their communities. A B4T business should help people flourish with integrity in a context of practical discipleship. B4T workers have clear ministry goals that may include social justice objectives but definitely include evangelism and discipleship.

There are many advantages and disadvantages for BAM, B4T, and tentmaking. For more information on advantages and disadvantages of each, read chapter 3 of my previous book, *Tentmaking: The Life and Work of Business as Missions.*

The following diagram reflects how BAM, B4T, and tentmaking relate to one another. Please note that all tentmakers and B4Ters are BAMers, and they are all engaged in business. Some B4Ters are also tentmakers,

---

[15] Brian Walck, "9 Missiological Insights into Business as Mission," Work as Worship Network, February 23, 2009, http://www.workasworshipnetwork.org/9-missiological-insights-into-business-as-mission-brian-walck/.

[16] OPEN Network, http://www.opennetworkers.net.

meaning they earn their entire salary from their job. However, most B4Ters are not tentmakers, since roughly 75 percent get some financial income from their job and some from donors back home.

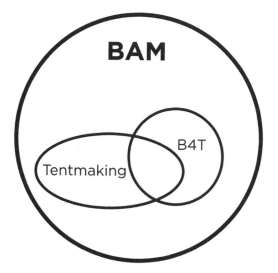

While the modern-day tentmaking movement was the start of rebalancing missionary efforts towards a more holistic approach in response to increased difficulties in gaining access to unreached areas, BAM has since begun to develop as a wider movement. This is logical because business will always be proportionately the largest component in an economy. By their definition, B4Ters will always be fewer in number, but at the cutting edge of reaching into unreached people groups.

Final Reminder

In considering each of the practical steps in this book, remember to start your thinking and planning with prayer. Jesus is the CEO of our businesses. This is not just lip service; we are serious about this. We tell our employees and Muslim friends that this is Jesus' business. We take our directives from Him. God tells His people through Samuel, *"Those who honor Me I will honor."*[17] That may raise eyebrows, but it often leads to softened hearts and open minds that have previously been hardened and closed to Jesus. In starting a B4T or BAM business, every step must

---

[17] 1 Samuel 2:30

be bathed in prayer. Every day, every meeting, every conversation needs to involve the Holy Spirit at all levels and activities of our business.

Now let's get started with the business of getting started.

"Commit your way to the LORD; trust in him, and he will act."
—Psalm 37:5 (ESV)

DISCUSSION QUESTIONS

1. What are some reasons doing B4T appeals to you?
2. Explain the statement, "Transformation begins with us."
3. Describe the differences between BAM, B4T, and tentmaking.

When business is done in godly, Christ-centered ways, there is also a spiritual return on our investment.

Chapter 3

STARTING THE BUSINESS— CHOOSING THE CAMPSITE

Start with Ministry

On the first morning in Calcutta, John Kavanaugh, a brilliant ethicist, met Mother Teresa. She asked, "And what can I do for you?" Kavanaugh asked her to pray for him. "What do you want me to pray for?" she asked. He voiced the request that he had borne for thousands of miles from the United States: "Pray that I have clarity." She said firmly, "No, I will not do that." When he asked her why, she said, "Clarity is the last thing you are clinging to and you must let it go." When Kavanaugh commented that she always seemed to have the clarity she longed for, she laughed and said, "I have never known clarity; what I have always had is trust. So I will pray that you trust God." In craving clarity, we attempt to eliminate the risk of trusting God. Fear of the unknown path stretching ahead of us destroys our childlike trust in the Father's active goodness and unrestricted love.[18]

Business for transformation is an adventure with God. He will use your business to prune and trim you into the person He desires you to be. *"In the beginning God created the heavens and the earth"*[19] He clearly had a plan—a seven-step plan you might say. In the beginning of the B4T adventure, we too want clarity to know His plan for us and, as Mother Teresa points out, that requires trust. Clarity and trust call for information. While gathering information, remember a big part of acquiring clarity comes from asking the right questions.

---

[18] From old personal notes, source unknown.
[19] Genesis 1:1

A friend's mother used to work as a clerk in a supermarket. One morning a little boy walked up to her with big, sad eyes and told her he was lost. This mother took his hand, gave him a reassuring hug, and told him not to worry, she would help him find his mother. They looked up aisle after aisle. At each aisle the woman asked, *"Do you see your mother?"* and each time the boy answered, *"No."* Finally, she took the boy up to the front of the store and stood him on a counter. She told him to look around very carefully, and once more she asked, *"Now do you see your mother?"* *"No,"* answered the child, *"I just keep seeing my daddy!"* We may be asking many questions, but are we asking the right questions?

No one B4T business model exists that is more successful than another. No one church planting strategy exists that is more effective than another. This book is written to help you ask the right questions as you pursue the plan God has for you in doing B4T. So the place we need to begin is with ourselves.

Know Yourself

Oscar Wilde said, *"The final mystery is oneself."* The biggest asset and the biggest detractor for any business can be its owner. Oswald Chambers writes, *"My vision of God depends on the state of my character."* That is a lot to think about. He goes on to say, *"Before I can see the Lord, there must be something corresponding in my character."*[20] The fact is that character matters. My dear friend Doug writes,

> Who you are is what counts. What you do can sometimes create a sense of false security. I'm a pastor, I help people, I preach—but that's not who I am, that's what I do. What I do is a good thing but it's my character that allows me—or, in some cases, keeps me—from seeing and experiencing the resurrected Jesus. It's my character that gives me my connection to Him, and allows others to experience that same Jesus through me.

Solomon also teaches us about ourselves. He says: *"To acquire wisdom is to love yourself; people who cherish understanding will prosper."*[21] Business owners must be people who can think clearly and critically, who know themselves, and who have the ability to listen to others and interact

---

[20]   Oswald Chambers, *My Utmost for His Highest* (Grand Rapids: Discovery House Publishers, 2012).

[21]   Proverbs 19:8 (NLT)

respectfully. Business consultant and author Andrea Kay adds: *"The best way to prepare yourself for the marketplace is to . . . discover who you are."*[22] *"Wise choices will watch over you. Understanding will keep you safe."*[23] As we move forward we need guides, coaches, and data to help us think through our next steps before forging ahead. Some people gather like-minded friends to give them input. Will Rogers had some great advice about starting a new project: *"It isn't what we don't know that gives us trouble; it's what we know that ain't so."*[24] To gain a broad understanding of the business, cultures, and the people that God is assigning you, gather advice from a variety of sources. Don't read only Christian books, don't only talk to Christian businesspeople, and don't speak only with friends. Talk with competitors, suppliers, and whatever other sources God brings to mind. You cannot learn too much, and the wider the variety of ideas the better.

The research tells us that those who go overseas primarily to work a job and secondarily to do some ministry are not effective at evangelism, discipleship, or church planting.[25] Ministry needs to be the driving motive for doing B4T. A passion for both business *and* ministry is needed. Thus, you need to develop a business that fits your ministry calling—and not one that fits your support strategy. However, once you have learned the language, you need to invest most of your time and energy in starting your business. In time the business will create numerous relationships that will generate opportunities to witness. In the beginning it will feel and look like you are only doing business, but that's okay. Business and ministry must be in step with one another. Like legs of a body, you cannot stand long on one without the other. Ministry needs to be the alarm that wakes you up; nonetheless, as you get out of bed and start to walk, one leg must go first, and that leg should be business.

In choosing the right business, you first need to understand God's assignment for you. Is He calling you to do a business and bless others through that business? Or is He calling you to minister to a specific group of people through business? Dan Gibson suggests two different

---

[22] Andrea Kay, "Learn to Think If You Want to Get Hired," *USA Today*, June 8, 2012, http://www.usatoday.com/money/jobcenter/workplace/kay/story/2012–06–09/learn-to-think-listen-interact/55467614/1.

[23] Proverbs 2:11 (NLT)

[24] http://www.brainyquote.com/quotes/quotes/w/willrogers385286.html.

[25] Patrick Lai, *Problems and Solutions for Enhancing the Productivity of Tentmakers Doing Church Planting in the 10/40 Window* (Department of Intercultural Studies, Asian Graduate School of Theology, 2003). 42

biblical perspectives of doing business for transformation: a Pauline model motivated by the strategic requirements of a place and time, and a Priscillan model, which emphasizes the value of the work itself. In other words, Paul used his profession to facilitate ministry, while Aquila and Priscilla were tentmakers by both trade and nature, engaging in business wherever they went with their ministry. Gibson says, "The Pauline tentmaker looks for a job where the ministry is, whereas the Priscillan tentmaker looks for ministry where the job is."[26]

You need to trust and know what God is calling or leading you to do. When times get hard, it is your relationship with God and the certainty of your assignment that will carry you through. Sam worked for six years to build a factory and reach profitability, only to have an earthquake destroy everything after only two full cycles of production. He writes, "Only God's call will translate into perseverance to face all the challenges that are part of the process in serving the unreached." Hoping any business will become your meal ticket does not constitute a call. You need clarity that the life of B4T is His assignment for you.

As you determine His assignment and select a business, be aware that not every business works in every location. Caleb was called to reach Ansari Muslims in India. The Ansari are craftsmen, skilled at working with their hands. Caleb, like Paul, designed his business to fit the skills of the Ansari people. Today, his handicraft factory employs sixty-two people, and several have come to faith in Jesus. Caleb followed a Pauline model. Ben, on the other hand, is passionate about three things: Jesus, his family, and bikes. He moved to a city in the Muslim world that was suitable for all three, set up shop, and is using his skills to impact people for Jesus. Ben followed a Priscillan model. Both are biblical models and both have the same B4T objectives, but the starting point for each is different.

Each B4T worker's calling and situation is unique. Therefore it is natural to expect each ministry and business to be unique. If God is sending us, we can rest assured He will use us where and how He desires. Yet we are told to count the cost, so it is a wise person who asks, *"Am I cut out to do B4T?"* A missionary friend in India had witnessed thousands turning to Jesus. Due to a change in visa laws, he switched to doing BAM. Being a good speaker, he recruited numerous people to come work for him and raised over US$350,000 to get off the ground. He was bankrupt in four years and is now back in the States. Many others have also failed

---

[26] Dan Gibson, *Avoiding the Tentmaker Trap* Fort Washington: PA (WEC International, 1997), 35.

and returned home. The point is that a dynamic Christian speaker/ evangelist/missionary may be a terrible businessman.

Knowing yourself involves three additional points to think through: recognizing the tap of God, speaking from your passion, and inviting others to join you.

Tap of God

Peter Marshall, former pastor and chaplain of the US Senate, described his decision to work for the church as a *"tap on the shoulder."* Nearly all B4Ters can relate to this. You will not have the energy and the focus to persevere in both outreach *and* work without such a tap. People who love their job rarely build a ministry through it and, likewise, those who are called to church work rarely succeed at B4T. B4Ters need that *"tap on the shoulder"* for integrating both their job and ministry. Most people choose their profession for one of three reasons: money, self-satisfaction, or calling. People who work for money quit working when the paycheck stops. Those working to satisfy themselves have a goal in mind, perhaps to gain an identity or to obtain prestige or power from their work. As long as the job fulfills their perceived needs, they will keep working; however, once the attention dissipates, so does the will to work. On the other hand, those who have been *"tapped on the shoulder"* (sometimes referred to as a "calling") have a passionate commitment to the task at hand. Self-worth, identity, and material benefits are unimportant. Whatever we do, we do to the glory of God. Whatever we have accumulated in life—education, skills, money, and so on—all are from God. We are to be stewards of these gifts so that we may multiply them and give them back to Him.

Whatever your vocation, you must be able to ask and give an answer to God, *"Why do I do this?"* Remember this: *God is more concerned about the worker than the work.* He does not use engineers, accountants, teachers, pastors, and so forth; He uses *people*—people who *deny themselves* and *take up their cross daily.*

Be certain of God's leading. God taps each of us in different ways. Before embarking on the B4T journey, you need to be sure that you are following Jesus' plan and not your own. Every B4Ter, BAMer, and tentmaker sooner or later hits a wall. Wives seem to hit the wall more often than the men. My wife will tell you she has quit a thousand times. Faith—the confidence in what the Lord has led us to do—has been the wings that have lifted us over those walls and kept us moving forward.

In birthing any kind of business or accepting a job overseas, remember to begin with prayer. This seems obvious, but it is easily overlooked. We need to move forward at God's prompting rather than because *"it is a good idea."* The assurance that God is leading you in the business will help you to keep your sanity when things don't seem to work out as planned. Count on opposition and obstacles to your objectives. Satan will not take your encroachment on his territory lightly. Opposition may come from a variety of sources: competitors, the government, religious leaders—even other mission workers. Scripture teaches that trials are a part of God's refining process in us (1 Pet 1:6,7). As such, opposition and obstacles are opportunities for our growth in character and spiritual warfare. Remember, God is more interested in His worker than in His work. Too often workers place too high a value on the importance of starting or operating a business venture for Christ, neglecting the greater work He is doing within them.

Speak from Your Passion

First and foremost, you need love. Jesus makes it perfectly clear that it is our love—the love He has given us—that is going to draw people to Himself.[27] Every day of our life, everything we do should flow from His love. Before developing the skills of a B4Ter, ensure that your love originates from and seeks to return glory to Jesus. The source of your vision has to come from your personal walk with God, not someone else or some organization.

Speaking from your passion is accomplished by opening up to what is in your heart. Your passion works much like the fuel in an engine; it keeps you going. Your passion will also energize others to help you in the business. From your passion, people begin to understand that it is not just a dream, but a reality. When people grasp your passion—your heart—God will begin to draw them to share your vision and goals and then seek ways to work with you.

> *"Whatever your hand finds to do, do it with all your might, for in the grave, where you are going, there is neither working nor planning nor knowledge nor wisdom."*[28]

---

[27] John 13:35
[28] Ecclesiastes 9:10

Invite Others to Join You

Learn from the experience of others. Continually ask others for input. Invite ideas on the best ways of starting a business. Obtain input regarding books and websites to peruse. Ask business owners from different industries what steps they took to succeed. Introduce yourself to local small business owners and request their advice. While learning what people did right, remember to also ask about the mistakes they made. Everyone's path is different. Invite others to share their wisdom and blend their ideas with your own.

Since outreach, discipleship and church planting flow through the business, prepare yourself for ministry first and then develop the business plan. What ministry skills do you need to competently reach the unreached? The basic ministry skills include the following: language, evangelism, an understanding of the religion and culture, and the ability to recruit like-minded team members and investors. Find people who are experienced in these areas and sit at their feet for a few days or weeks. Once you begin the business, you won't have time for much else, so you need to be sure you have the ministry training necessary before beginning the business. Recruit these people to be ongoing coaches, guiding you through the process of learning their skill as you move overseas, begin language learning, and then start a job or a business. The first book I wrote, *Tentmaking: The Life and Work of Business as Missions*, has much to say about ministry preparation.

Job 1—Profitability and Impacting Lives in Jesus' Name

The mantra of the B4T worker is this: *church planting is paramount, and profit is paramount*. Though we have already discussed the four aspects of BAM, a B4T business is ultimately going to be judged on two factors: its impact on the local community and its profitability. For a B4T business to be considered a success, it must be striving to be profitable and impacting the local community in Jesus' name.

It is essential that you make the necessary adjustments and, if needed, sacrifices to adapt your business strategy and processes to achieve these two objectives. Not all decisions are made on whether you need to make money or not. Sometimes it is a matter of giving service to your customers at odd hours, and even for a lower profit. Nor are all decisions based upon winning people to Jesus. There will be prayer meetings, conferences, and so forth that you will have to miss, as someone needs to keep the doors of the shop open. The B4Ter is seeking to fulfill both objectives: profitability and reaching people for Jesus. To fail at one is to fail at both.

There are challenges, pleasures, and rewards in starting a business at the ends of the earth. All of these challenges, pleasures, and rewards come at various times in the forms of a job well done, lives being touched, money being made, and hearts being reborn. But these rewards only come as the result of hard work, diligence, and absolute commitment to both the business and the ministry. Understand that business and ministry have their foundation in relationships with people—your customers, suppliers, vendors, and neighbors. The complexity of it all makes it even harder to predict the outcome of any venture you may start, but the opportunity and the challenge is there if you are willing.

Pros and Cons of Starting a Business

Starting a business means jumping into the great unknown. It is good to work through the simple old-fashioned list of pluses and minuses before starting a business. Here are some pros and cons that we have discovered; more are listed in chapter 3 of my first book.

Pros

Much of the payback people get from their entrepreneurial ventures is personal. Probably the biggest draw a B4Ter has toward starting his own business is gaining control of his time. Having the independence and flexibility with time for discipleship of others, family, and other activities is huge. A business can pave a path for others to get visas and join in the work. Operating your own business also enables you to locate your life and work in a particular city or village among the people God has assigned to you. Starting your own business enables you to hire those people God has put on your heart, creating an abundance of chances to bless the people with work, income, and status, as well as precious moments to observe your own life in Christ. As the owner, you can invest the business's profits in the further education and training of employees, social justice issues, needy locals, or your team members as God leads. Business owners are challenged and surprised every day, resulting in our faith spiking in ways that only explorers and entrepreneurs can understand.

There are personal benefits to starting a business. Running your own business provides an opportunity to do something for which you have a passion. You get to spend the majority of your waking hours working for the benefit of people and for objectives about which you are excited. Rather than simply carrying out other people's ideas or implementing their visions, you reap the professional benefits of attempting any exciting insights you get. You can aggressively pursue new ideas for products and/or services. Being the boss frees you to fully leverage your creativity, ingenuity, and dependence upon God. A feeling of great satisfaction is derived from working with the King of kings as he uses your knowledge and skills to solve the day-to-day challenges that business generates.

Cons

While starting a new business venture can be invigorating, it is also a tiring pursuit. The hours you set for yourself may grow exponentially as you try to launch the company. You cannot simply put in your eight hours and go home; if there is a problem or important unfinished business, then it's your job to attend to it. Expect to put in many extra hours, especially the first two or three years.

As the owner, you will be required to wear many hats. When you open a business, you need to have the ability to complete every single job in the business, since you never know when someone will quit or call in sick. If there is a problem, it falls in your lap. There is no one to blame but yourself; it's your business and you are at the controls. In addition, due to the fluctuations of business, your income may be unsteady the first two to four years.

You may have a deep understanding of your professional field, yet it is a given that every day you will be confronted with unanticipated challenges. Your ability to learn the ropes, delegate, and adapt quickly will be central determinants to your success. You need to be able to make decisions, handle pressure, and be flexible. You must be a disciplined self-starter. No matter how good your business plan, your team, or the size of your bank account, there are no guarantees that your business will succeed. Furthermore, all your employees are counting on you to succeed, since their own families' prosperity depends upon you.

Many stories exist about people who fail in starting a business because of numerous shortcomings. But if you look around the marketplace, obviously plenty of successes exist too. As you start out, listen to the Lord, gather a team of coaches, and understand your own heart and motives. Ignore the naysayers.

The worst detractors cite statistics about small-business failure:

They tell you 90 percent of small businesses fail within five years
… Be careful about who you talk to, because if all that negativity
hits you on the wrong day, it can be very potent. You have to
be the kind of person who says, "I'm not going to listen to it."
The small-business failure legend purports to show that half
of startups fold in the first year, and 80 percent to 90 percent
succumb after five years. But nobody seems to know where this
stat originated. In fact, several well-documented studies indicate
that starting a small business offers a much more reasonable
chance of success. For instance, the SBA, using U.S. Census
Bureau data, reports that almost half of all new firms with at least
one employee survive beyond four years. This urban legend also
suggests that businesses that closed were all failures. But the SBA,
using another set of Census data, says a third of new businesses
that closed in their early years were financially successful when
they shut down. "When I was researching my business concept,
I interviewed owners of 100 businesses that had closed," says
Williams. "I found that three-quarters were nowhere close to
failing financially. They closed because of highly personal reasons,
such as a health crisis, or they just woke up one day and [realized
they] didn't enjoy it any longer."[29]

The Risks

Risk is a constant in business. So what are the risks of starting a B4T
business? In reviewing the pros and cons of B4T, although you can reap
many benefits by starting your own business, there are two important
risks or costs (Luke 14:29–32) that must be seriously prayed through and
discussed with those involved.

1. *Losing Money.* You are going to need money to get your
   small business started. Whether you raid your savings
   account, borrow from friends and relatives, or acquire
   a loan from a bank, there is a real possibility that your
   business will not succeed and that you, your friends, and/
   or the bank will never see that money again.

---

[29] Mark Henricks, "Have These 5 Myths Been Holding You Back from Starting a Business?
Time for a Reality Check," *Entrepreneur's Startups Magazine,* March 2006.

2. *Personal Sacrifice.* Business success can come at a high personal cost. Getting your business up and running may consume most of your time and energy, including your precious evenings and weekends. You may not have much time for family or friends, or the extra cash to return home for your best friend's wedding. Be certain that your wife, children, and team members are fully on board and that they are also ready to make some of the personal sacrifices necessary for your business to succeed.

Do You Really Want to Work?

While doing business in general, we need to heed the words of Kriegel and Patler:

> The most accurate predictor of success is a strong preference for the work. Aristotle said, "Pleasure in the job puts perfection in the work." But he didn't go far enough! Research reveals that the more you love what you do, the better you'll do it and the more money you'll make. The key ingredient in most successful projects is loving what you do. Having a goal or a plan is not enough. Academic preparation is not enough. Prior experience is not enough. Pleasure and productivity are Siamese twins in these unconventional times.[30]

The emergence of BAM/B4T is a major development in missions. More and more mission workers are discovering the advantages of starting, working in, or operating a business. Yet there are real challenges to combining business and apostolic church planting. You need to prayerfully ask yourself the question, *"How much do I really want to work?"* Many B4Ters average sixty-plus hours a week for the first two years. In addition, if one is going to start something or grow an enterprise, they must ask this fundamental question: *"Am I committed to doing my work with unadulterated excellence, no matter how arduous the task or how long the road?"* Consider what percentage of businesspeople actually own part of their own company. Most work for someone else. They risk losing their job, but not their business. Personally, I have always found working for the Lord to be more demanding than working for a boss.

---

[30] Robert J. Kriegel and Louis Patler, *If It Ain't Broke . . . BREAK IT!* (New York: Warner Books, 1991), 259.

B4Ters are distinguished from traditional mission workers by much more than financial self-support, especially in terms of training, function, and their intended mission. B4Ters are specialists. They take on both the jobs of a businessman and a minister and do so in a cross-cultural setting. It requires passion and focus—God's assignment/calling.

Jack, who works in India, states:

> When I started my business, I was told to hire a great accountant. I couldn't justify the expense, so I dug into the financial aspects on my own. While working hard to find real solutions, I discovered that as long as I was willing to adapt, I could conquer any challenge. Every entrepreneur faces a similar situation. As your business grows, you encounter new responsibilities that are beyond your current abilities. Fortunately, we entrepreneurs are a special breed. Our conviction to succeed drives us to achieve what others may see as impossible. We move forward against almost any obstacle, even our personal limitations. Rather than stopping in your tracks when new challenges appear, conquer them with confidence.

You don't become a B4Ter to become safe and reasonable. If you are looking for a visa, an income, and an identity in the local community, you do not want to do B4T or start a business. World champion boxer George Foreman says that what makes a great entrepreneur is *"someone who's never going to give up."*[31]

Failure is a frequent companion of B4Ters. You need the discipline to pick yourself up and move forward, whatever the problem. One B4T worker summed it up this way: *"Inside the chest of every successful B4T worker beats a heart full of passion for business. Our passion, our calling is key to picking ourselves up when we fall and keep moving forward."* Another B4T worker writes, *"Let people know the only 'comfort zone' that they should expect and truly yearn for is the 'Jesus zone.' And we know that when we are in the Jesus zone, joy abounds."*

After helping dozens of small firms get underway both in America and Central Asia, Marshall, a coach with NexusB4T, told me,

> Having a true passion for the business is essential. Business is so demanding. It almost always takes longer and more work than you think to achieve a payback. Business requires passion. You

---

[31] "What's Online," *Inc.*, November 2009, 10.

must truly love the product or service you offer, love the selling, love the customers, and you don't even mind customer-service problems.

Jon, a B4T worker whom Marshall coaches, adds, "You'd better be tenacious and you'd better be determined to make that business successful no matter what—even if it requires a lot of sacrifice and late hours." Matt, a seminary student who took my B4T course, wrote me:

I have recently realized in my own life a good deal of laziness. Sometimes this manifests itself in a reluctance to do work, but more subtly perhaps, it comes out in an overemphasis on protecting leisure time and leisure activities. I do tend to be a laid back person, but as a friend of mine recently commented, "A lot of people seem to think of themselves as laid back, but really they are using it as a cover for laziness." It comes in many forms, but laziness (or the classical sin name, sloth) is a real problem that will prevent many from becoming effective tentmakers. Part of the solution, I believe, to my own struggle and that of my peers in this regard is realizing that <u>work is a holy institution</u>. When God designed the paradise of Eden for Adam and Eve, the activity description of the place was not a list of leisure activities or exercises in self-actualization; it was productive, <u>old-fashioned work (Genesis 2:15)</u>. I, like so many others, have grown up in a world where it often seemed that work was in competition with God. That is, work was using time that could have been used to serve the church or draw closer to God in personal worship. It is easy to view work in this way when we don't view God as the creator and establisher of work. However, He wants me to find actual joy and enjoyment in my work, not just view it as a necessary and sanctifying experience. In a culture that is consumed with the aspect of worship as a feeling or an experience of God's presence, we must step back and redefine worship as something broader. Worship is the way we live our lives. Work—exercising our natural God-given abilities of dominion and creativity and productivity—glorifies God. Most likely, when we struggle to embrace work we also struggle to truly enter into worship and surrender to God.

"<u>*Work is worship*</u>" is something I hear repeated by B4T workers around the world and often repeat to myself. When we view our work as being done unto the Lord and not man,[32] it releases a weight that both the church and the world may hang on businesspeople, freeing us to praise Him in and through our daily work routines.

Timing

We are often asked when the best time to start a business is. Seth Godin speaks to this:

The best time to start is when you've got enough money in the bank to support all contingencies.

The best time to start is when the competition is far behind in technology, sophistication, and market acceptance.

The best time to start is when the competition isn't *too far* behind, because then you'll spend too long educating the market.

The best time to start is when everything at home is stable and you can really focus.

The best time to start is when you're out of debt.

The best time to start is when no one is already working on your idea.

The best time to start is after you've got all your funding.

The best time to start is when the political environment is friendlier than it is now.

The best time to start is after you've got your degree.

The best time to start is after you've worked all the kinks out of your plan.

The best time to start is when you're sure it's going to work.

The best time to start is after you've hired the key marketing person for the new division.

---

[32] Colossians 3:17

The best time to start is before some pundit declares your segment passé. Too late.

The best time to start is when the geopolitical environment settles down.

Actually, as you've probably guessed, *the best time to start* was last year. The second best time to start is right now.[33]

I agree with Seth, with the exception of restaurants, that the best time to start a business was last year—so get going! With restaurants, the best time to start is any month other than Ramadan. Some countries' visa application will dictate when you need to begin the business. *"If you are too lazy to plow in the right season, you will have no food at the harvest."*[34] *Now* is the time to get going.

DISCUSSION QUESTIONS

1. Describe the "tap of God" on your life.
2. Explain why evangelism / church planting and earning a profit go hand in hand in doing B4T?
3. What "cons" may cause you to hesitate in doing B4T?
4. Answer for yourself, *how much do you really want to work?*

---

[33] Seth Godin, "When to Start," *Seth's Blog,* November 15, 2006, http://sethgodin.typepad.com/seths_blog/2006/11/page/3/.

[34] Proverbs 20:4 (NLT)

"If you are where God wants you to be, then it will all turn out alright . . . in His plan and in His timing. He is often last minute, but never late."

—A B4TER

Chapter 4

THE INTANGIBLES

Successful B4Ters blend a passionate belief in the destiny of their venture with practical realizations. Carsten in Central Asia said, *"Without the passion, going into business would be a mistake, but to have only passion is not nearly enough."* Before even beginning to start a business or working in an overseas company, there are a few additional intangibles that are worth reviewing.

Get Wisdom

"The fear of the LORD is the beginning of knowledge; fools despise wisdom and instruction."[35]

Steve Forbes' famous line is a favorite of mine: *"With all your 'getting'—get wisdom."*

Ecclesiastes 4:9–12 also teaches us:

> Two are better than one, because they have a good return for their labor: If either of them falls down, one can help the other up. But pity anyone who falls and has no one to help them up. Also, if two lie down together, they will keep warm. But how can one keep warm alone? Though one may be overpowered, two can defend themselves. A cord of three strands is not quickly broken.

Solomon talks frequently about seeking advice and getting coaching. In doing B4T, my research[36] shows that those who have at least one mentor or coach are significantly more likely to succeed than those who have none. Jon has one mentor and eight coaches. Seven coaches assist with various aspects of his business, while one works with his culture and language learning. Throughout most of my career overseas, my wife and I have had two mentors and a variety of coaches. Having two mentors who have different backgrounds enables us to bounce ideas around and glean

---

[35] Proverbs 1:7 (ESV)
[36] Lai, *Problems and Solutions.*

input different from our own perspective. Our mentors have proven to be a significant help in our marriage relationship as well. When my wife and I cannot agree on something, we regularly decide to ask our mentor, and he becomes the tiebreaker in what otherwise could have become a heated discussion.

Often, you will need to do something in which you are not knowledgeable or skilled. You can spend many hours learning the skill, but at what cost? There's a time trade-off. You can give the job to a volunteer from your church, but often you get what you pay for. You can also hire someone who is conveniently available and at a cheap price, but this often proves more expensive in the long run. Having to micromanage an untrustworthy consultant or oversee getting something accomplished three times before it is done right has a time cost. If your time is precious, this is a false bargain. Or you can seek out the best available expert, pay his fee, and get the best advice or service. This gets the task done right the first time, so you can concentrate on higher priorities.

Proverbs teaches, *"Whoever walks with the wise will become wise."*[37] In seeking mentors and coaches, learn there is value in pursuing the best. To get the best, be prepared to "overpay" in order to be their client. I began this practice when it was a financial hardship. Now when money is less of an issue, it is less difficult to hire the best. Good, experienced coaches are available for all areas of life and work, but they don't come free. *You get what you pay for.*

It is common for B4Ters to have a coach who acts as sounding board, confidante, advisor, creative muse, and accountability partner. The money you spend for a coach can be a bargain. The small amount of time given to a focused discussion with an exceptionally knowledgeable coach can save valuable time.

When you are considering hiring a consultant or a coach, here are three things to consider:

1. *Has the coach actually done what he is advising you about?* Or is he an academic theorist who is a speaker or writer but not a doer? Generally speaking, I want my financial advisor to be a successful investor. I do not want a fat doctor who smokes. In missions, especially in B4T, there are a lot of people talking about it who have never succeeded at it. Be wise. You can waste a lot of time on self-appointed experts

---

[37] Proverbs 13:20

eager to take your money.

2. *Is the coach current?* There are a lot of "former" and "ex" folks who hang out the expert advisor shingle after exiting the field and are soon advising from waning memory rather than up-to-date practical experience. Make certain their expertise is not more than five years out of date.

3. *Does the coach have satisfied clients?* Avoid experts without satisfied clients. Ask for references and then *check* the references. A good, general, time-saving, disaster-preventing litmus test that entrepreneurs should apply to anybody they consider relying on for advice is:

    a. Are there at least three other successful B4Ters who have been helped by this coach?

    b. Are there at least three other successful B4Ters who have utilized the coach over a period of time or repeatedly?

    c. How recent has the coach been active in coaching B4Ters?

Jon in Central Asia summarizes, *"One coach is not enough. You cannot do B4T without first considering what intellectual capital is available to you."*

"How much better to get wisdom than gold, and understanding than silver!"—King Solomon [38]

Mentoring

Business for transformation is a destination. Most journeys are more enjoyable and more productive if we travel with others. *"Plans fail for lack of counsel, but with many advisers they succeed."*[39] No wonder Jon's business has helped birth several new churches and has created jobs for over three hundred people!

Coaches tend to focus on specific tasks or issues, like developing a new accounting system, smoothing out a difficult relationship with a team member, or finding new markets for a product. However, mentors engage in every area of our life and work. Good mentors will track our relationships with God, our spouse, children, team members, and coworkers, in addition to our language and culture learning, the business, evangelism, and church planting issues. By understanding the big picture

---

[38] Proverbs 16:16

[39] Proverbs 15:22

of our life and work, a good mentor helps us to integrate each area of our life in ways that bring balance and keep us from putting too much on our plates.

Doing business overseas is never the same as doing business domestically. Apart from having to deal with different ground rules, language and local cultural factors often shape the work of a B4Ter. Hence, it is important to work with a competent and experienced cross-cultural mentor. Mentors give us another set of eyes and ears to guide us. A mentor's wisdom and experience can help us to avoid many potholes—even cliffs—in the path of life. By looking at the challenge through other, more experienced eyes, we can discover alternative solutions that will save time, money, plus physical and emotional energy. Good mentors ask the tough questions about assumptions they hear us making and will work with us to discover the action steps that enhance our ability to glorify God in our life and work.

A mentor needs to be proactive in looking ahead to uncover potential potholes before they become real problems. This means a mentor needs to get to know those with whom you associate on a daily and weekly basis: your family, team members, key nationals you work with in the business, or others whom you are discipling. Mentors should press for reality and transparency in all areas of our life and work. Good mentors do not hesitate to ask the taboo questions about finances, thought life, sex life, team dynamics, and more.

A relationship demands interaction. To build and keep trust, a mentor needs to communicate with you regularly. Assisted by the new technologies and demanded by the needs of a new generation of workers, mentors should communicate as regularly as feasible, but OPEN Network mentors would strongly recommend that it be at least monthly by voice and weekly by email.

Mentors work with people based on a personal covenant relationship, not an assigned task. We are all individuals, so no mentor will fit all areas of your life and work. Still, select one or two who have strengths in your areas of need. The mentor's experience can be a great boost for lifting us over the walls we encounter in both our relationships and jobs. A mentor will become a trusted confidant who can be actively involved in problem solving and will guide you around the land mines of life and work before they detonate. As Proverbs says, *"Mockers don't love those who rebuke them, so they stay away from the wise."*[40]

---

[40] Proverbs 15:12

Whatever business you pursue, remember that *people* are your real product. God's assignment for us is all about reaching and serving people for His glory. Mentors assist us in our relationships with others. People will require the greatest amount of your time and effort. Witnessing, modeling, teaching, and training individuals until they do their jobs well and/or are mature in Christ—these are the kinds of relationships that must exist to make a business for transformation succeed. If you are looking for a mentor who understands the B4T world, I suggest you check out *www.NexusB4T.com.*

Spouse

The number one reason B4Ters fail overseas is not because of a poor business plan, weak language, or disobedient team members—it is marriage problems. My research[41] shows that if you and your spouse are not in agreement about doing B4T, you are very likely to fail. I discuss these issues thoroughly in *Tentmaking,* but it is such a vital issue that it is worth a few paragraphs here.

It is often said that marriage is hard work, so care needs to be taken when you decide to combine the work of a marriage with the work of B4T. Many wives of B4T business owners do not work in the business. Yet if you are considering working together, recognize that running a business together and being a family are two different things. Make sure that you both are working together because you enjoy being together, the working relationship is pleasurable for both of you, and it adds so much to your marriage that you want to extend your relationship from home to work.

Ask yourself, *"Do I want to be with my spouse 24/7? Can I see myself working side by side with my spouse? Do we share the same values and vision?"* These questions need to be discussed, and if you can't come to a clear agreement, then that is a yellow light.

A business plan is vital for any business. However, before you create a business plan, create a *life* plan—then you can see where your job/business fits on your list of priorities. If you determine that you can start a business with your spouse, then map it out with him or her. Married couples planning to do a B4T together need to discuss and determine what roles each spouse will play in the business. Before you start out— just like when you planned your wedding in advance, from a budget to a guest list—this is the time when you delineate everything in the business,

---

[41] Lai, *Problems and Solutions.*

from your respective roles to your financial plan. Be clear about what the roles are going to be within the business and which ones you will hold. Most arguments center on roles and finances; you have to sort out the "who does what" within the business. It is the same with running your household. Choose business roles based on each partner's strengths, and be willing to defer to one another's strengths. Understand what each of you contributes to the business, and understand what each of you needs to take from the business. It is essential that you articulate these things with one another before you commit to working together.

Tenacity is a key to success, and often it is the wife who wants to quit and return home. What is more, nearly half of those interviewed said they had little time for family or personal interests and personal passions. Although many wives do not work in the business, their *being on board* with B4T is essential. Whatever role a wife is going to play, whether at home or in a business, both spouses need to understand their roles and agree with God's vision and plan for doing B4T. B4T will either strengthen your marriage or tear it apart.

Generosity

God is a generous God and as such we need to be generous in our jobs too. Riza, a Muslim, had worked for us for eight years. She had availed herself of an offer where our business paid for half of her master's studies. One week after completing her degree, she received an offer for her dream job in her hometown and decided she should leave to take it. She came into my office and asked what would be the terms for paying back our share of her master's degree. When I told her that I did not invest in her education for the business's sake, but for her sake and that she owed us nothing, tears streamed down her cheeks. She knew our business is based on the Bible, and she knew where that generosity came from. Riza could not stop telling others what had been done for her.

"The generous prosper; those who refresh others will themselves be refreshed."[42]

We want to try to create a win-win with everyone we deal with. Whether it is a supplier, a customer, or an employee, be sure each feels blessed or respected as a result of that interaction. God wins and we win when our customers win too. The most creative thinking comes from asking, "What can I do so that both of us gain the most from this

---

[42] Proverbs 11:25 (NLT)

situation?" The goal is to create a beneficial relationship so that both parties are constantly rooting for each other.

Flexibility

"Business in a box" or other such systems have their place in the world, but realize that step-by-step techniques often do not allow you to veer off course or think outside the box when opportunities or conflicts arise. You need to approach every customer every day as a unique person who requires solutions based on your life experiences so far. Once you have covered the basics (such as researching the matter and asking open-ended questions), you can open your mind to questions or solutions that will lead you to a place you might not have previously explored.

Business is a living organism. It is growing, dying, and always in a state of change. If a business is not changing, it is dead. It is not uncommon for a B4Ter to start out in one direction, only to have that idea morph into something else. Whether you employ two people or two hundred, fluctuations in the marketplace, economic crises, and natural disasters all impact your multiple bottom lines.

Sam had a factory in Indonesia. After four years, he was making a good start. Several Muslims had come to Christ, and the business provided jobs for over a dozen people and was nearing profitability. Then an earthquake hit and it all collapsed—literally. However, this allowed Sam to pursue another business that is already proving to be more profitable, and in addition he's seen over three hundred come to Jesus. If something is not working, pay attention to nearby opportunities. We all know that when God closes a door He opens a window. Several B4Ters have failed because they wouldn't flex with the time.

We must be learners and quick adapters. Strong-willed entrepreneurs often power around a challenge or blast through it rather than face it. Instead, review your processes and metrics biweekly, uncover any new challenges, and be flexible enough to revise your path to success. Address the issues. Find and use shortcuts that will make your work even more enjoyable.

Are You an Entrepreneur?

I am frequently asked, *"How do I know if I am an entrepreneur?"* Estimates vary but on the average only 10 percent of all people are natural entrepreneurs. Many non-entrepreneurs have succeeded in starting B4T businesses, but in most of the successful cases they had a great coach or mentor walking with them through the start-up process. So if you are not an entrepreneur, be sure to get a mentor and form a team of coaches to advise you. Be sure to listen to them.

If you are not sure whether or not you are an entrepreneur, here are ten signs many people might consider to be liabilities or character flaws but can actually be indicators that you are an entrepreneur:

1. ***Out of the Box***—It doesn't make sense to you that something has been done the time-honored way with no explanation of why. New is better. You change things just to change things. You are not someone who wants to just go through the motions or sit by idly. Nor do you like following the pack. You know that greatness resides outside the lines of conformity; and you don't think that policies, laws, and regulations apply to you.

2. ***Passionate***—You are hot or cold; no lukewarmness is in your thinking or actions. Your passion is fed by an intrinsic drive that provides the internal reward that can sustain you through hard times and between paydays. This God-given passion may be for a vision, product, or service, yet the opportunity to solve this problem will make life better for others and yourself. Most entrepreneurs believe they will change the world. They believe they will overcome any and all obstacles that lay in their path to success.

3. ***Risk Taker***—You don't take uncalculated risks, but you are not bound by a fear of stepping into the unknown either. Where others succumb, you know how to control your fears. There's a deep belief in God working through all that you do that will ultimately lead to good.

4. ***Visionary***—You see things others just don't see. You feel things others don't feel. You spot opportunities and imagine results that others cannot imagine. You like to improve things—everything. You don't go along with the agreed-upon norms of the group or community you work and live in. You always see how things could be done better. In addition, you are opinionated and freely give your two cents about your better way of doing things, even when you're not asked.

5. ***Flexible***—You readily adapt to new circumstances and situations. You love new ideas. Change is your friend. Being a Steady Eddie is difficult for you because you want to create something others can be inspired by and contribute to. You're too creative for your own good when it comes to working for others, so you have difficulty keeping a job.

6. ***Easily Bored***—You find yourself easily bored, and others start viewing you as a problem. But nothing is wrong with you—you are simply bored with activities that aren't up to your abilities and aren't challenging. That's why you hated most of the classes you ever attended. You have difficulty making the kind of small talk that so many people get comfort from. This social pattern of relationship and rapport building seems like a waste of time to you and makes you uncomfortable.

7. ***Tenacious***—You may have been labeled obsessive, because when you get started on something, you have difficulty letting go. Don't let anyone convince you that this is a disease or deficiency. All of the great entrepreneurs become completely immersed in their vision.

8. ***Workaholic***—You find it difficult to unwind. There's always something to do, something to improve. You can't go to sleep at night because you can't turn your thoughts off. An idea may even manifest itself in your dreams. The next morning you find yourself still consumed with that idea, distracting you from the job you're supposed to be doing.

9. ***Rebellious***—You have been described as a rebel and rule breaker. You have a lifelong record of resisting authority. It's not that you don't like authority, it's just that you see better, faster, more efficient ways of doing things.

10. ***Don't Fit the Norm***—You have always been a bit uncomfortable in your own skin. Until you get used to the idea that you are in fact different from most people, it could prove to be a problem—or be exactly the motivation you need to acknowledge the entrepreneur screaming to get out.

Building a Solid Foundation

Building a solid foundation is going to take a significant amount of work and much personal sacrifice, so count the cost now before you begin. You cannot wish your business into being a success—you have to do the legwork. You can begin with an idea or a product in mind, but test it thoroughly. *Do not get input only from Christians.* Tom, the head of a business in India, says, *"Do not rely on missionaries for business-related help or information. Missionaries don't have a clue about doing business."*

Seek balanced input. After each step in your business plan, evaluate. According to Luke 14, we need to discern if we have the money, people, and personal energy to build the tower of which we are dreaming. Ask questions of everyone so that you may ask more questions. Is my idea viable? What risk is involved? Do this yourself, so you can observe people's responses. You cannot outsource the preparation. Sam Walton, founder of Walmart, was famous for visiting his stores across the country two to four days every week. There is much you can learn over the Internet, but nothing beats talking with people face-to-face and seeing how they feel and react to your idea.

Contact the embassy of your home country in the land to which you are moving and glean what information or in-country contacts they can give you. Go there and meet the people. Wine and dine them—they may introduce you to some key people who can open doors for you in the future. Many countries have business and tourist bureaus overseas. Perhaps one is in your country. Talk to these people about your idea, even if they are not in your area of business. Then ask them about your product and if they believe your idea is viable. Ask for contacts back in their home country.

Plan at least one exploratory trip to the land to do the needed research. The following chapters are full of practical pointers of what needs to be researched, but the implementation is up to you. If it is difficult to get a visa for the country from your home country, explore getting a visa from their embassy in another country. Several OPEN workers have been denied visas when applying from their home country. An American, whose application for a visa to Libya was rejected in both the Libyan embassies in Washington and London, got a visa for one year through a Libyan embassy in the Middle East. A Korean, who could not acquire a visa into Pakistan in Korea, tried the Pakistani embassy in Singapore and was successful. Embassy staff are often trained to reject people from the country in which they work but assume that if you are already abroad, you must have money, and they are therefore sometimes more lenient.

Sometimes you need to take a job with an international or local firm just to make a beachhead among the people you are seeking to reach. That is fine, but strive to give yourself nine to eighteen months of language learning in a nearby country before taking on such a job. Once you begin work, expanding your language is hard. Overseas contracts tend to last one to two years. After that, a person must renew or find another job.

Though working with an NGO or development agency is a great way to reach out to people. NGO jobs tend to be limited in time because the work is tied to government grants and specific projects. In addition, national organizations want expatriates to equip their own people so that they can take over as soon as possible. This results in international jobs and careers evolving unpredictably and requiring ongoing changes. So sooner or later, you may wish to start your own business. But NGO's have proven very effective in reaching people for Jesus.

In many Middle East countries, your workplace may be full of other expatriate experts, and your home may also be isolated from people you wish to live and work among for God's glory. Finding a good fit is difficult, so networking is indispensable. Again, ask many questions. These factors are reasons for starting and owning a business.

Education, training, experience, and local contacts account for the way most people choose their jobs overseas or the businesses they start. However, none of these are as important as having the drive to do something that inspires you enough to want to get up in the morning and do it. If you are sure God is in it and others agree that the idea is worth pursuing, the tips in the following chapters will assist you in investigating the idea more thoroughly. Clearly grasp that this is not an easy or wide path. Although gaining the knowledge, experience, and contacts you need may take six months or more, it is well worth the time. If you follow through on learning all you can about the business, there is a good chance you will have the perseverance that is necessary to make a difference for Jesus among the unreached.

DISCUSSION QUESTIONS

1. Explain the value of having coaches and mentors.
2. In starting out, should you look for the cheapest coaches? Defend your answer.
3. What are three questions you want to ask any coach before you ask them to work with you?
4. What is the value of having a "life plan"?
5. Are you an entrepreneur? How many of the ten characteristics of an entrepreneur do you believe you have?
6. List the factors that favor starting your own business. How many apply to your current situation?

"The illiterate of the 21st century will not be those who cannot read and write, but those who cannot learn, unlearn, and relearn."
—ALAN TOFFLER

"Hand outs do not give dignity—jobs do."
—MATS TUNEHAG

"God doesn't call the qualified, He qualifies the called."
—HENRY BLACKABY

"Whether you think you can or whether you think you can't, you're right!"
—HENRY FORD

"We work to become, not to acquire."
—ELBERT HUBBARD

"Always do right. This will gratify some people and astonish the rest."
—MARK TWAIN

"There is no faith without risk; no grace without cost; no love without pain."
—PETER LORD

"A B4Ter . . . grabs all the fragments and pieces of their life and work, brings them together, and aims that straight at God."

—*A B4TER*

Chapter 5

DESIGNING YOUR TENT

"Your job is to make something happen."[43]

Remember waking up before dawn to jump into the lake at summer camp? The hardest part was the moment right before you jumped, when you knew the water would be freezing cold, but you didn't yet trust that your body would acclimatize. For would-be entrepreneurs who want to follow their passion but haven't made the leap, the fears about starting a new business can feel just like staring at that frigid, early morning water. Dawson Trotman, founder of the Navigators, hit the nail on the head when he said, *"The greatest amount of wasted time is the time not getting started."*

As you design a business, remember the old saying, *"The devil is in the details."* When we are designing something new, we begin by seeing the big picture, yet it is in getting the details right that the overall effect becomes convincing, viable, and God-honoring. Given the vast differences in geography, cultures, and economies of the countries and people groups within the 10/40 Window, it should come as no surprise that there isn't just one typical strategy for doing B4T. There are hundreds of models within the OPEN Network; some are succeeding and others are failing. Few of these businesses have been in operation more than ten years. But in our study and interaction with these various models we have discovered some fairly common factors that, if applied correctly, may help make your B4T experience a success.

Gathering ideas for a job or developing a business begins with you. Who are you? What has God designed you to do? Ask yourself: *Do I have the ability to convert an idea into something tangible? Do I have a track record of visualizing an idea and then bringing it to life?*

Starting a business is not the exclusive domain of entrepreneurs—managers and technicians have successfully started B4T businesses too. However, whatever type of worker you are, you need to recruit to your

---

43   Seth Godin, *Seth's Blog,* http://sethgodin.typepad.com/seths_blog/.

weaknesses. It is important to know yourself and recruit those who can do the things you cannot in order to help the business and ministry succeed.

Entrepreneurs find idea generation and implementation relatively easy. Most often, their weakness is following through and developing systems for efficiency. When starting out, ensure that you have coaches, a mentor, and team members who will bring the skills, perspective, and balance you need to your plans.

Think!—Be a Learner

Be a learner. Ask questions. Ask everyone questions. As you begin your new job or start a business, leave no rock unturned in seeking information. Don't begin with what you can do or what you can make, begin with what you can sell. If are starting a business and you don't know how to sell something, then hire or recruit someone to join you who can.

An OPEN worker writes:

> The first thing we often ask ourselves when starting a business is, "What can the locals produce?" Later, often after the production has begun, we ask the question, "Who will buy this stuff?" We think about production first, the consumer second. This is backwards and often the reason that we cannot sell what we make to anyone other than our friends who buy our goods as charity.

A seasoned businessperson never stops asking questions and never stops listening for answers. Whatever comes your way, you need to evaluate it and ask, *"What could I do with that? Is this an opportunity God has given me?"* Planning must be based on inquiry. Questions can keep a business alive. You must have your eyes open all the time. Take copious notes. Learn to listen. Opportunity sometimes knocks very softly.

Many B4Ters have found out too late that nobody wants to buy hand-quilted Christmas stockings at $24.99, and no buyer will even look twice at low quality goods. You need to be committed to creating top quality goods and services, delivering them on time, and selling to reputable buyers.

The marketplace will not react sympathetically to missionary products; the B4Ter must make products and offer services that fit the market.

In testing a product's ability to sell, do not test-market it among churches or friends. Of course they will buy your junk—they want to encourage you and help the ministry. But this is not reality. You need to test the quality and sale-ability of your product in the real world. Be open to criticism. Critics should be your close friends when starting out.

Never stop learning. Phil Parshall, a close friend and former mentor, has written eight books on evangelism and church planting among Muslims. One day I was at his center in a Muslim area talking with Muslims. After one exasperating discussion with a Muslim evangelist, Phil exclaimed, *"I love talking to that guy! I learn so much from him."* No matter what our age or experience, we need to always be learning. Solomon clarifies, *"To learn, you must love discipline; it is stupid to hate correction."*[44] When people rebuke or correct us, learn from it.

Start Small

"Start small and grow big. Start big and go broke."—Malcolm S. Forbes[45]

In the beginning think small. Figure out how to achieve your goals on a tiny budget—then cut that number in half. Cash disappears much more rapidly than you'd expect. It really will cost twice as much and take twice as long as you think. From day one, strive to be lean and mean. No fancy offices. Buy only the office equipment you need. No fancy, full-color business cards. Your goal is to stay alive until you can nail your secret formula for success. If you run out of cash, you have run out of gas—meaning you aren't going anywhere.

Ed started his IT business in Malaysia, guided by businessmen in the West. Since these friends were funding him and because he didn't know the market, he started big. He bought equipment he never used and created services that never sold. After three years he was almost bankrupt. But God rescued Ed and his business in a surprising way. With an influx of cash? No. A huge new client? No. He burnt Ed's office down. With the insurance money Ed was able to start over. The second time around Ed started small, purchasing only the equipment he knew he needed. Within five years he had thirty-three employees and his business was a success.

There are many great stories of how big businesses started small but grew to become giants because the founder never stopped learning. William Wrigley's company started out selling soap. As an extra incentive for merchants to carry their soap, they offered stores free baking powder with every purchase. When baking powder proved to be more popular than soap, they stopped making soap and started selling baking powder.

---

[44]   Proverbs 12:1 (NLT)

[45]   http://www.forbes.com/global/2005/0523/080.html.

Then Wrigley got the idea to offer merchants free chewing gum with each can of baking powder. The rest, as they say, is history.

While there is a handful of B4T workers who began big and made it, there is also a handful who started big and failed. Most of the largest B4T companies around today, including forty five of the top fifty, started with less than a $40,000 investment and a handful of employees.

Having said that, there are times where it is impossible to start small. One worker writes, *"Several people have suggested a small start. The problem is that the government will not give us accreditation if we start too small."* Ultimately, you want your business to make an impact on the community. Size matters, but you should not be *too small* at the start, lest no one take you seriously; nor should you be *too big*, lest you use up all your capital too quickly. Again, the key is to know what you can and cannot do, but as a rule, start as small as you can. It is easier to grow, adding new employees and space, than to cut employees and downsize.

Grace Is Sufficient

It is not a sin to fail. For most of us, we learn the more from our failures than our successes. So do not be afraid to fail. As I tell my employees, *"Get out there and fail! The faster you fail, the faster you learn; the faster you learn, the faster we'll succeed."*

The workplace is a school of life, given by God. We need to fail forward. Take a proactive approach—lead. One B4Ter succinctly states, "This is your business. If you don't do it, it isn't going to get done." Read everything you can about your profession, your industry, and your products and services. Find out what other companies similar to yours are doing to get business. Buy and use your competitor's products. Meet with people who have special skills and talents and share information with them. Keeping your mind fine-tuned sharpens your edge and helps you eliminate future mistakes. But in the end, remember: it is better to make a mistake than to take no action at all. Every mistake provides you with valuable information to make a better choice for your next move. As Irish playwright George Bernard Shaw said, *"A life spent making mistakes is more useful than a life spent doing nothing."*

Be Creative

"Imagination is more important than knowledge."—Albert Einstein

An important biblical principle that is germane to B4T is the understanding that man has been made in the image of a very creative God. Though this image has been defaced and horribly corrupted by sin, it is yet an integral part of who we are. Because our Maker is the Creator of all things, being in His image we engender creativity in our work. For this reason we enjoy being creative—making new things and starting new ventures. Like our heavenly Father, we find meaning in creating new things.

As B4Ters, part of the job is to create productivity; often this involves inventing new things, bringing new ideas to life. You have the time. You have the skill. It is an essential first step in achieving success to accept responsibility and finish what needs to be done. Some people may believe that they don't have the talent, the skill, or the guts to create and implement the innovations needed to do B4T. Yet one thing that every successful innovator has in common is the will to get things done. If you want to succeed, you probably will. If you don't believe you can do it, you probably cannot.

Several times a year I pick up a car magazine, read a random person's blog, or browse a copy of Better Homes and Gardens. I drop in on a hunter's convention, IT show, or trade fairs outside of my normal interests. I do this to pick up creative thoughts and new ideas that I may be able to rework in order to fit my context and customers. Be learning, and do it in new environments. Miles Laboratory first exploited this after developing a chewable vitamin. Initially the market for vitamins was small and stagnant until the idea for Flintstones vitamins came along. Chewing on Wilma and Dino is not a gimmick as far as kids are concerned—it's the only reason to take a vitamin!

If imagination is the master of great strategy, implementation is its servant. First dream and then ask, *"How can we reach our dream?"* Henry Ford first imagined a car everyone could afford. Then he designed the assembly line, cutting the price in half as the means to accomplish his dream. When it comes to creating value, imagination wins out over forecasting and prediction.

"But be doers of the word, and not hearers only, deceiving yourselves." —James 1:22

It is not how many ideas you have, it's how many ideas you make happen. I have met many B4Ters who had a good idea—several have even built award-winning products—but they did not have the focus and perseverance to bring their good idea to bear fruit. When gathering information determine which way the future of your local market is moving and then go in that direction. As you move ahead, don't listen to the naysayers. For fourteen months my team told me not to purchase the suite next door to our office, which would have expanded our business. But with the encouragement of a word from the Master, and without anyone's permission, I purchased it. The result was many years of steady income.

Be alert to unexpected successes and put your emphasis there. Often your first idea is not your best idea. As doors open, be flexible to pursue new opportunities. The job we do—the ideal of reaching others with the gospel and of genuinely loving people—does not change. But some business principles and BAM strategies *will* change from place to place— different cultures and different environments often require a completely different approach. Zinzendorf rightly noted that, *"our economic systems cannot maintain the same course for more than a generation . . . They must be capable of being poured into as many different molds as it pleases the Savior for eons on end."*[46] Each of us must always be learning, always be making mistakes, and always be adjusting our approach to find the best fit.

Risk Equals Faith

"God works as long as His people live daringly. He ceases to work when they no longer need His aid."—A. W. Tozer[47]

Jesus regularly asked people to do difficult things. To the paralytic He said, *"Pick up your bed and go."*[48] To Peter He said, *"Drop your nets and follow Me."*[49] He tells us to love our enemies, go the second mile, lose our lives, and pick up our cross daily and follow Him. His love is not a wimpy love. His faith was not for the faint at heart. His faith is a hard-nosed, risk-filled, dangerous (in a worldly view) kind of faith.

Mark Twain put it this way: *"Why not go out on a limb? That's where the fruit is."* Twain is also known to have said, *"A life without risk is not a life worth living."* For a believer, the same can obviously be said about faith, for we know that *"without faith, it is impossible to please God."*[50] As a traditional missionary, I was told I had the gift of faith. Yet as a businessman, no one has ever said to me that I have the gift of risk. But, may I ask, what is the difference? The missionary must trust God to supply the funds for his support to feed his family. Likewise, the businessman

[46] William J. Danker, *Profit for the Lord: Economic Activities in Moravian Missions and the Basel Mission Trading Company* (Grand Rapids, MI: William B. Eerdmans, 1971), 21.

[47] http://business4transformation.blogspot.com/2014_06_01_archive.html

[48] Matthew 9:6

[49] Mark 1:18

[50] Hebrews 11:6

must trust God to cut the deal and make a profit so as to feed his family. Both require trust. Both depend on God. But in church we call it faith, and in the secular world we call it risk. <u>Faith, simply put, is risk ordained by God.</u> God wants us to live by faith as it makes us more dependent upon Himself. Nonetheless, we are usually trying to make our lives secure and safe. But when we are safe and secure, we often neglect or forget God. Thus, He is constantly trying to tear down our worldly securities to cause us to rely more upon Himself. Risk/faith is good because it causes us to be more dependent upon Him.

I have studied the concepts of risk and faith for several years, coming to the conclusion that, as a Christian doing business, risk and faith are the same thing. I conclude this in that everything I do must be done in faith. Paul clarifies, *"Whatever you do, work heartily, as for the Lord and not for men"*[51] and *"whatever does not proceed from faith is sin."*[52] So whatever we do, we do unto the Master and not ourselves. And if we do anything, including taking necessary risks in our life or work, we are doing that with God by faith. When we hesitate to "risk it," we are also hesitating to step out in faith. Now I am not advocating that we do foolish things, but when you have written a solid business plan and have experienced B4Ters and coaches check off on the plan—*move forward!*

We had just purchased our office unit for our business. The team gathered together in the shell of the building to pray and bless the building, committing it to Jesus' purposes. While we were praying I was hit with a sudden panic. My mind raced, *"What have I done! How is this all going to work? What kind of idiot am I? Lord, help!"* While others were still praying and I was struggling with this panic attack, the Lord brought to mind a similar situation twelve years earlier. I was sitting in a rocking chair in the hospital, rocking my one-day-old son. At that time my mind raced, *"What have I done! How is this all going to work? How am I going to raise, feed, and educate this precious child! Lord, help!"* He reminded me then that this is His child, and if I steward his life to the best of my ability, God will bless my son to His glory. He reminded me that this too is His business, and if I steward the company to the best of my ability, He will also bless it to His glory.

When each Israelite took that first step onto the seabed of the Red Sea, I am sure many had a few fears. They were literally entering new grounds. But they heeded the word of God and stuck with one another.

---

[51] Colossians 3:23 (ESV)

[52] Romans 14:23

God protected and provided for them. For the Israelites, and for us, faith and risk are one in the same. A big part of being a B4Ter is learning when to take risks and when to play it safe. When those times of panic hit, there are two things to do: one, draw close to God and remember His promises to you. And two, find brothers and sisters whom you can share your fears with so that they can encourage and minister to you. Having the perspective of God and godly people helps bring us back to reality.

In Jesus' parable of the talents the servant whom Jesus deemed as "wicked and slothful" replied, "I was afraid, and I went and hid your talent in the ground."[53] Seth Godin nails it when he says, "The harder you try to play it safe, the more likely you are to fail."[54] Most Christians would agree that stepping out in faith is a good thing. May I argue that for the B4Ter, stepping out in calculated risk is also a good thing? Taking wise risks builds faith, and as mentioned, faith pleases God.

As you begin taking risks, as with business, start small. Jesus says, "Whoever can be trusted with very little can also be trusted with much, and whoever is dishonest with very little will also be dishonest with much. So if you have not been trustworthy in handling worldly wealth, who will trust you with true riches?"[55] Do not step out and risk a million dollars when you have not learned to trust Him for one hundred dollars. As with learning any new skill, seek opportunities to develop your talent in taking risks. An essential step in the process of learning to take larger steps of risk requires us to incorporate a medley of spiritual, intellectual, emotional, physical, and financial risks. These many new experiences build us up toward maturity in Christ, as well as in our sacrifice and service to Him.

"Unless there is an element of risk in our exploits for God, there is no need for faith."—Hudson Taylor[56]

Failure

I have been lost on more than one occasion in the woods. In those situations, given the choice between someone who says, *"I'll tell you the way,"* versus someone who says, *"I'll go with you,"* I will always choose the latter. It is always best to travel with someone who knows the way. Jesus said, *"I am the Way."*[57] Take note that He did not say He was the

---

53 Matthew 25:25

54 Seth Godin, *How to Make a Purple Cow* (Google ebook: Penguin, 2004).

55 Luke 16:10, 11

56 http://sermonquotes.com/post/40179656415/element-risk-god-faith-hudson-taylor.

57 John 14:6

destination or the goal. Life in Christ is a journey. Sometimes we freeze up because we fear making a mistake. At such times we need to remind ourselves of the journey, and if we don't get lost once in a while, we are not really exploring.

People are too afraid of failure. Yet if you stop and think about it, the majority of us would agree that our most important learning experiences often are the result of failure. One of the reasons mature people stop growing and learning is because they become less and less willing to risk failure. If you are not making any mistakes, you are not risking enough. Much of what we call experience or wisdom was learned from our failures. Most successes are built on a foundation of failures. But when we fail, we feel weak. Nobody likes to feel weak. Yet Paul points out, *"For when I am weak, I am strong."*[58]

The Chinese have a word *kiasu*, which means "afraid of losing." This refers to a person who is afraid to move; even after completing the plan and having all the resources in place, he is ever worried that it is too dangerous to move forward. The B4T leader must face the uncertainty that arises, fully aware that, as a pioneer, there is often no previous model to learn from or depend on. There is an element of uncertainty and potential loss that could create fear, causing us to hesitate and not act.

Think of Moses at the burning bush, Joshua being anointed to be leader, Gideon in the winepress, Elijah fleeing Jezebel, and Peter before the cock crows. Need I go on? God keeps us weak so that His strength can flow through us, enabling Him to receive all the glory. As leaders, we need to adequately prepare, listen to God, and then, in faith, boldly execute the plan. Such boldness is not to be equated with recklessness, but rather is a matter of confidence and risk taking determined by God's leading and adequate planning. When God has spoken and all the planning has been done, it is time to act.

Thomas Edison explains, *"I have not failed. I have just found 10,000 ways that don't work."* The most successful B4Ters do two things differently than other people: First, they are more willing to take risks and, therefore, fail more often. Second, they use their failures as a source of motivation and feedback on how to do things better. Society teaches us that failure is something to avoid at all costs. Fear of failure causes us to be tentative or inactive. Don't become stuck on a failure. The toughest problems teach the best lessons. Learn from each failure. What you learn informs your next action.

---

[58] 2 Corinthians 12:10

Bouncing Back

Perseverance is an essential trait of a disciple of Jesus. Some of the most successful businesses in the world only came into being after a few serious failures. From a prototype that doesn't work to a service that doesn't sell, your first business can quickly turn into a first failure. But as an entrepreneur you can bounce back into the fray and start again. Business failure is part of the B4T learning process. The brightest minds allow themselves to make mistakes, learn from them, and start again. Getting past that "once bitten, twice shy" mentality is a big challenge, but essential for second-time entrepreneurs.

If there is no risk *in* a business, then the chances are there is no risk *of* business. A business plan needs to be developed with a full description of potential customers and competition. B4Ters may enter a town and see vast potential for business when in reality they are only seeing business done differently, or their own demands not being met. Just because you cannot find a barber and everyone has long hair—i.e., there is no competition and many clients—does not mean you should set up a barbershop in a Sikh community!

Galatians 6:1 says, *"But watch yourselves, or you also may be tempted."* We need to seek wisdom and have many counselors; we need to know ourselves. We need to understand our personal risk-taking style. As you move through the necessary steps of preparation, give yourself permission and space to proceed forward at the pace you are comfortable—but keep moving forward!

Despite their image, entrepreneurs are not the daredevils of the business community. Nor do entrepreneurs focus much on risk, wealth, power, or failure. If you do not like risk, are terrified at the prospect of becoming an entrepreneur, or believe starting a business is the path to fame and fortune, you are probably not going to be a successful creator of businesses.

Richard Branson, the British billionaire who started Virgin Records, Virgin Atlantic Airlines, and several other businesses, says, *"Paradoxically, entrepreneurs with the greatest appetite for risk also have a healthy respect for it. In everything I do, I examine the downside, the danger, and what can go wrong."*[59] Branson bought just one plane when he started his airline, and he had an agreement with Boeing to take it back if things did not work out. Understand that shrewd entrepreneurs attempt to place risk

---

[59] Brian O'Reilly, "What It Takes to Start a Start Up," *Fortune*, June 7, 1999, 140.

on others while maintaining their freedom to lead and make decisions for the business. Jesus put it this way, *"Be wise as serpents and innocent as doves."*[60] Never buy what you can lease. Never lease what you can rent. Never rent what you can borrow. Good entrepreneurs reduce risk while increasing faith.

The bottom line is that you want to minimize the risks you, your employees, and your customers are exposed to. You also should limit the impact that an unexpected occurrence can have on your business.

Trust God

One OPEN worker said, *"Begin every day, every project, everything with prayer."* God is the CEO of our business, but it is all too easy to leave Him out of our day-to-day activities until we need Him for some big problem. Our business and our faith need to be integrated, lived out, and modeled daily for all to see.

We had been struggling with our two businesses for nearly three years. Even so, I felt from day one that we should expand beyond what our current facility would allow. However, the team was adamantly against expansion. One day as I was driving home the Lord gave me a distinct word to buy the unit next door to ours and expand. Without asking anyone's permission, I did. Although that created some problems with the team, come the end of year, the business we expanded made more money than ever before while our main business, in which most of the team worked and got their visas, lost a lot of money. However, the surplus of the one bailed out the other allowing everyone to remain in the country.

Trust God in the midst of your daily routine. We know and agree He is there, so involve Him in practical ways.

Make the Journey Fun

The more fun a person has, the more she will learn and the better she will perform. Treat each discovery like a present: unwrap it and see what surprises it has in store. Fun is success undefined, so enjoy the journey. Continually redefine what you consider to be success.

Faith is innovative. The house was full, a crowd blocked the door, but faith found a way of getting in. If we cannot get sinners to where Jesus is by ordinary methods, we must use extraordinary ones. If the door is

---

[60] Matthew 10:16

closed, go through the window. If the window is also closed, go through the roof. And if that is to the discomfort of some believers, then so be it; the salvation of the lost is a greater priority. Sharing the gospel on any level, among any people, involves risk. We must never mind running some risks for the sake of the gospel. Bold action is necessary if the lost are going to be found.

The world is constantly reinventing itself. Creativity serves all the purposes and desires of the human race. Faith, too, should be innovative, reaching some by unusual means—including the unreached that live behind closed doors. As Charles Spurgeon puts it,

> Through door, through window, or through roof, let us break through all impediments [and] labor to bring poor souls to Jesus. All means are good and decorous when faith and love are truly set on winning souls. If hunger for bread can break through stone walls, surely hunger for souls is not to be hindered in its efforts.[61]

Have you ever wondered what the boundaries are for Christ in you? Historically, great people of the Bible have been uninhibited risk takers. They enjoyed God. They loved His assignment for their lives. They were not afraid to break the barriers of customs and culture. They dove into life headfirst. Let the herd graze where it will. But for you, put a little Tabasco sauce on your "Kentucky Fried Duck" and step out in faith, or rather, *risk it.*

"If we are not living scared, we are not walking by faith. Faith includes risk."—George Verwer[62]

---

[61] C. H. Spurgeon, *Morning by Morning* (Peabody: Hendrickson Publishers, 2006).

[62] https://plaiblog.wordpress.com/category/success/page/2/.

DISCUSSION QUESTIONS

1. Do I have the ability to convert an idea into something tangible? What evidence can you give to back your answer?
2. What are your weaknesses that you need to recruit team members or coaches to help with?
3. Why should you *not* be afraid of failure or making mistakes?

"Everyone then who hears these words of mine and does them will be like a wise man who built his house upon the rock; and the rain fell, and the floods came, and the winds blew and beat upon that house, but it did not fall, because it had been founded on the rock. And everyone who hears these words of mine and does not do them will be like a foolish man who built his house upon the sand; and the rain fell, and the floods came, and the winds blew and beat against that house, and it fell; and great was the fall of it."

—JESUS [63]

[63]   Matthew 7:24-27

Chapter 6

LAYING A GOOD FOUNDATION

Jesus said, *"Yet it did not fall, because it had its foundation on the rock."*[64] Foundations matter. We cannot start wrong and expect to finish right. Whether erecting a tent or building a business, we need to remember first to start with a solid foundation.

As your idea takes shape, ensure that the foundation you are laying is sound. Being an entrepreneur usually means not only having a dream, but also wanting it to happen *now*. This sort of over eagerness can lead to skipping steps and laying a weak foundation that may crumble at the first sign of adversity. Do not miss a chance to get the best advice you can from folks who have already established a similar business.

When you think you have learned all there is to learn in your adopted city, go to another nearby town and find a business that is similar to yours. If you are not going to be in competition geographically, the owner will have less to lose by sharing with you. Ask what he has learned. What are the tricks of the trade? Discover ways to shorten your setup process and avoid costly mistakes. Also try to find entrepreneurs who did not make it in your line of business. Why were they unsuccessful? Get a reality check by talking to potential customers. What are they expecting? Can you deliver what they expect better than the competitor down the street?

Often we are asked, *"What is the best business to access lost people so they can be exposed to the gospel?"* The answer is that there isn't one. Never forget the *business* does not communicate the gospel, *people* do. We have seen MBA students with terrific business plans fail while Bible college grads make millions at their business. We have seen seminary students never lead a soul to Jesus while engineering grads plant dozens of churches. As we learned in *Kung Fu Panda*, there is no secret sauce. That is why this book was written: to make it perfectly clear that our Lord rarely works in the same way twice, be it to prosper a business or plant churches among an unreached people group. So as you work to lay a good foundation,

---

[64] Matthew 7:25

emphasize and apply workable principles. My first book, *Tentmaking*, covers the key *ministry* foundations. Here, we are focusing on the most important *business* foundations.

Choosing a Campground (Look on the Fields)

Jesus says, *"I tell you, open your eyes and look at the fields! They are ripe for harvest."*[65] Before choosing where to start your business, you need to first determine who you are marketing your product. Are you specifically selling to the people you are trying to reach or to all of the people in the city or region? Are you constructing a product you plan to export? In the midst of doing your research, your ideas about your target customer may change several times. As you answer each question, do not hesitate to adjust them to fit your God-given situation and assignment. Add explanations and qualifiers under each category as they occur to you; this will document your thought processes and be a reminder of how you got to the final concept.

Your "target customers" are those who are most likely to buy from you. Resist the temptation to be too general in the hopes of getting a larger slice of the market. That is like firing a dozen bullets in random directions instead of aiming just one bullet dead center on the mark. Instead, try to describe your clientele with as many details as you can based on your knowledge of your product or service and the people. Gather anyone you can into visualization exercises to get different perspectives on who may be your customers. The more input the better. Here are five questions to get you started:

1. Gender: Are your target customers male or female? Both?
2. Age: How old do you expect your clients to be? Late twenties? Retired?
3. Location: Do they live in a big city? If so, what kind of neighborhoods do they live in? Or do they live in rural villages? Is geography a limiting factor for any reason? Where do they regularly travel? By what mode of transportation?
4. Income: How much money do the people generally earn? And what are their spending habits? Is your business supplying a basic need or something that requires having

---

[65] John 4:35

disposable income?

5.   Occupation: What do people do for a living? Does their lifestyle fit within your marketing scheme?

Beware of manufacturing carpets, trinkets, or souvenirs with the goal of selling primarily to churches and friends back home. This is a limited market; it is building a foundation on sand. Usually such businesses start off well. However, after two or three years, though churches and friends may buy from you, they will not market your idea/product to others. They see buying from you as charity. Initially you may create enough sales, but this is a very limited market that will soon dry up. Then, after a strong start, those you have employed will not have any work. You will have built up their expectations and trust in you, but now you cannot pay them. They will get bitter with you and your Jesus if they find you cannot sustain their jobs, thus making you seem unreliable.

Location, Location, Location

Finding a location that is suitable for your business and people group can be challenging. Securing your first commercial real estate lease can be downright scary. Here are eight tips to consider in picking a location:

1.   Evaluate the space you need. Do you plan to grow your office? Your lease term will likely be for several years, so make sure you have enough space for the duration of the lease.

2.   Do a study of hte traffic patterns. Is the location easily accessible? Is public transportation available? Is there ample parking? Is there visibility to the street so customers can find you easily?

3.   View a lot of properties. Do not make a decision after just one or two sites. Make sure you are comfortable with the price in comparison with similar spaces before making your final decision.

4.   Ask for concessions from the landlord. Depending on the strength of the market, you can ask for things like a few months of free rent or a "tenant improvement allowance," which is basically compensation for the dollars you agree to put in to improve the place. This is generally easier to get if there are a lot of locations available to rent.

5.   Look for hidden expenses in the agreement. Charges above

your fixed or base rent, like operating expenses and service charges, can surprise novices. They may not be in the term sheet, so ask specifically for this information.

6. Do not choose a space based solely on the landlord's word. One OPEN worker found the perfect location at an excellent price. The only drawback was that in order to enter the land, they had to drive ten meters across someone else's property. The landlord insisted, *"It's no problem; I have been doing it for years."* But the worker checked, only to learn the owner of the property was planning to expand his building, which would eliminate his access. No wonder the price was so good! Get everything in writing.

7. Do not review documents on your own, especially if you are new to the language. Have your lawyer review the lease.

8. Are market shifts or demographic shifts occurring? Is the area growing?

When picking a site to locate your business, consider the nature of your product or service. Understand culturally appropriate negotiating techniques. Consider having a trusted local insider scout out some possible locations and get initial prices before letting the landlord know a foreigner will be renting the property. Clarify who is responsible for repairs and maintenance.

You must pick the site that offers the best possibilities of being profitable. Sometimes it is better to pay a higher rent in order to have access to great traffic flow, street visibility, and parking. Consider McDonald's— they will always try for the best location with the best footfall to have the best chance of making a profit.

Rent or Buy?

When it comes to determining whether it is best for you to rent or buy your business's property, *do your homework*. There are several factors to take into consideration. The first is your cash situation. If making the down payment consumes cash needed to expand your young business, buying now may be unwise. Also consider that you will need to have reserve funds or credit for unexpected repairs. These can be large expenses in the case of air conditioning systems, roofs, foundations, etc. Carefully examine the tax consequences of becoming the landlord. Most are positive, but it varies from country to country. Do not expect the laws in your home country to resemble in any way the laws in your adopted country. In many places, if you purchase the property in your own name, the business can pay rent back to you, which generates income without incurring double taxation.

Another thing to look at is your business's future. How much space are you going to need five years from now? If your business is growing quickly, owning your own space is probably not a good idea. If you are going to buy a building and occupy it all by yourself you are losing money on the empty space. In such cases it is better to rent space to tenants giving you more flexibility, as you may be able to take over their areas as the business grows. Finally, consider your exit strategy. Try to pick a building that fits with the rest of the properties in your area, so when the time comes to move, you will have less trouble selling it. Remember that real estate is not a liquid assest. It can take months or years to sell the property. If your business strategy calls for you to someday be on the other side of town, it can slow you down.

If you purchase, you need to figure out how much you would pay on the mortgage versus how much you would pay in rent. In addition, calculate the effects of appreciation, amortization, taxes, and repairs. When you calculate the rate of return, there is no guarantee you will like being a landlord instead of a tenant. But owning your own place can be a good way to lock up a desirable location, avoid future rent hikes, and get a good grip on controlling your own future—all while making a potentially profitable investment.

Generally, if you have the opportunity to either rent or buy, it is better to buy. Owning your property offers many benefits. With each mortgage payment, you will build equity in the property instead of just lining the landlord's pockets. That equity may be enhanced if the property value appreciates. And as the landlord, you control the space, enabling you and not someone else to determine the design of both the inside and outside of the building. When you own you also control costs, since you decide on financing and maintenance and upgrade schedules.

Do not preselect a specific location. Shop various locations to discover what support and practical help the local government or other businesses may offer. You must aim to be the best at what you do. Only the best can maintain market share and financial stability. There may be a small niche market for the second best, but the business will not flourish—and in business there is no third place. When you are buying a property—as with everything, ask good questions, ask lots of questions, listen carefully, and take good notes.

Renting on the other hand is wise on two accounts: First, if you are strapped for cash, it is better to rent. You need to ensure you have enough cash to last the hard, initial start-up years. If you blow most of your reserve cash on a property down payment, you may not be in business after one year. Second, if your people or government or adopted city are unstable, or have a hatred for your homeland, it may be wiser to rent. More than one B4T worker has purchased land for their business, only to lose it when the government threw them out—because of their nationality, not their outreach activities.

When you rent, you should pay for what you see, not what you envision the building becoming. When negotiating with an experienced landlord, be sure to read the small print. As with everything you do, be sure to involve your lawyer whether you are buying or renting.

Work for Others or Self?

Should you start your own business or work for someone else? This is a common question, and obviously there are pros and cons to each answer. If you own your own business, then you control your own time. If you work for somebody else, then you are locked into working the hours your boss dictates. If you own your business, you are responsible for everything and have no guaranteed salary. If you work for somebody else, you only have to focus on your job, plus you have a set income. So what are the pros to each?

Advantages for owning your own business:

1. Freedom to try new ideas. You can innovate and be creative.
2. Satisfaction of creating a business and providing jobs for people (remember, these people are then your dependents, counting on you to make the business succeed so they can feed their own families).
3. Independence (but for at least the first two years you will feel like a slave to the business).
4. Flexibility. You set your own work hours, you can choose the location of your business, and you pick the people you work with.
5. Challenge yourself and your walk with God. Like having a child, starting a business teaches you many new things about yourself and God.
6. You set the vision and core values that establish the corporate culture, ideally creating an environment founded upon kingdom values.

Advantages for working for someone else:

1. It is free training. You learn how to work and operate a business at no cost. You can learn from your mistakes at someone else's expense.
2. You can discover if business is the right approach for you.
3. While you are learning how to operate a business, you can also be saving for when you start your own business.
4. Networking, while working for someone else, you can build your own business network.
5. Not being the boss is a lot less stressful than having to make many decisions every day.
6. It's a safe income.

When I weigh the pros and cons, it comes down to the individual. As a coach, I try to work with each person to determine how God is both leading and gifting them, so as to determine what is the best choice for them. Michael Gerber has written a very helpful book, *The E-myth Revisited: Why Most Small Businesses Don't Work and What to Do about It.* Gerber describes three types of workers in business: entrepreneurs, managers, and technicians. To simplify, entrepreneurs start businesses, managers run or manage businesses, and technicians are the skilled workers who do the technical work of the business. As Gerber points out, most of us fall into one of those three categories, and if you are an entrepreneur, you are naturally going to want to start a business. Gerber states that most people are managers or technicians, and that there are few true entrepreneurs.[66]

If you are a manager or a technician, get a mentor who is an entrepreneur to work with you. Why must non-entrepreneurs have a mentor who *is* an entrepreneur? I recall this story from my days in business school: Mozart was once approached by a young man who was interested in Mozart's advice on how to compose a symphony. Since he was still very young, Mozart recommended that the young man start by composing ballads. Surprised, the young man responded, *"But you wrote symphonies when you were only ten years old."* *"But I didn't have to ask how,"* countered Mozart. If you do not know how to start a business, you need a mentor who does.

---

[66] Michael Gerber, *The E-Myth Revisited: Why Most Small Businesses Don't Work And What To Do About It* (HarperCollins; Upd Sub edition, October 14, 2004).

Joe an OPEN worker writes,

I started my first business in 1993, after spending fifteen years learning the language and being an employee of four different companies working in the region. Being a model to your MBB community is a noble goal. But to open a successful business in a new country, you have to overcome several major obstacles:

1. *You must have excellent language and a solid understanding of the culture.*
2. *Accept that all your competitors will have a relative or close friend working for the government who are giving them under-the-table help.*
3. *Startups require a ton of work, adding major stress to your family life.*

Jonathan adds,

My recommendations to young workers who want to run a B4T business are:

1. *Obtain the language and culture well.*
2. *Seek employment in a national firm for a few years.*
3. *Find an almost-bankrupt business and buy it. This saves you much time and money since it already has a license and place of business. Or, if that is not an option, find a national you trust and offer to give him a share of the business. You will be the GM and he will receive 5+% of all the income depending on what services he is willing to do. Lease all assets from an offshore company until fully capitalized. The national business partner should know how to navigate the tax system and fire employees without going to court.*

Bob says,

How often have you heard an entrepreneur or a want-to-be entrepreneur say they want to run their own business? It is almost as if they are starting with the end point and working backwards. They want to run a business and so they look for an idea. Sometimes they are clever enough to at least look for a real problem to solve, but not always. Instead of focusing on what you want to be or what you want to achieve, think about what it is that someone else truly needs. You and your ego should be beside the point.

Whatever you decide, whether to work for others or yourself, be sure you are following God's leading.

Work for a Local Company or the West?

Mainly four entities provide work to Westerners overseas:

1. International or local corporations.
2. Indigenous national institutions like colleges, universities, and government agencies.
3. Relief and development agencies.
4. New start-up businesses.

These are the arenas in which to look for jobs. But keep in mind the Four Steps and Eleven Building Blocks, which will be discussed in Chapter 12. If the business does not engage the people the Master is assigning you to reach or meet all of the eleven building blocks, you may wish to keep looking for a more suitable job.

Within these four arenas, there are essentially two overseas job markets: expatriate and local.

The expatriate market pays Western wages in order to obtain qualified Western expertise, and job openings are advertised publicly. This arena is mainly the domain of international corporations. These companies often hire their Western workers in the home office and move them overseas. But if someone has the skills they need and are willing to work for a local salary, these firms usually prefer to hire them rather than a local.

The "local hire" expatriate market consists of local corporations, small-to medium-sized enterprises (SMEs)/businesses and indigenous institutions that are open to hiring Westerners who are willing to work for local wages. Jobs in this market are not generally listed but are discovered by networking or making a personal visit. I have met numerous individuals who had difficulty landing a job from their home country, only to find job offers abound once they arrived in their adopted country, just because they were there.

Most local companies would rather hire you onsite than when you are back home, as they do not wish to pay your moving costs. Understand that few local companies will pay anything close to Western wages. If you work for a local company at local wages, you need to take care to live at the level of your income. If you live above your level of income, it may harm your credibility. In addition, government officials are watching and can discern the true motives of most foreigners working in their community.

A Filipino English teacher in China was not paid by the university she worked in for five months, so she resigned. The department chairman came to her amazed that she would resign for not being paid her salary, as no other Western teacher had resigned. The department head told her, *"You mean you are really here to earn a salary? All of the other English teachers in China are missionaries and receive income from their friends back home!"* Government officials are not dumb. They often turn a blind eye because they value the service and quality of work we bring to our jobs. If we think we are fooling them, we are really fooling ourselves. The point is, live at the level of your known salary.

Many companies and institutions want to hire Westerners since it gives them prestige and helps them to land overseas business. However, few can afford to pay Western salaries. So when Westerners are willing to work for less, they hire them. Why do Westerners work for less? Locals assume it is for one of four reasons:

1. They desire to explore and travel. These people rarely stay longer than a year unless they marry a local.
2. They are a government agent or working for the CIA. During the years my visa was supplied by a platform (a cover business), one Indonesian asked me, *"Are you with the CIA?"* Surprised, I asked, *"Why would you think that?"* He replied, *"Well normally the only ones who learn our language and have money to travel like you do work for the CIA."*
3. They are running away. There is something in their past that they are trying to hide or forget.
4. It is for religious motivation. They are here to convert people.

Dean writes,

A person can find numerous jobs that provide adequate income to live in China, though low by western standards. In some situations, however, a person will need supplemental support. In such settings, it is vital to negotiate hard for other forms of compensation like housing, in-country transportation rates, health care, etc. This lowers a person's need for support and enhances credibility. Be sure to live appropriately to your role in the community. Identifying and connecting with the people is one of the great blessings of BAM. When BAMers live beyond the means of their job, they undermine credibility and distance themselves from the people.

The crucial secret to finding a job is to take initiative and doggedly persist at it. No one has your interests more at heart than you do. You can try, but rarely does outsourcing your job search lead to a suitable fit. Since there is no organized, centralized job market, but only a web of needs and personnel, no single firm has knowledge of all the contacts or openings in your field. Many jobs are never advertised, and over 80 percent of job acquisition involves some networking. I recommend that you take two weeks or more to travel to the cities where God is leading you, and personally visit companies to search for jobs. You may also contact NexusB4T for job opportunities in a variety of fields at www. NexusB4T.com

The vast majority of jobs are obtained through some kind of networking. Ultimately, people connect with people, not paper or computer screens. Managers are much more likely to hire someone who has been referred to them than someone who is only a name on a resume. Researching jobs will alert you to companies in which you have contacts. Having no contacts is not a problem; simply make your own. With the interconnectedness of the world today, experts claim that we are at most six handshakes removed from any person we want to meet on the planet. In other words, you know someone who knows someone who knows someone. If you persevere, you can meet any individual on earth.

The first place to start networking is with NexusB4T. NexusB4T is linked with people working in most Muslim, Hindu, and Buddhist countries, as well as experienced coaches who have connections in a wide variety of fields and locations. One new worker headed overseas to his adopted city in search of a job. There were no other foreign BAMers in this city. At the suggestion of a NexusB4T coach, he learned where local officials liked to have lunch and went to that restaurant repeatedly for several days. Finally he got to know one official who became his friend.

He explained to the official his desires to work and the types of work he could do. The official then introduced him to a number of people, resulting in his finding a job.

If you are looking for a job in a larger city, check out the business centers / executive suites offices. These businesses deal with foreigners. It is easy to meet other foreigners there who will have ideas and contacts, plus the local staff is usually well aware of the local business situation and opportunities. This is also helpful when local business or government leaders ask how you learned about them. It is logical that you make connections this way.

Naturally, make use of the Internet. Set aside regular times to surf for job openings. In addition to the NexusB4T, there are several like-minded organizations that will assist in placing B4Ters. You will find that Global Opportunities (GO) can significantly shorten your initial research, because it has researched and organized many job sites already. GO and other helpful agencies are listed in Appendix D.

Do not be shy about contacting the top dogs. Tom and Dan set their sights high as they went to the city of their calling in Asia and met with the CEOs of the three foreign-owned companies. After a day of knocking on doors, they had no bites. In fact, they described their three job interviews as a "fiasco." By God's grace they met one of these CEOs at the train station as they were returning to the capital city. The CEO greeted them and in brief, told them he thought they were clueless about how to interview. To his surprise, they quickly admitted he was right. Because of their honesty, he hired them to do a simple job for him—it was a test of their ability to get things done. They succeeded, and so the CEO started giving them additional business. Today their business is worth ten million dollars, has people working in six different countries, and they have baptized over nine hundred new believers.

Have your resume, and if appropriate, your portfolio in order. Follow up every reply and every meeting with a note of thanks. When you are onsite, see as many people as you can, even if they are not the biggest players in the industry. These people can still provide valuable information and may even be able to refer you to more influential people.

Most contracts with local or foreign-owned firms last one or two years and then have to be renewed. Many jobs are tied to specific projects. Therefore, international workers frequently change jobs. Performing your job with excellence and genuine servanthood will help to make you so valuable that your contract will be renewed. Daniel was the youngest employee in a Middle Eastern oil company's office. He worked hard and excelled at his job. In 2014, when the oil prices began to drop, many of his more experienced expat co-workers were let go, but because of the value he created for the business Daniel retained his job.

In some settings, two-year contracts may be renewed for decades. Yet, because many will have to find new jobs, it is wise to continually be networking and seeking for leads on new job openings in the area where you live.

> I worked for various schools teaching English. Having a Masters in TESOL was very helpful, but still I found it frustrating having to change jobs every two or three years. I would be hired to train the staff and once they were trained my contract would end, then I would be let go to restart the job-hunting cycle.—Karla in Southeast Asia

B4Ters also need to update their skills and knowledge. Many companies tend to pass over people who have been overseas too long, because they fear they are out of touch with current knowledge and technology. Therefore it is important to read widely in one's area of work and find ways to keep updating your skills. Consider using some travel time to take cutting-edge courses in your field, wherever they may be offered.

Sharing Your Tent

If you choose to start your own business, you need to determine the best ownership model for you. Sole proprietorships, partnerships, and limited liability companies—each has its pros and cons. Hire a lawyer or company secretary and discuss the matter with them. Gather advice from other businesspeople, both locals and foreigners.

Start small. When possible, sub-contract anything and everything. Companies that invest as little as possible will be more responsive to a changing marketplace, reducing costs, and providing flexibility, which is helpful for doing ministry while enhancing the business's competitive advantage.

A fuzzy partnership can be disastrous. I have witnessed many B4Ters choose partners circumstantially or for convenience, and then fail miserably. It is essential, whether your partner is a local or a foreigner, a Christian or a Muslim, a team member—whatever—that you hammer out an agreement in the beginning as to how the company will be run and ultimately dissolved. I have witnessed nasty team splits and seen local partners take everything the B4Ter brought into the business. Start with the end in mind. Someday you will return to your home country or retire from the business; plan for that from the outset.

Owning Your Own Business

> I needed to learn as a boss what it takes to make a profit. Before, I always reported to someone and helped them make a profit, for which they paid me a salary. I didn't know how easy I had it, and this is compounded by the fact that I have to consider my model as a Christian in all the personal, legal, and administrative sides of a business enterprise.—An OPEN worker in Southeast Asia

Many B4Ters want to work ten hours a week. They are looking for the business to provide an identity or a cover without really working. The mentality is, *"How can I fool the government and the people into believing I have a job, so that I can do real missionary work?"* Such thinking centers on what we can get away with, rather than how we can serve the people. As slaves of Jesus, we are not to go the half-mile, but the *second* mile. I have had two directors of mission agencies call me and ask, *"Can you help us to start businesses where our people only need to work five to ten hours a week?"* My reply to both was, *"If I could do that, I would be a billionaire!"* Work is not a penalty, but a blessing. Bill puts it this way, *"I love my job! When I am at work I get to be with all these people. It's eight hours of opportunities to be Jesus to my employees—I wouldn't give that up for anything!"*

"We have two objectives with every business we start: first, each business is to clearly contribute to doing church planting, and secondly, each business must be profitable."—Andrew

Every business is all-consuming and labor intensive in the beginning. So, though we are equally committed to transforming the community in Jesus' name, we cannot make this our actual working objective until the business is profitable. As Scott, a NexusB4T coach points out, "At the end of the day, if there is no margin, there is no ministry." If the business is not profitable, you will lose the business, your visa, and the opportunities to reach the community for Jesus. Thus, plan to invest the first one to three years, or as long as it takes, focused on making the business succeed. It is common for the B4T business owner to initially invest fifty to eighty hours a week to build the business up until it has a consistent positive cash flow. At that point, the B4Ter can afford to hire more locals and thus reduce the time working in the business, as well as create opportunities to bring other areas of her life and work into balance.

We need to work to make money until we are profitable. Once we are profitable, then we can emphasize the transformational priority and, if needed, decrease the amount of hours in the job. But as Bill so clearly points out, the work and the ministry are the same thing. We should not need time away from work to do evangelism and discipleship. When we see evangelism and discipleship as separate from the workplace, it indicates that we do not have a clear understanding of how Jesus and Paul did evangelism and discipleship. Jesus and Paul did life together with their disciples. They never sat around in a circle with the Bible open on their laps discussing the Word and how to apply it. Rather they lived life together, discussing and applying the Word while they lived it.

The jobs we work or create need to connect us with the people we are trying to reach. One of the disadvantages of working solo can be a disproportionate amount of time spent seated, whether on the phone or in front of a computer. Business owners must discipline themselves to get out and talk to people. Have someone hold you accountable for how you spend your time each and every day.

Partnership

When starting out, seriously consider having a partner. Generally, start-ups that have two or more cofounders do significantly better than lone entrepreneurs, and the bigger the cofounding team the better.

If you decide to enter into business with an expat friend or teammate, whether you have known one another for twenty years or twenty days, you need to have a partnership agreement. Making a legal partnership agreement is wise, because you are starting a business together and it is simply good business practice to have these agreements in place. If you have any desire to grow the business to a point where you might sell it to somebody else, you want to make sure that the partnership arrangements are spelled out from the beginning. Otherwise there is the potential for litigation or worse; sin.

A partnership agreement sets expectations. When everybody is happy about the partnership, it is a lot easier to agree to what is fair. In your start-up plan, you need to include an exit plan. Someday, one partner or the other will choose to leave the business. At that time you will be dealing with emotional tension, frustration, fear, and despair—not to mention money. Having these discussions well in advance gives the partners a fair baseline for what to do. Just as clear job descriptions help us know what to do as we open a new business, an exit agreement clarifies what to do when we close down the business.

When you actually cut a deal, there are certain issues every partnership should negotiate—most notably, the partners' respective obligations, how they will split profits, how they will exercise authority, and how they will deal with a change of ownership.

As you value the business in the beginning, remember that an idea is not worth anything. The value comes from tangibles, such as the effort, cash, and persistence put into the business. When valuing the business, use fixed percentages. A 50/50 split of a company that is not thoroughly thought through is usually a bad idea. Even paying someone five percent for some sort of contribution can come back to haunt you. Instead, build the partner's ownership around a shifting percentage based on contributions over time. Do not assume that the money you start with is going to be enough. If you and a teammate each put in $10,000 and each own half the business, what happens when the money runs out and only one of you is willing or able to put in the next block of capital?

In addition, who has real control of the business? Sooner or later, control matters. Do you have it? And if you don't, are you okay with that? The myth of most partnerships is that the world is going to stay the way it is, or that the world is going to change exactly the way you expect it will change. However, it won't and it doesn't. It is also likely that at some point one partner is going to want to grow the business rapidly or take it in a different direction. So build in a clause that says, *"At any time, one person can offer to buy the other out. The second person then has the chance to either buy the first person out at the same valuation, or sell."* Money can solve some problems, and this is one of them.

Business partnerships can be complicated, just like romantic ones. Understand who your partner is so you know what you are getting into from the beginning. Check out a prospective partner thoroughly. Even good friends may not be good business partners. Talk details. Check references. After all, the best time to find out whether your partner is a crook or a kook is before you start. Do not take his word for it; personally check out his references.

When we opened our first business, our mission pushed us to partner with another worker who was already doing traditional mission work in the area. Rather than immediately agreeing, I checked out his references and learned that, though he claimed to have a good working history, two former employers told me he was "inconsistent and lazy." I asked them both to put that in writing so I could show the mission leaders, which they did. As a result, the mission leaders withdrew their pressure on me to partner with him. Less than a year later the mission fired him. Checking out references saved me a lot of headaches.—Andrew, Southeast Asia

The sins (and debts) of one partner can afflict the other, and even the tightest contract will not protect you from an incompetent colleague. So before you start negotiating any partnership, double-check your decision to take on a partner. Be straight with yourself. Are you looking for expertise, money, contacts, or just someone to compensate for your weaknesses? Make sure your prospective partner is really bringing something to the party. Perhaps what the partner brings into the business can be readily found by hiring a coach or an employee.

Some organizational leaders recommend that entrepreneurs who are good at business, partner with someone who is good in evangelism or is theologically trained. This works as long as both the business is struggling and the ministry is having minimal impact. If both the evangelism and the social ministry begin to grow in step with the business, it will also work. However, I have never seen that happen. What usually happens is either the business takes off and the ministry is stuck in the mud, or the ministry grows rapidly and the business struggles. The result is the relationship becomes imbalanced and often one becomes jealous of the other leading to a nasty split.

Consider going into business with a partner who complements your strengths and weaknesses. If you are thinking about asking someone you know to join forces with you and start a business together, before you make that offer there are a few questions you should ask yourself:

1. Is this a person I can work with every day, and who complements my skill set? Always recruit to your weaknesses. Think about the person, and ask if she will make the highs even better and the lows more tolerable. Will she bring out your strengths and compensate for your weaknesses? Whoever your partner is, they should have strengths in the areas of your weaknesses. But whatever a partner's strengths or weaknesses, both partners must be actively working in the business thirty-plus hours a week. Unless both partners

are working in the business, neighbors and government officials who are watching will assume something is wrong, and over time it will impact you both.

2. What are my core values? Does the person share the things that are most important to me that can glorify God and grow the business? Be sure that any potential partner agrees on the essentials. Are you in sync on issues like integrity, business ethics, work ethics, transparency, outreach, discipleship, and passion? Jon told me, "*I have a strong work ethic, but my partner comes from a mission background. He goes home early most days, while I put in sixty-plus hours a week. It's creating a lot of tension in my soul. I think I am going to ask him to leave the business.*" Be honest and realistic about your expectations. Your values are a reflection of you, so they go beyond just the business or the ministry. You cannot compromise on your personal core values.

3. Must all partners have equal shares? Should there be an odd number of partners so you can break ties by majority vote? Does it make sense to have a national or a partner of the opposite sex if they are a good fit? Will everyone work like an owner if they have a stake in the business? In my experience, the answers vary with the individual.

Take the time to pray and think about each of these questions. Understand that there are people who think like owners whether they have a stake in the business or not. Leadership and work are about attitude. It is not about the job title. If someone needs a big title to be happy, you probably do not want him or her on your staff. Related to this, you need to decide how partners divide responsibilities. I have seen it split by inside person / outside person and also by function, but there are, of course, other good ways.

There are many ways to structure an organization. Even as a solo entrepreneur, you do not have to go at it alone. You can set up an advisory board or a board of directors to hold yourself accountable. Working closely with a mentor is also another way to keep yourself on track.

Local Partners

The handful of OPEN workers who have local partners have generally limited their ownership to 33 percent or less. Limiting the level of influence that a national partner has enables you to have a controlling say in how to operate the business. The national partner's role needs to be clearly understood to provide local and cultural insights and facilitate relationships in the community. Clearly state the expat's role in the partnership before you discuss working together. For example, my own Muslim partner agreed not to be involved in the business but to use his influence to enhance the business. He signs official documents as needed and opens doors with people who help provide insight to the culture and build favor with distrusting government officials. For each of his services, I pay him for the work he does, plus an annual fee of $600. When the business began to prosper, we gave him an additional annual bonus of $400. I made a legal contract with this local business partner and had a lawyer witness it to ensure the partner understood his role of *partnership* while the majority ownership, decision making, and money was mine.

Normally what you are asking of local partners is an investment of time, not money. By limiting their financial investment, it reduces the risk of their running off with the business. I suggest that you do not look to national partners for money, but for their local knowledge of the market and relationships both with other businesses and government officials who can help you grow the business. If they have a large percentage of ownership, they could affect the ethos of the business.

Local partners who have little skin in the game rarely seek to have any influence on the direction or running of the company. Some local shareholders will want regular updates on the business, but many will not. However, if the local partner invests money in the business, then you will need to treat him as a partner according to the percentage of his investment.

Do not worry about your witness in taking on a local partner. My good friend Roy who works in the Middle East says, *"If your local partner cannot figure out what your real purpose is for being in the country, then he should not be your partner."*

I have had a Muslim partner, but he was a silent partner who was not involved in the operations of the business. I know of others who have Muslim partners as well. Some worked, some did not. One key is to make sure your local partner is a lot richer than you are. If he is, he has little reason to rip you off. If he is poor, though he may be honest with you and be a good friend, even a believer, he is likely to have someone in his family put pressure on him to cheat you. Sometimes, often several years into the business, you will discover you are being cheated and then things get messy. Even if they do not financially invest in the business, remember the best partners need not be friends. In fact, that often does not work. Keep in mind that local partners should be wealthy and highly respected in the community.

If you opt to have a local partner, you do not want to go into this quickly or without good background checks, references, and personal understanding of their local involvement. A good functioning relationship is needed in any partnership. Particularly, issues of money and power need to be watched very carefully. Corruption is a problem in most countries. Talk through your values in these matters with a potential local partner before committing to partner with one another.

Let me repeat: *choose a local partner who is wealthier than yourself.* Just because a local is a believer does not mean they share your values. Multiple times I have seen local pastors run off with the business or a business vehicle simply because they could. In each case, the pastor was pressured by family members to take advantage of the "rich American," and as a result they succumbed. Do not place national leaders under such temptation.

As with every aspect of the business, ensure that a lawyer has checked off your partnership documents. You should also consider:

- The financial and tax liability of partners.
- Initial and later contributions of cash, property, and services to the business.
- What will happen if a partner wants out or dies.
- How to value partnership assets.
- Admitting new partners.

Franchises

There have been a handful of successful B4Ters who brought a franchise overseas from back home. The franchises that do best overseas are less known, have lower standards of quality control, and give greater flexibility to the franchisee.

Understand that though more and more franchisors are open to franchisee creativity, the basis for a successful franchise is a standardized system. Before committing to a franchise, study both the franchise's systems and the local culture to discern if the products, services, and business of the franchise will fit the local context. In addition, explore the franchise's values and work ethics to ensure they too fit the local culture. Remember, most franchisors are controlling and are sticklers for consistency and following their rules. Can you work under such constraints? You also may be required to share confidential information about your business operations. It is likely that headquarters will pay you an annual visit, so be sure that your franchisor understands and is in agreement with both the "B" and the "T" of B4T—your complete agenda for doing business abroad.

One of the reasons for starting your own business is to be your own boss, but when you buy a franchise you are still answering to someone else. The franchisor tells you who to get your supplies from, in what areas you may do business in, and with whom you may compete. Two advantages dominate the practicality of franchising. The first is a relative independence for each business and, with it, a sufficient adaptability to allow each business to meet the cultural, circumstantial, personality, and ministry needs of its location. The second is the advantage of a strong product or service already proven so that the huge start-up costs in energy, time, and money are not disabling. The guidance, company policies, procedures, supporting communications, troubleshooting, and training are easier to follow when you work from an existing company manual than they are to invent when you start a business from scratch.

DISCUSSION QUESTIONS

1. In selecting your people group, what are the initial questions you need to answer concerning who you will target your products or services?
2. List several reasons why the location of your business is important.
3. What are some advantages of renting a business location over buying?
4. Name the advantages of working in a Western-owned company over a locally owned business.
5. Would you take on a local, non-Christian partner? Explain your answer.
6. What characteristics and skills would you want in a business partner?

"Don't sit down and wait for the opportunities to come. Get up and make them!"
—C. J. WALKER[67]

[67] http://inventors.about.com/od/wstartinventors/a/MadameWalker_2.htm

Chapter 7

SELECTING A TENT

Each of us has our own way of entering a pool. A few of us stick a toe in to test the temperature, while some timidly walk into the water, trying to slowly adjust to the water's temperature. Still others jump off the diving board, plunging right in and creating a giant splash. Starting your own business is much the same; each one of us must develop our own way forward. Just because a start-up strategy works for one entrepreneur does not mean it will work for you. For every B4T worker who starts out having a detailed business plan and a strict timeline, there is another who succeeds by appearing to break all the standard business rules.

In determining what business is the best fit for your people group, your city, and your calling; remember, you need to begin with yourself. Solomon tells us, *"The wisdom of the prudent is to give thought to their ways, but the folly of fools is deception."*[68] The highest wisdom is for a person to understand his own way—in other words, to know oneself. Understanding our way refers to realizing our calling, gifts, talents, skills, and experiences. We need to understand how God has interwoven these things into our lives so that we know both how He would have us abide in Him, as well as how He would have us manage these things in and through our lives, so as to bring maximum glory to Him. God created us in His unique way for His unique purpose; He's not going to expect us to depart radically from the way He has formed us.

Factors to Focus On in Selecting a Tent

Now what kind of business should you start? There are eight factors to focus on in selecting the appropriate B4T business for you.

---

[68] Proverbs 14:8

1. Study Yourself—Consider Yourself as a Customer

Sally loved chocolate. She moved to an Arab city to study the language. During her two years of study, she was out of sorts in that she could not find good chocolate anywhere. There was chocolate in many of the stores, but it just wasn't good quality chocolate. The country is not poor and people spent money on many luxury items, so she felt there would be a market for quality chocolate if it were available. She tested the market by bringing varieties of chocolate back when she traveled abroad. Her Arab friends enjoyed these delectable delights. However, Sally had no idea how to make chocolate. She knew she loved chocolate and she enjoyed cooking, but making chocolate as a business was taking it to another level. Sally asked her friends, *"Who makes the best chocolate in the world?"* The most common answer was Switzerland.

So Sally went to Switzerland. She visited chocolate shops until she found one she really liked. The owner was not a Christian, but she boldly approached him and said, *"I'll work for you for six months for free if you'll teach me how to make chocolate."* The owner replied, *"What's the catch?"* She said, *"No catch. I love your chocolate and I want to open a shop similar to this one in the Middle East. I'm not going to compete against you, and I won't make or sell chocolate in your country—I'll even sign papers affirming that. I just want to learn from you."* He agreed, so she worked there for six months, taking detailed notes. She learned all there is to know about chocolate, including the business's financial system and marketing strategies. Then she returned to her adopted Arab home and opened her chocolate shop. Today she has a growing business.

Sally focused on the first factor: she started with herself as a customer. Later, as she found that her friends shared her tastes, she developed a product to meet the wider needs of the community. Keep in mind, if you are not going to buy the product, why would anyone else?

A bakery was opened in Central Asia because Francis, the wife of a tentmaker, loved making cakes for her neighbors. Her neighbors loved her cakes and thought she should try opening a bakery. Today, she has four shops selling six hundred cakes a week. Whenever I visit Francis' city, I go straight to her shop. She will tell you how the bakery has created hundreds of opportunities to share her faith and how there has been spiritual fruit, too. Remember, you begin by being a customer.

As you study yourself, pray, ask lots of questions, and be sure to listen.

2. *Enjoy Your Job*

Note that both Sally and Francis loved their product and their jobs. It is essential that you enjoy your job. One of the keys to a successful business is finding the right business for your passions and personality.

Mark, whose business now has branches in several countries, once told me, *"God has called me to reach Muslims and do business. I couldn't be having more fun."* Whatever business you do, make sure it is something you enjoy doing. Taylor, a B4Ter working in South Asia explains, *"It's really a fact finding, due diligence type of exercise. You start with yourself to see if this is something you enjoy doing."*

James, in Central Asia, was depressed. He was certain it was related to his business, but he could not figure out why. Whenever he was away from work he was fine, but at work he felt pressurized with a dark cloud hanging over him. James had started a language school. His business was profitable, had four full-time employees, and had seen one employee and two neighbors come to Christ. When I visited him, I evaluated his records and his relationships, which all seemed fine. Maybe there is something spiritual causing the depression, I thought. However, when I asked him if he enjoyed teaching, James' reply surprised me, *"No, I hate it!"* *"Then why did you start a school?"* I responded. He replied, *"Because everyone told me that was the best way to get into the country."* I encouraged him to sell the school and go into another line of work. He did and within days his depression lifted.

Don't fall into the trap of starting a particular business just because someone tells you it's a "sure thing." You need to enjoy your business; after all, you are going to be doing it for weeks, months, and years. In fact, for the first two or three years you are going to be working in the business for ten to twelve hours a day. If you do not enjoy the job, you will become bored or depressed, feeling trapped. The people around you—both coworkers and customers—will sense your attitude. This will impact your sales, but more importantly it will impact your witness.

For example, don't open a restaurant if you don't love food. Currently I am facilitating the opening of a restaurant, and I have found that these people are crazy about food and cooking. All they talk about is food! All they want to do is cook! While going through five weeks of training in a restaurant in Mexico, a young man with a phenomenal testimony worked an eight-hour shift every day. When his eight hours were up, he often chose to stay and work longer. He said to me, *"I don't want to leave, I love being in the kitchen."* While that seems crazy to me, he is the kind of person who will succeed at B4T because he enjoys his work. We have all been around people who loved their work. It's infectious and it's a wonderful witness. And yes, I hired him.

As you find joy in setting up the business, be sure to pray, ask lots of questions, and listen.

3. Be Adequately Equipped

Though Francis already knew how to make the world's best cakes as a hobby, Sally set aside time to learn the skill of making chocolate and running a chocolate shop. Both approaches work, but whether you already have the skills or need to learn them, it is important to select a business you know intimately. When you start out, you don't need to know everything about your business, because you can learn as you go. However, you do need to know what to do. It is the rare owner who is the expert at every job in her business. Nonetheless, you need to know how to do everything in the business as a generalist so you can guide and train people, as well as be aware when people are cheating you or doing something incorrectly. Thus, you will need to know what you are doing, no matter what the task.

Jeff Bezos states, *"One of the huge mistakes people make is that they try to force an interest on themselves. You don't choose your passions, let your passions choose you."* As you study yourself to determine what kind of business is a good fit, make a list about yourself. Ask for input from others as you consider the following:

- Passion or calling
- Strengths
- Weaknesses
- Skills
- Spiritual gifts
- Education
- Job experience
- Awards or achievements you've received
- Things you do that others compliment you on

Starting a business in which you already have experience has many advantages. You can use your knowledge about the industry, your training and skills, and your network of contacts that might help you find financing, suppliers, and customers. However, if you don't have these advantages, a lack of experience shouldn't stop you from opening a business.

Caleb, in India, had no business background and admits, *"I didn't even know how to use an Excel spreadsheet when we started. In other words, I learned by doing it."* Caleb went on to share that when he first started out he put in fifteen-hour days learning his trade. Today he's a successful B4Ter.

Rob, who works in Southeast Asia adds,

> I did not know much about my business when we started, so we started small. This left us some wiggle room. We knew we would make mistakes, but being small, when our aim was off we could easily fix it and fire again and adjust again as needed. If you are willing to fire before you aim perfectly, you probably won't hit your target precisely but you will have taken that first step in the journey of a thousand miles.

We succeed in doing things because we know what we can and cannot do. Many B4Ters fail because they plan to do things they are not equipped or called to do. For instance, a worker decides he wants to open a coffee shop. He writes a good business plan, raises some money, and recruits three others to work with him. Yet no one understands or has worked in the coffee business, and what is worse, no one is putting in the hours to learn how to operate a coffee shop. So when the shop is built, they do not know how to operate it well.

If you do not know how to operate a business or are not willing to learn and put in a ton of hours, there is no point in starting the business. Jesus tells us,

> For which of you, desiring to build a tower, does not first sit down and count the cost, whether he has enough to complete it? Otherwise, when he has laid a foundation and is not able to finish, all who see it begin to mock him, saying, "This man began to build and was not able to finish."[69]

On the road to success, knowing yourself is part of being adequately equipped. So before you make a plan, you need to diagnose your own ability to carry it out. There is a free and helpful business profile test you can take to help understand your strengths and business affinities. You may find the link at the end of appendix C.

As you seek to be adequately equipped, remember to pray, ask lots of questions, and be sure to listen.

---

[69] Luke 14:28–30

4. Profile the People—Consider the Community You Are Trying to Reach

God assigned Brandon the task of reaching the Mab people of a modern European city. The Mabs make up about 20 percent of the population, are generally less educated, and work blue-collar jobs. Most live on the south side of the river. Brandon and his team tried various approaches for reaching the Mabs. Over time they decided business would be a great approach. Since Katie, one of the team members, had highly developed computer software skills, they opened a computer software business. They targeted American businesses and, after struggling a few years, they found a major American client and soon the business was flourishing.

Needing local programmers, they advertised for help—only to learn none of the Mab people had the skills they needed. All of their clients were in America, and all of their employees were Western, Christian-background people. Their business created zero natural touch points with the Mab people. Soon team members who were working forty-plus hours a week began to despair over the business. It was a successful business, but it was not a good B4T business since it did not engage in reaching the Mabs—their assigned people group.

Recognizing things were not going to change, the team decided to use the monies from the computer business to open a bakery / coffee shop on the south side of the river. Today the shop has hired five Mabs and most of its customers are Mabs.

It seems obvious, but it is surprising how many people start a business based on hearsay or input from other expats. When you profile the people, get input from *locals*. Ask questions and then be sure to listen. In doing research, first talk with the people you want to reach and who will be your employees and customers. Get their thoughts and reactions on what you want to do. Then conduct a survey with people whose past experience has taught you, would be likely customers for your business. The local newspapers may also prove useful and search the Web for ideas.

Try conducting a survey. Whether you do it in person or by using a written questionnaire, make sure the questions are clear and mean the same thing to everyone. If you use a written form, make it visually attractive, easy to read, and brief. Multiple-choice and forced-choice questions (such as ranking 1 to 10 or answering with yes or no) work best, but allow one open-ended question for people to comment freely.

For example, Jesus knew His clientele well. Initially people followed Jesus for His provision of food and His miracles. The people were primarily focused on the pursuit of self-gratification and happiness. Jesus fed the hungry. He healed the sick. Through these "attractions" people came to understand who He was. There are many ways we may attract people's attention. Discern the needs of the people and then determine before the Lord how you can uniquely meet them.

Your business should create opportunities to interact with your people group on a daily basis, be that via your employees, customers, or suppliers. The best B4T businesses create touch points with all three of these groups. What goods and services do the people want or need? What skills do the people have to offer? In most communities around the world, people want three things: jobs, education, and leisure. You need to consider your business in terms of the needs of the people you are reaching. Generally, the kind of jobs the country wants depends on the stage of development of the country. Learn and then give the community what they want.

The needs of people groups, countries, and societies usually fall into one of four simple categories:

- Basic needs
- Jobs
- Education
- Leisure

All societies have basic needs (food, water, shelter, health care, and safety). If they do not have these needs met, determine how you can meet them. Often an NGO model is more effective in providing for these needs than a business. Once a country has its basic needs met, the people want jobs. Once they have simple or semiskilled jobs, they want a higher education to enable them to get better jobs. And once people have good jobs, they want to spend their money on leisure. This is the basic way that an economy develops.

The majority of people in undeveloped countries like Afghanistan, Chad, Laos, and Mali struggle to provide for their basic needs. Providing training in health services, water projects, and the building of homes will grant you entry into these countries.

Turkmenistan, Tajikistan, Algeria, and parts of Indonesia and India are richer, but can be described as underdeveloped countries. What people want in these countries are jobs. Small manufacturing companies and building basic service-related businesses like taxis, hairstylists, bakeries, restaurants, or other simple retail businesses, will create these jobs.

As mentioned earlier, when people have jobs, they want better jobs that give better pay and better working conditions. To qualify for such a job, they need a higher education. Developing countries like China, Turkey, Malaysia, and Morocco need education. Setting up schools— whether it be English, computer, or business-type schools—will endear you to these governments and give you excellent opportunities to meet people while you work.

Saudi Arabia, Oman, and Singapore are developed countries that want leisure activities. Operating tours, clubs, hotels, up-market restaurants, or even providing services that reduce their workloads are good entry strategies for these and other wealthy countries.

God may assign you to reach a wealthier section of society in a poor city so that your business may meet a higher need. If so, align your business plan to fit the profile of this segment of the city. Study the specific people you are to reach to discern what their particular needs are, and then design a business to meet those needs.

Jesus tells us, *"Lift up your eyes, and see that the fields are white for harvest."*[70] We need to *see* the people. Every country, every people group, every language has its distinctives. Take time to profile the people and learn these distinctives. Learn their interests and needs. Language fluency is an essential step in accomplishing this.

The best B4T businesses are designed to engage and meet the needs of local employees or clients. Design your business for the market and the skills people have available first and *then* according to your own personal interests. David, in Central Asia, was spot-on when he said, *"The best B4T businesses are designed to fit the people group, not only the worker."*

As you profile the people, pray, ask lots of questions, and be sure to listen.

5. Consider the Culture

Another helpful way to find the right business for you and your situation is to study the cultural trends of the people and the country. What businesses are shaping your people or country? Or what business can you launch that may impact the country? You need to operate a business that is a good *fit* with the culture. Contextualizing the business is as important as contextualizing your lifestyle.

Starbucks succeeded in China in ways Dunkin' Donuts and Krispy Kreme did not. With rising costs and increased competition, Starbucks contextualized their products. Instead of trying to force onto the market the same products they serve in the United States, Starbucks developed

---

[70] John 4:35.

flavors that appealed to local tastes, such as green tea–flavored coffee drinks. Rather than pushing take-out orders, which account for the majority of American sales, Starbucks adapted to local consumer wants and promoted dine-in service.

C. V. Prahalad says,

> There is a tremendous amount of debate in the United States about [the need for] a level playing field. I think a level playing field is a fundamentally wrong notion. Strategy is not about a level playing field. Strategy is about a differential advantage. We must . . . ask the question, "How do I change the rules of the game in my business so that I hold the high ground on a non-level playing field?"[71]

God intended humans to be diverse. Although it is true that the kingdom of God admits Jews and Gentiles on an equal basis, it is equally true that in this present life they are distinct. Realize that Muslims buy from Muslims, Chinese buy from Chinese, Jews buy from Jews. It is natural for people to support their friends and countrymen through the purchasing of their wares. All evangelism and all businesses must have a high appreciation of the local culture. People take their own culture and traditions seriously. Violating or denigrating cultural norms closes doors to both the gospel and business. Like Starbucks adapting to China, a good businesswoman does the same in selling her wares.

We should not be intimidated by the differences that exist in this world but instead embrace those differences. One business succeeded in winning a big client in South Africa by simply translating their documents into Afrikaans. The chairman, who was an Afrikaner, could not believe it, saying he had never heard of a foreign enterprise that was thoughtful enough to have documents in English and his own language. Remember, human beings are human beings; recognize and honor their humanity.

We also need to study current trends to learn the direction the people and their culture are moving. How does the culture function? What motivates the people to work? Does religion have a high profile? Asking and answering these questions will help in developing appropriate business and ministry strategies.

There is a saying my mother often quoted to me, "*The early bird catches the worm.*" Often the first to start a new type of business in a country or city succeeds, where those who follow fail. One friend entered

---

[71]   Kriegel and Patler, *If It Ain't Broke*, 99.

China in 1985, just as China was opening. He had no teaching credentials or experience. More by accident than design, he found a job teaching English at a university out west when English teaching was hardly known in China. Twenty years later he was still working there. Others coming in nowadays need higher degrees to get a teaching position, but since he was there first, he became known. He has become a friend of the university. As a result, he has been able to stay and has seen many come to know the Lord. People coming in later—after a need is well established—will need higher and higher degrees and greater experience to be accepted.

There are several countries that have been closed to the West and the Good News but are now opening up for trade and tourism. There are many opportunities if we open our eyes and look. For example, some of these countries have terrific beaches that, if developed wisely, could become major tourist destinations. There is an opportunity there for both business and the gospel. Understand the trends of the community. Be first. Be a market leader. Try and anticipate where the economy and the community are going to be five years from now, and start a business that will fit the future. Besides, it is going to take three to five years just to get the business going.

Countries are generally categorized as being undeveloped, developing, or developed. As already discussed, the kind of businesses each of these categories of countries need is different. In addition, each of these types of countries may be further categorized as regressing, stagnant, or progressing. Is your adopted country moving forward or backward? Consider the trends of countries worldwide compared to your adopted land, as this may suggest the future of the economy for your chosen people group. Learn the needs of this country in all areas: educationally, socially, economically, and materially, as well as spiritually. Knowing the direction the country is heading may spawn ideas for a business. Many countries will compare themselves to another country that is on their same level of development but are a few years or steps ahead. Study what is happening in these model countries and who the people or leaders compare themselves to. This will help to anticipate the future needs of your new country.

Watch and *see* the trends of countries worldwide. Poorer, less developed countries look to similar yet more advanced countries as a model. These countries learn from the more developed nations' examples and struggles, both good and bad. India, with its huge population problems and diverse cultures, often compares itself to China. Singapore is small yet has four main cultures and languages. Singapore tends to emulate Switzerland, which is also small and has three diverse languages and cultures. Some North African countries pattern themselves after France. If you know the economy, education, and transportation industry of your country, as well as who they are patterning themselves after, you may easily determine where the country is headed and what type of businesses they will need five years from now. If you can, try and visit one or two countries that have recently (within the last decade) come through the stage that your country is now passing through. If time or monies limit you, then study these countries on the Internet.

Read online news about the country and the people God has assigned you. Learn local customs. How do people greet one another or pass business cards? What is the work ethic of the people? What is considered to be "on time?" How do women and men relate to one another in public and in private? Become a student of the people and their culture.

Jesus points out that we know how to tell the signs of the weather; in the same way, we should learn to accurately forecast the economic, educational, spiritual, and other needs of the countries we are reaching. Talk to the people who are there. If there is a minority Christian population, do not rely on the Christians alone for your information. Christians often want to please you, so they tell you what they think you want to hear. They want you to come to their country. Instead, get input from both the non-Christian and Christian leaders. Non-Christians will see you as a competitor or foreigner. Often they will point out the reasons why you should not come, which is more helpful. If you can overcome the problems, you can surely begin a business.

Doing business cross-culturally is very different. There is much to learn when considering a culture, and this is one of many places where it is invaluable to have a mentor. You may have to relearn how to advertise, or how to rent a building. You might hang banners, and people may steal them for clothes. People will not register until they see classes in session. So how do you get your first class started? Maybe offer free tuition to the first thirty students.

As you consider the culture, persevere in prayer, ask lots of questions, and listen to what people have to say.

6. Survey the Society

It is essential to any good business initiative to receive input directly from customers. Generally, governments want to bring in investment money, technology skills, exports, and specialists. Specific information can easily be learned by meeting with government officials. Most officials will supply you with free information.

Another underutilized resource is the library. University libraries are often the best. My business application was rejected and, as with most government officials, no one would tell me why. The best answer I could get out of anyone was, *"Your papers are not correct."* Did they want a bribe? Something else? I went to the national library and read up on my line of business. There I found a government document with the application form for applying to register my type of business, and it had all the answers! I reapplied using the answers given in that book and my visa was approved right away.

Sometimes the people or customers cannot tell you what they want, so you need to invest time to observe them. Henry Ford is known for his statement, *"I did not ask people what mode of transport they wanted, because if I did, they would have said they wanted a faster horse."* One OPEN worker heading to a progressively modernizing Muslim country recognized that more women were moving into the workforce. These women used to take care of their parents but now were busy at work. This meant that there were a number of elderly people who were staying at home alone. He studied the issue and learned that many middle- to upper-class people were hiring sitters for their parents, because they could not trust them to stay at home alone all day. So he created a daycare center for elderly people where adult children can drop off grandpa and/or grandma at eight in the morning and pick them up after work!

Build a business that meets a need or creates an attraction within the community. Such a business will ensure your longevity in the country. Businesses that put you face to face with the people in natural settings are best.

Yet if this is not feasible due to government or personal limitations, do not be discouraged. One worker in the Middle East told me,

> In nine years of living in a Muslim country, only four times have I actually done business with a Muslim. I build friendships and create witnessing opportunities through social contacts with neighbors and people I meet at clubs, gyms, community centers, community events, and coffee shops. However, my business is essential since it provides me with credibility and respectability that I would not have otherwise.

Plan ahead. Survey the society. Think through where your target country is today in order to know where it will be going tomorrow. Don't prepare yourself for jobs the government currently needs, but for jobs they are going to need three to five years from now. Why? The training needed to qualify, plus the application process to find or set up a business, often takes one to three years and sometimes longer. Unless you already have the skills and/or degrees needed to set up a business or school, by the time you are ready your opportunity may be gone.

As you survey the society, remember: pray, ask lots of questions, and listen.

7. Research the Resources—Look Over the Land

Research the resources of the people you are trying to reach. A la Caleb and Joshua, it is essential to invest time in physically scouting out the land. This may require two or more trips to your future home to gain a clear understanding of the challenges and opportunities that are there. Learn from NGOs or companies that have conducted similar businesses in the region. If available, attend local seminars and trade fairs. Engage local consultants in formulating and, later, in reviewing your business plan. Ask what resources or natural products are developed already that can be exported, especially back to your home country where you already have connections. What products don't they currently have that are made in your own country and can be imported?

Based upon the location of the country, the climate, and the geography, you can determine the factors that would be beneficial for you to begin a business. Consider the water, soil, and temperature. Everyone needs water. Can you dig wells or create irrigation systems or develop other systems for obtaining water? Is the temperature and soil suitable for a crop that is presently not available in this land?

When Cal received his assignment from God to reach the Muslims of northern India, he traveled to their homeland and invested time studying the people. He quickly learned that the people loved to work with their hands and were known for their artisan gifts. They already had local markets for the products they were making, so he explored opportunities to market their goods overseas. He quickly discovered there was a small but big enough market for the people's goods abroad. Cal knew little about this type of work, so they started small with just a couple of employees, and he studied and learned the trade as the business moved forward. He learned the skills and work habits of the people and built a business to fit their abilities. Today Cal has more than ninety employees, factories in two locations, and two groups of believers gathering in budding house churches.

Some B4Ters pay little attention to their surroundings. In setting up shop, one man decided to sell imported corn since it was easy to import from his home country. But nothing sold. Only when he looked around did he realize no one was buying because his shop was in the middle of a rice field! There was food in abundance and the people preferred rice to corn.

Based upon the raw materials available in the country, what can be exported to other countries? What locally made products can be exported to other countries? Are there useful items in your focus country that you have never seen in your homeland or the United States or Europe? Send a few samples to friends in your home country. Ask them if they like it and, if so, how much they would pay for it. If they would pay a price more than what you can buy and ship it for, you could have yourself a business.

What products in your home country are needed or would be beneficial in your adopted country? Find out why they are not presently being sold there. Have a few shipped to your new country and try selling them in a friendly market or to friends. Again, if the price that people are willing to pay is more than your costs, you could have yourself an import business.

My favorite B4T story about someone studying the land was more by accident than intention. It's a story about strawberries. Jack went to Japan with a traditional organization doing traditional missions. He studied the Japanese language for two years in Tokyo and then was assigned to work in the Tochigi region of Hongshu Island, the main island. It is a mountainous area where a lot of rice is grown. When Jack and his wife moved there, they tried to meet people by riding buses, hanging out in tea shops, and going to the parks. After two years, Jack had good language but no friends.

This was traditional missions 1960s-style, so after four years Jack and his family returned home for a year's furlough in Michigan, an area that happens to have a lot of strawberry farms. Jack got home and started eating strawberries, which he had not eaten in four years. Then it dawned on him, *"Why don't we have strawberries in Japan?"* The answer: they are all imported so it's too expensive.

Jack got out his map. Japan and Michigan are at the same latitude and have similar weather. He asked himself, *"Why can't we grow strawberries on our farms in Tochigi?"* Jack was not a farmer, but that did not deter him. He thought the Japanese farmers in his area could grow strawberries and sell them in Tokyo for a good profit; people were already paying a lot of money for strawberries in Japan.

So Jack got some of his friends in Michigan who were strawberry farmers to donate about one thousand strawberry plants. He invested much of his furlough working in the fields, learning how to do everything to grow strawberries so he could have a successful harvest. The Michigan farmers shipped the strawberry plants and timed it just right for the growing season and for Jack to be back in Japan.

What happened? Jack arrived back in his Tochigi community and said, *"Guys, I've got these strawberries coming—who wants to grow them? We're going to make a lot of money. It's going to be a great opportunity."* They all looked at him like he was from Mars and then told him, *"Jack, you are the world's biggest idiot. We Japanese do not eat strawberries."* Nobody would grow the strawberries.

The shipment was already in route. So what did Jack do? He said to two farmers who had enough land, *"How much money did you make growing rice last year? I will pay you right now that same amount to use your land for one year to grow strawberries. You can get a whole year's salary, guaranteed, even though everything might fail."* The Japanese farmers were delighted to have a year off with pay. They gladly took Jack's money.

So he rented the use of those two farms for one year and planted and nurtured each plant. When the strawberries were ripe, Jack hired a few people to help him with the harvest. At the end of the year, he shipped all of the strawberries to Tokyo and sold them in the market for the high foreign price. Jack made more than a lot of money. Upon returning from Tokyo, it was just a matter of days before the local farmers came to Jack asking, *"Can we grow strawberries?"*

Jack went from no friends to lots of friends in four years. Today, that part of Japan is known as the strawberry capital of Japan—but even more importantly, despite Japan being a pretty tough ground for the gospel, today there are two churches in that community. Two churches, because Jack researched the resources.

When researching the resources, attend community events and visit business associations. Nearly every country has annual trade fairs to showcase their products. Attend a fair to see what products the country has to offer. Only at trade fairs can you find such a large concentration of people that know about local resources in one place and time. At a trade show you can talk to people in distribution, marketing, sales, and manufacturing. Take a notebook along and ask questions that will help you understand their businesses and the industry as a whole. It is an exhausting process, but well worth the effort. After the last trade show I attended my feet were killing me, but I came away loaded with literature, a pad full of priceless information, and a significant number of new contacts. It is an invaluable day-long lesson you cannot get anywhere else.

When moving into a *high-risk* area, even though many Westerners may be fearful, gauge things by what you see the nationals doing. Studying the government's view on growth and business should reveal what businesses they might be favorable toward. In many countries, relationships—not money or your business plan—are what make the difference. You need to go there and meet the officials yourself. Whatever business you are in, work to develop good relationships with government leaders.

Don't rely on what you read in the international papers, and don't listen to American businesspeople, and definitely don't listen to the people at the American embassy! Talk to the local government officials, talk to the people. And don't do what they say to do—do what you see *them* doing. Jesus tells us to be *"wise as serpents."* It is acceptable and natural for many businesspeople to lie about things. So never trust just their words, but observe what they do.

To scout out the land initially, I recommend that you go as a student. Most countries welcome foreign students, so use that opportunity to study the language and the land. If there is no school available, take several short-term trips. One is not enough to get a balanced picture; you need several trips to gain a well-rounded perspective so as to reflect and ask better questions on the next trip. Do your homework first and then establish your business.

Al, working in Central Asia, writes,

> Because of the severe shortage of roofing tiles and the reputation of the quality of our product, we have had numerous requests by mayors of different regions to help locals start small roofing tile enterprises in their economically depressed areas. The most recent request was from the mayor of F. They have no way to get roofing tiles to repair structures in their region. Through this, we will be able to impact this and other regions the way we have already done in the ones that the Lord has placed us in. In this way, we are helping to revive the region spiritually through the starting of churches. It is significant that in these regions

where no churches exist and where no Christian workers have gone, we are actually sought after and being invited in by the local government. We have similar invites from the mayors of two other cities.

Read, read, read. You can readily do research online. You will find many sites offering extensive information. Gather every magazine and industry publication you can buy, download, or subscribe to. Read about what's new and what is changing in the country. Learn about the movers and the shakers, where they are, and what they are doing. Make yourself familiar with many aspects of the industry you are considering, so that when you do meet people, you will know the jargon and understand their interests.

As you research the resources, it is important to involve God in your thinking and ask lots of questions and listen.

8. Evaluate the Educational System

Based upon where the country is in the world—undeveloped, developing, or developed—what are their educational needs? English, computer, and business skills, as well as engine repair, are just a few of the types of schools that can be opened to serve the people. Even as the missionaries of the 1800s used elementary and high schools to influence people for Jesus, we too may use specialty schools to bless and influence people today. Such schools are welcome in most developing countries. In many Muslim and Asian countries the position of a teacher is an exalted position. Schools also create contacts with a large number of people.

The first business I ever opened was a kindergarten. The idea came from a meeting with local village officials. They were concerned as the city kids were getting into the better government schools because they had opportunities to learn to read and write by attending private kindergartens in the city. With their encouragement we began one, then two, and today there are four such rural kindergartens teaching roughly two hundred children each year. Over eighty Muslims have come to Christ, all because of teaching their three- to five-year-olds.

If you do not have the degrees necessary to teach or to accomplish what is needed, be committed to getting such qualifications. Be well prepared. Again, do not get degrees for today. Rather, look ahead. If electrical engineers are needed today, will they still be needed after you complete the four to six years of study that is required to get such a degree?

When you evaluate a country's educational system, you are anticipating the future. When looking at this system, learn where the country is so you can project where it is going to be. Again, know which countries your country emulates. For example, Malaysia looks to Japan for ideas and as a model to emulate. If you are moving into Malaysia and looking ahead, ask what Japan is doing now—because those are the things Malaysians are going to want to do. Then, when you go to the government, take articles from the newspaper and point out, *"Here is what Japan is doing, here is what the prime minister said about Japan and how the country wants to be like them."* The government officials will see that and likely give your business approval.

As you evaluate the educational system, make it a priority to pray, ask lots of questions and listen.

When beginning the process of selecting your "tent" (your business), remember to bathe every step with prayer. Study yourself, profile the people, consider the culture, survey the society, research the resources of the land, and evaluate the educational system. Implement these points, and you will likely set up a tent that will make an impact for eternity.

DISCUSSION QUESTIONS

1. What are the things that you will miss most while in your new nation? Is this a possible business?
2. What are the things that you are most passionate about?
3. What do others say is the preparation that you need to undertake to be able to do each of your business ideas?
4. What do others say about your business ideas or skills that might help you to engage with your people group?
5. Assess the economic development of your people group. What will be their needs in the next five years? Ten years?
6. How might your business be contextualized to the local culture?
7. Which nation does your chosen people group seek to emulate? What does that tell you in regards to your work goals?
8. What needs are unmet due to the consequences of recent changes in your people's culture?
9. What are the locals famous for? Is there a market for this elsewhere?
10. Can you spot any happy coincidences, like Jack's discovery with the strawberries?
11. What is it that the locals really must have?
12. How might your chosen people group be missing out on some foreign product or service?

"You don't learn to walk by following the rules, you learn to walk by doing and falling over."

—*RICHARD BRANSON*[72]

---

[72] http://www.brainyquote.com/quotes/authors/r/richard_branson.html.

Chapter 8

SETTING UP YOUR TENT

Arnold, a NexusB4T coach emphasizes, "It is essential to ensure there are buyers for your product or service *before* starting your business."

When setting up your B4T business, there are many issues and approaches to researching which products or services your customers will desire. This chapter highlights seven key issues that a B4Ter should research. Many of these issues are common to doing business anywhere. Nonetheless, all should be investigated to ensure your business enterprise will both glorify God and earn an income for yourself. Remember, *"The wisdom of the prudent is to give thought to their ways, but the folly of fools is deception."*[73]

Issues to Investigate in Setting Up Your Tent

1. Check Out the Competition

The first step to understanding your competition is to know who they are. While this may seem obvious, it is often more complicated than it appears. There are two primary ways to define competitors. One is to strategically group competitors who use similar marketing strategies, sell similar products, or offer similar skills. The second, more obvious way to group competitors is by their customers—how strongly do other businesses compete for the same customers' dollars? Using this method gives you a wider view of your competitors and the challenges they could pose to your new business.

Suppose you are considering opening a coffee shop. If there are no coffee shops in the area, you might think there are no competitors. Wrong! Any business that vies for customers' leisure time and social interaction is a competitor. That means kiosks, restaurants, parks, children's play centers, and bookstores could all be competitors. Ask yourself why someone would

---

[73] Proverbs 14:8

stop going to the other places and come to your coffee shop. Free Wi-Fi, perhaps? Then ask which of those people you would want to attract.

You can learn what a good business is and what a good business is not by studying your competitors. Visit their websites and look at their prices, services, testimonies from customers, and special offers. Spend some time analyzing their advertising and sales literature. What do they emphasize most? What are they not mentioning? Do you see aspects you could improve? Try calling or emailing them to ask for their rates and services. If they have a store, visit and browse around. Write down your impressions as soon as you have hung up or left the building. Keep a record for each competitor you visit. Examine what all or most of them have in common, why that is, and how you can set yourself apart. Discuss your findings of each competitor with other people, particularly locals and potential customers, to learn what they think.

Examine a significant number of your potential competitors on a local scale and, if relevant, the regional or national scale. Study their strategies and their everyday operations. Your analysis should reveal a clear picture of the potential threats and opportunities, and weaknesses and strengths of your potential competition. Try to discover what the trends are in the industry you want to enter and whether there is an opportunity or advantage for your business. Utilize the library, the Internet, and other secondary research sources—such as government data, reference books, and industry associations—to learn as much as you can about competitors' tactics and goals. Role-play. Visit their store as a customer and assess their strategies and operations through the eyes of each customer segment. Never underestimate the number of competitors out there. Try to spot potential future competitors as well as current ones. If you don't limit yourself to the obvious definitions of competitors, then you will be less likely to get sideswiped by an unexpected rival.

Knowing the competition is key before selecting any business. If possible, while you are still studying the language, do a market survey for each of the types of businesses you are considering to start. Make sure there is a market for the product. Jim writes, *"We put the cart before the horse, in that we started producing handicrafts and then we went looking for markets. We naively assumed if we had a good product that people would buy it."* So allow me to restate this to make it perfectly clear: it is essential to ensure there are buyers for your product or service before starting your business.

The purpose of a market survey is to determine if anyone will buy your product or service. You need to be sure there is a market before you go into production. Note: do *not* lock yourself into one business idea too early. You may have to survey many products, services, or ideas to find a winner, and it may not be immediately obvious.

As you compare the competition, make a list of key contacts—suppliers, competitors, and buyers. While asking questions, remember that ideas are context-dependent, so we need local cultural input. We need nonnationality-, nonethnicity-driven ideas, as this leads people to deal with truth within their context. Test your questions and surveys with locals and language tutors to ensure you are communicating what you intend. And do not trust language tutors alone to get it right, because if they are an educator or young person, they may not know the correct business terms. This would result in you asking poor questions and thus leading you to make decisions on poor or wrong information. Validate everything with more than two people. Do not get input only from Christians; they tell you what they think you want to hear because they want you to move to their city. Instead, you must get input from those who don't want you to open shop in the city, for they will tell you the truth. You need to know the problems, not just the blessings, about what you are seeking to do.

One wise approach includes going to the government officials and seeing if they are on board with your business idea. If so, then go straight to the competition and tell them your intentions to compete against them. Having a relationship with key government officials is helpful in explaining to the competition that you have their support so they cannot easily blackball you. When the competition hears your idea, they will give you all the reasons why you will fail. And if you have a solid solution that solves each of their reasons, your business idea should be a winner.

When you are gathering data from the competition, go to more than one competitor. One may lie to you or have different priorities in running their business. Go to several competitors and always ask the exact same questions. Usually you will have forty-plus questions to be answered, so do it over a period of three to five days. Engage the owner or manager and become his or her friend. Buy something from them on each visit—and not the cheapest item! If they cannot talk at work, invite them out for dinner, dessert, or even breakfast, depending on their working hours. Go to expensive places—this is market research!

Discover the strategies that have worked for the competition in the past, and let the competitor or her customers take you through the process that is used to acquire new products or services. When you get inside information about how a company works, you can come up with strong solutions tailored specifically to help the business grow. If you are considering manufacturing or reselling a product, find out how they are marketed and packaged.

Think about your competition and the type of consumer who would want your product or service the most. Make sure your business will either employ and/or sell to the people group you are seeking to reach. Talk to real customers. Make sure your product or service is valued in their eyes.

What can you produce, or what service can you offer that will also enable you to glorify God in tangible ways?

Study your market audience also. What is the size of the group that may purchase your product or service? Do you have a large enough working market? If there are eleven competitors in the city, is that too many for 19,000 target customers? If you do not like the numbers, explore doing another business and be happy that you saved yourself from a potential financial disaster.

Determine where the local business system creates difficulties. This requires a critical analysis of the business system. Look at the economics of the business system, the individual components that add value, and the dynamics of the business system. Where do you see your business making a contribution that will earn money and glorify Jesus?

Figure out the sustainable competitive advantages that your business brings to the community. Can your competitors readily copy these advantages? Sustainable, competitive advantages exist when the customers perceive a consistent difference in valued characteristics between your company's products and those of your competitors. The perceived difference is a direct result of a difference in capability between you and your competitors. Both the difference in valued characteristics and the difference in capability can be expected to last for some time.

One thing I like to do when starting a business is to visit those whom I am soon to compete against. I ask them to lunch and when we are eating, I tell them, *"I'm thinking about coming in and setting up a business that is going to compete against you and what you're doing."* Some of them try convincing me not to do this, giving me a list of the reasons why this is a bad idea—meanwhile, I am furiously taking notes. Then I look at the list and say, *"I can do that, I can do that, I can do that. Okay, I can do this business."* Or there have been times when ticking off that list I think, *"I can do that, I can do that . . . Uh oh, I can't do that."* This is a way to learn from your competition all the things you can't do and shouldn't do; and if you can do them, then you are okay. If you cannot do them, then you know not to start that business.

Robert explains,

I'm starting a restaurant. In the beginning I went to seven competitors and asked to meet with the manager. When the waiters asked why, I would reply, "I just want to meet him to ask him some questions." They usually told me he was busy. So in each place I sat down and ate, and then I gave the waiter who served me a 40 percent tip. On the way out, I also gave every employee I saw a five-dollar bill. When I came back the very next day, guess what happened? People were running to serve me; everybody wanted to wait on me. I sat down while they were all fighting over me. "How can we help you sir? Anything we can do for you?" I told them before ordering anything that I would like to see the manager. "Oh, yes sir!" Then they rushed to the back and soon the manager came to see what was going on. "Hello," I greeted him, "I want to open a business that's going to compete with you in this area, and I'd like to talk to you." After the manager said he didn't want to talk, I thanked him and got up to leave, but the employees said to the manager, "Hey, you need to talk to him. He is a good man!" So what does he do? He sits down and answers my questions! Half the managers ended up becoming friends with me and have been very helpful. Though a few of them gave me minimal information and were not very helpful, the point is that I learned some very informative things. You have to adopt that kind of persistence. It is just good business! I would have had to pay a market researcher much more to learn what I did, and I got that information directly myself. I didn't have to get somebody else to do it.

2. Develop a Distinctive

God gave Clay an unusual assignment in a remote part of the country. He visited a key city in this remote region and learned that it had many computer training centers, but not one computer business. Once the young people learned how to program computers, they needed to move to the capital city seven hours away so as to utilize their new skills. Clay recognized an opportunity and he started Clay's Computer Programming, selling his services to business friends in America. He started small, hiring only the top graduates from the best training centers. Clay's American clients found his employees' work to be top quality and at half the price of what they were paying in the United States. Clay's friends were telling

others, so CCP's reputation and clientele began to grow. Today they have over forty programmers, are one of the largest white-collar employers in that city, and have a key witness in a remote unreached area.

"Most recent analyses state that combining a global reach with local adaptiveness is now the primary strategic direction of multinational corporations," says professor of international business Gunnar Hedlund, of the Stockholm School of Economics. As cross-cultural workers, we know the language, culture, and people better than other outsiders. We need to integrate our knowledge of the world, with our insider insights to develop a distinctive that can be marketed locally.

What is unique about you or your product? What ability, skill, education, or experience do you have that can be marketed to the people you are reaching?

While doing a seminar in Korea, a young man came up to me at the end of the first day, saying, "I am sorry, I don't have any special skills. I don't have any special education. Really, I feel useless. I don't know what I can do. But I really feel like God wants me to go to the Middle East." I asked, "What's your background?" He replied, "I went to a Bible college, then to seminary, and then I was in the military." We continued to chat about his life, and we couldn't come up with anything for a while, but then an idea popped into my head, which God gets credit for, and I said, "You were in the military. In the military you are required to learn taekwondo, right? Do you like taekwondo?" He said, "Yes, I love it." "Okay," I went on, "I think you have to be a fourth-degree black belt to be an instructor, right? So can you be a taekwondo instructor?" He smiled, "Actually I'm a second-degree black belt now, and I'm very close to getting my third degree. Yes, I could get my fourth degree." I said, "Then I have an idea: get your fourth-degree black belt, become a teacher, and then go open a taekwondo studio in North Africa." And that is what he did! I have lost touch with him over the years, but he did start a successful taekwondo studio, which he ran for at least six years. He had a skill that he did not recognize as a skill to reach out to the lost. God can and will use most everything in our past to glorify His name.

Develop a niche by specializing; create extraordinary services. Try to do something that is remarkable, memorable, and unique. Get off the main road into the back alleys to discover something different that would appeal to the local clientele. For example, vanilla is a main-street flavor while rocky road is not. Though there may be just a few people who are unwilling to eat vanilla ice cream, there are legions of people who are allergic to nuts or marshmallows or are just plain uninterested in eating

an unusual scoop of ice cream. The safest choice for a kid's birthday is vanilla. But vanilla is boring. You cannot build a fast-growing company around vanilla.

In most markets, the boring slot is filled. The product designed to appeal to the largest possible audience already exists, and displacing it is difficult. How can you market yourself as "more bland" than the leading brand? Real growth businesses are built around products that cost too much, cost too little, are too heavy, are too complicated, are too simple—too something—but are just perfect for some.

Pedro and Martina opened an import-export firm in a poor Muslim country. It did not seem like a wise business strategy, because the country had nothing to export, and only two percent of the population had money to buy anything. Not surprisingly, the business lost money. For three years their mission agency helped make up their losses, but finally the mission pulled the plug. When they set up their company, Pedro had gotten to know several local officials and had many over for a meal. They loved Martina's Tex-Mex food—and an idea was born. Pedro and Martina asked their mission if they could stay and open a restaurant. The mission agreed, but told them they would not get any more financial help. Using some money loaned from a friend, they set up a restaurant in the neighborhood where the wealthy two percent lived. There were only three quality restaurants in this city of nearly a million people. Targeting both the expatriates in the city and the wealthy two percent, the business grew and prospered. In a matter of months, everyone in the community knew them. As they hired locals and expanded their network of friends, they began to see locals come to faith.

Differentiate yourself. Every human being is unique. When you make a connection with someone by being yourself (as opposed to trying to act like a salesperson), you build relationships. Customers feel comfortable dealing with you when you are relaxed.

When starting out, think small. No need to think about selling to the masses. Think of the smallest conceivable market and describe a product that overwhelms it with its remarkability. Go from there.

You can also enhance the commonplace. What can you do to make the ordinary seem special? Take a restaurant or coffee shop—nothing special since most cities have tons of them. But by enhancing the commonplace, B4T workers have opened fantastic restaurants, some with a theme from their home country or city. One worker in Asia who is from Texas opened a Texas steakhouse. Now, to me, the food looks very Chinese, but it attracts people. He has longhorns and all sorts of photos from Texas all over the restaurant. He told me he could not grill a steak if his life depended on it. He simply has taken local dishes and given them Texas names. People come because they like the Texas theme. There is nothing like it in the city.

3. Bring Back the Past—Bring Back Lost Standards

In many cultures and countries, especially those moving from the developing to the developed stage, the business community often loses some of its traditional standards and ways of working. One business idea could be to reinstate traditional business services. For instance, when I have gone into some hotels, people greet me by name. One time I asked, *"How do you know my name?"* The clerk answered, *"Remember when you came here last year and I took your picture? Well, here. Look . . ."* I looked around the corner at a file with lots of pictures. He said, *"When I saw your name on today's list of registrants, I checked my pictures. You were there. I review each day's list so when we meet I know who you are."* Despite having about a hundred people checking in each day, he remembers every returning customer's name. You can bet I have used that hotel again. That is a lost standard; in the past everyone used to know everybody's names. So consider what people used to do or value so that you can restore those standards.

About eight years ago, Carl launched a small loans business. It was in a highly relational, remote area. To receive a loan, a potential client needed to be recommended by an existing customer of the small loans business. This enabled the client to avoid an extensive credit check. Once a person is in, they are trusted. There is a relationship. If they overdraw or are delinquent on a payment, they will probably receive a personal phone call as a reminder before being penalized. The employees know their patrons by name. Carl did not create anything new, he simply re-created something that seems to have been lost: a loan agency centered on relationships.

Think customization. Customizing your product or service to your people group or clientele often brings surprising results. David writes, *"When we designed language programs to fit specific business needs, like courses for hotels, call centers, and business executives, our profits soared."* Even though your product or service may be similar to others on the market, it is your job to make it as customer-specific as possible. Call customers regularly to find out how they are using your products, what they like about them, what they don't like, what they would change, and how they would make them easier to use. Then make modifications and design new ones to match the information gleaned from these customers.

Update old ideas. Often you can find a workable business by taking an old idea and putting a new spin on it. Ask yourself, *"Is there a business idea that used to exist in the community but doesn't any longer?"* Is there any way to update an old idea and roll it out to a new audience? Ask older friends if there is a business or service they remember from their childhood that could be dusted off and reintroduced.

4. Upgrade the Norm—Raise the Bar

Take any business you are in—pet shop, flower store, window washing, or bicycle shop—and make it the most thorough, best-inventoried, highest-profile sort of business in the area. Become the standard by which the competition is measured. In many towns across America, for instance, Domino's Pizza sets a standard by guaranteeing quick home delivery—*"30 minutes or it's free."* Don't live up to a criterion, set it. In other words, raise the ante. You can do this with a product by designing it better, presenting it better, giving better instructions, or supplying better after-market support.

Service is what keeps you in business for the long haul. It is your track record that builds customers' confidence in you and attracts prospects to you. People do not care how much you offer them; they care about whether you exceed their expectations. If you want to delight people or create a remarkable experience or if you desire people to talk about you, the secret is simple: give them more than they expect.

Jack, a B4Ter in China, opened a Western-style restaurant that was packed the first few months. Soon, copycat restaurants were opened by locals, reducing his customer count. Jack responded by offering free English lessons during lunch—something his competitors could not do as readily. He also started showing free movies in English on a big-screen TV in the evenings. Then for those who bought a dessert, a follow-up discussion about the movie in English was offered. Jack keeps a library of movies onsite so people can choose what they want to watch. With both moves Jack took advantage of his natural English language distinctive to raise the bar, resulting in an improved bottom line.

If I walk into your store and it looks and feels like other stores I have been into before, my expectations are locked in. Now what? But if I walk into your office or store and it is like nothing I have ever experienced before, you get a chance to set my expectations. Marketing is not merely bragging; it creates a culture, tells a story, and puts on a show. Often in our rush to get picked or get noticed or build a buzz, the instinct is to promise our customers more. Perhaps it pays to promise less instead, to radically change expectations, and to reset what it means to deliver on the promise of satisfying the customer.

Consider ways to provide unique value for your services or products. Refocus your big idea for a specialized market. Break off a piece of a big market and refocus it to a different audience. For example, one entrepreneur started a language school that struggled until he realized many locals went to Korea for jobs. He recruited a Korean man to join his team and then added Korean to the languages the school offered. Within a year, the school moved from being in the red to in the black. Whenever you consider an idea that interests you, take a hard look at that category and ask yourself, *"What if I took a similar business and tweaked it to fit the local audience?"*

Another way to grow a business is to take a prosaic, bland sort of product and make it alive again. Hamburgers are a good example. There are so many bad burgers in this world. One restaurateur decided to make *"the best burger west of the Nile."* He did, and his clientele grew. I venture to say that anyone with a hot grill who makes an honest burger (or pizza) with generous portions and fresh fried onions will never lack customers.

The underlying concept here is that a distinctive system can give you a big edge. Virtually any part of a business system can be the basis for building a competitive edge. Change is the operative word, and the secret of change is to focus on the new path, not on the comfort of a worn trail. The new path is where you will find the challenges to be overcome, the freedom to create, and the space to maneuver. Yes, there will be adversity and hard times. Remember, the first one to plow new ground must also dig up the rocks.

Success came the hard way to Sam Meineke, founder of the popular chain of discount muffler shops in North America. When he opened his service station he worked from six in the morning till ten at night but was not making any money. One day a man came in for a dollar's worth of gas. Since business was slow, after he wiped the man's windshield Sam offered to wash the inside of the windows too. The driver said, *"Tell you what, son. Fill 'er up. I've never had this kind of service!"* Sam reported that at that moment he had an epiphany. *"Suddenly I found my business success formula: Treat customers right and give them extra service."* Soon the cars were lined up around the block.

Robert adds,

Raise the bar, raise the standards. When we started our English center, we set a high bar and we kept it there. Most of our competitors had forty or more students in each class. We allowed no more than twelve in ours. We offer ten different languages and all of our teachers are native speakers. We can charge our customers a little more than most of our competitors because they know they are going to receive a quality learning experience. Students know they are going to learn faster and better and be able to pass their entrance exams for the university if they study with us.

5. Restore or Buy Out an Old Business

Sometimes older businesses get shunted to the side due to competition by national chains or foreign franchises. Perhaps a particular type of business comes to be seen as outdated or mature, with no prospects for growth. Diners in the United States, for instance, were almost anachronistic in the 1970s and '80s, pushed aside by the onslaught of fast-food chains and convenience foods. Now they are being revived, complete with shiny chromium jukeboxes at the table.

A team in North Africa recognized this idea when they bought an aging hotel and remodeled and modernized it, attracting a new clientele. Similarly, an old bakery in North Africa was turned into a coffee and pastry shop. In Central Asia, two B4T workers bought a boarded-up restaurant and reopened it as an ice cream parlor.

Restoring or buying out an old business and refurbishing it with new life is a welcome strategy among politicians and the aged. Older people especially love to see old businesses come back to life, returning value and memories to the community. One thing that is becoming quite popular in the United States is remodeling businesses in older parts of the city. One of my personal favorites is a McDonald's in a run-down area in downtown Chicago, just a few blocks from Moody Bible Institute. Originally this McDonald's went out of business, which is surprising since McDonald's outlets normally do not go out of business. Yet this one closed its doors *until* somebody came along and upgraded it, adding a distinctive. They then filled the store with Elvis Presley memorabilia: guitars, albums, and music of the "King" being played all day long. The turnaround was instantaneous.

6. Import an Idea

Discover a business that is working somewhere else and import it. On a business trip to Europe, Howard Schultz of Starbucks noticed how Italians spent hours in cafés sipping coffee. He imported the idea of cafés to the United States. When you travel, ask yourself if a certain business is available in your adopted country. Could it work there? You could be a market survey away from a successful business.

Jon recognized that quality chicken meat was difficult to come by in his adopted country. He found some coaches to guide him and then started a poultry farm with birds imported from Europe. Today he operates two large farms with over thirty thousand chickens each and over two hundred smaller branches scattered around the country. He has created hundreds of jobs and has seen several new churches birthed as a result.

The next time you visit a new place, keep your eyes open. You just might stumble across the perfect business. When you relocate to a new area, look around to see what is missing. Or if you like a particularly successful business already in your area, why not move where it does not yet exist and establish one yourself? Not every business idea travels well, so be sure to put aside your own feelings for the product or service and examine it from a business viewpoint.

As the standard of living rises in a country, there will be more disposable income for people to spend on themselves. Specialty restaurants with foreign themes have been flourishing around the world. Exercise gyms, bakeries, and high-end clothing stores are just a few of the businesses B4Ters have imported and are finding successful. Offer guarantees on products or free returns for defective items. How many places offer free refills in your city? The things that are common to us in the West are often lacking in the marketplace in the East.

Add value through innovation. New products and services are created, and old ones are tweaked or revamped. Evolutionary marketers are always looking for ways to promote a "new wrinkle" to the old target group and to expand by taking on new niches that will be receptive to their innovations. Attempt new marketing approaches and uncover new ways to communicate the value of your company's innovations to your target audience. Evaluate the services and products offered in your city or village. How do they compare to those back home? Are there cost-effective ways you can upgrade?

Learn what is most important to your customers. For example, Chinese want low prices, Kazakhs want quality, and Malays want products that are easy to use. Even in the same community, different customers want different types of products. Do not try to be everything to everybody. Pick the customer group(s) that you want to target, and then aim to deliver the product or service they want.

Do not be afraid to stand out or try something new. John had been to numerous foreign cities and noticed they all had at least one thriving pizza business. He returned to his adopted city and told his friends of his idea to start a pizza parlor. *"Nobody here eats pizza,"* they told him. Undeterred because of what he saw in so many other cities, John responded, *"Maybe that's because there aren't any places that serve pizza!"* Today he has a thriving business and a couple of employees have come to faith.

Many business opportunities surface for the simple reason that many consumers are dissatisfied. Indeed, my main business started from being a customer and not liking what was offered. Is there a service or a product you cannot get overseas, or is the quality so poor that it is disheartening? With a service business it is not that difficult to raise the bar and develop a distinctive based on observations learned in other countries. Look, listen, taste, touch, and smell. You know what you are dissatisfied with and want to replace, improve, or change. So begin where the tool breaks, the service slips, or the shoe pinches—then import an idea that makes it better.

7. Be Professional

"Clothes don't make the man, but they go a long way toward making a businessman."—Thomas Watson, Sr.[74]

There are many ways to make an impact. If you think a bit, you already know how to use at least one of the most effective methods to gain the attention of officials and leaders. Think back to your days in high school. Who were the coolest kids? Weren't their friends automatically cool, too? It is all about perception—and perception becomes reality. If I perceive you as just a small businessperson or having no money, I am not going to give you much time or attention. If you are going to be a businessperson, then you must dress, live, and act like a businessperson. People do not believe what you tell them; they believe what they see. Being professional is an integral part of doing business.

Jesus tells us to strive for perfection. In the Master's office there is no room for sloppy *agape*. Your lifestyle and presentation must fit the role you are fulfilling. You cannot claim to be a businessman and then

---

[74] Ros Taylor, *Work/Life: Develop Confidence* (Google eBook: Penguin, 2006).

live among the poor. You cannot claim to be a regional director for a company and then never leave the country. Dr. Steven Rundle, professor of business at Biola, told me,

> In my own "fact-finding tour" in Turkey a few years ago I met almost no one who would admit to using a platform or business as a cover. They all thought they were bona fide businesspeople. However, I discovered that almost without exception they were very confused about basic concepts such as profit. They thought they were profitable, or hoped to soon be profitable, but had little understanding of what their costs were, and therefore had no clue about profit.

Business by definition is a profit-making entity. If your business is not making a profit or striving to make a profit, you are operating a platform, not a real business.

Who are the key people you should know and develop relationships with as you start a business? Government officials are surprisingly tolerant of businessmen who "love Jesus." What they are not tolerant of are *surprises*. It is important to have one or two government officials who are friends, whom you can keep informed of your plans and activities. In addition, you will need a trusted lawyer, tax consultant, and banker; each has the potential to make or break your business.

As you present yourself as a serious, professional businessperson, first find a lawyer. Local friends are well meaning, and some, even the most helpful, cannot help you through the juggernaut of legal technicalities in the same way a good lawyer can. My standard recommendation is if you wish to save time and present yourself properly, find a lawyer recommended by a non-Christian Western businessman. If you do not know any businesspeople, find where there is a business center in the city and ask them for help in finding a lawyer or company secretary who deals with setting up organizations and new businesses. Most lawyers grant you one free session before they begin charging for your time. Take advantage of that by visiting at least three lawyers to learn their backgrounds, costs, and to determine with whom you will feel comfortable working. Using a lawyer to register a business will cost anywhere from $1,000 to $5,000, yet it is essential. If you do not have a lawyer, government officials and even friends will be suspicious of your real motives.

Seek out other expatriate businessmen—both Christian and non-Christian—as well as locals to learn which lawyers, accountants, and bankers they retain and why. Most lawyers will have tax accountants and banks they can recommend. Be sure to discuss these needs during your initial interview to glean as much insight as you can in order to have a broader perspective on what your business needs from each person. Remember, in many countries a language school, restaurant, coffee shop, and manufacturing or retail business could all have a completely different registration process.

Regarding meeting with a lawyer or any person, one B4T worker had some good advice:

> We learned never to ask a lawyer "Can we do this?" Instead, ask, "This is what we would like to accomplish. What is the best way to do it?" Too often we assume our Western legal strategies and structures are the best or right way, instead of letting the local lawyer inform us of the best tactics. Many things are possible in most countries yet our preconceived structures are typically not the best in foreign lands.

Let the lawyer process your application papers. The lawyer does not have to be a Christian, and in some cases it is better if she is *not* a Christian. One coworker hired a well-known Christian lawyer who was locked into doing things one way. Because she was successful in getting Christian service organizations into the country, this tentmaker was encouraged to use her for her business registration as well. After three rejections by the government she tried a different, non-Christian lawyer. Soon afterwards she was granted a work visa. A good lawyer will introduce you to the right people and pave the way for the approval of both your business application papers and your work visa.

It is likely you will also need a local business address. Most governments frown upon using your home address as your business address. More than a handful of aspiring B4T workers have been kicked out of their country for working at home, even in the initial setup stage of the business. In some countries you cannot set up a business address without first having your business legally approved. This is kind of a "Catch-22," in that you do not want to rent a business facility without knowing if your business registration will even be approved. The solution is utilizing a business center or executive suites office to temporarily serve as a business address. Nearly every capital city has a business center. And if there isn't one, maybe that should be your business! Even if you are planning for your business to be in the hinterlands of the country, it is normative to have an office address in the capital. Choose a business center that is both affordable and has a well-known street address, preferably in the center of the city on a main thoroughfare so it is easily recognized as a true business location. Jim reported,

> Recently one of our coworker's visa applications was rejected. We learned the reason was because the stationery did not have a local office address on it. Within two days, we went and found a local business center, rented a mailbox, and using their local address on our stationery, resubmitted our papers with the exact same wording. The visa was granted the very next week.

Business centers are places where you can rent an office or a mailbox. They are cheap, helpful, and professional. Since they are geared toward providing temporary business services, they are a good place to begin gathering information when you first arrive. You should be able to find them on the Internet. An average business center will know where to find a lawyer and other key people who can advise you on setting up your business. This is where "normal" businesspeople begin exploring new markets. Another professional way forward is to attend trade shows or trade fairs in the city. There you can ask all the questions you wish without raising any suspicion.

You will need a phone number and a website. The business center may provide you with a phone number, but it is okay to use your cell phone too; just be sure you answer it in a professional way during business hours. Nowadays it is pertinent to have a decent website set up in advance. The last time I went to submit my papers to reregister my business, before the guy at the counter even took the papers, he looked up the website on my business card, then turned to his computer terminal at his desk and typed in the site. He explored the site a bit to see how it looked and *then* took my papers.

You must have a good website, stationery, and especially business cards. Business cards are very important in most countries. Look at the business cards of others in your country to make sure your cards are of the same quality as theirs. Make quality two- or three-color cards. Your business cards should have your name and title, the company's name, and, of course, the company address, telephone, email, and website. It is good to use English on one side and the national language on the other side.

Stationery is needed too, but these days you can build a template into your computer; there is no need to print up hundreds of stationery in advance. It is helpful to print some sharp two- or three-color brochures or pamphlets of your product or services as well. These brochures should picture the product and clearly sell it or the service to a customer. Keep your resume up to date, ready to email or give a hard copy to those who ask.

Finally, buy and wear quality business attire. Today business dress varies from country to country. If you are not certain what is appropriate for your people group, sit in a café in the heart of the business area of the main city and observe what people wear. It is smarter to be better dressed than the locals, rather than underdressed. Buy a sharp business suit. In some cultures "power suits" are a part of doing business. When you meet with government officials, you must look real. You must dress better than they do. "Dress for success" is not just a saying. If you look like you have money, people will believe you do. Governments and businesses wish to deal with individuals whom they perceive will succeed—meaning they have money. In some Southeast and Central Asian countries, Western suits are not appropriate. Look for what wealthy businessmen wear, and dress like them. First impressions are important.

As you investigate opportunities, be open to all the possibilities you discover. Remember, prayer is the starting point for setting up your tent (business). Invite Jesus into every conversation, and ask for His input on every decision. Work *with* Him, not just *for* Him. As you work together, consider how to develop a distinctive. Prayerfully discern ways to bring back the past, raise the bar, restore an old business, or import a new idea while being professional. No one will utilize more than a few of these pointers, but when starting out each will help move you toward getting your tent in place.

DISCUSSION QUESTIONS

1. To differentiate your product, state three things about it that make it stand out from everything else in the marketplace.
2. List seven factors you should investigate when selecting a new B4T business.

"Where you start is not as important as where you finish."

—ZIG ZIGLAR[75]

[75] http://www.ziglar.com/quotes.

Chapter 9

STAKING YOUR TENT

Often I am asked, *"What is the best kind of B4T business to start?"* or *"What is the most successful B4T business?"* Frankly there is no one business better than another. In the OPEN Network there are so many different kinds of businesses—and so many different kinds of people—that it is impossible to give specific advice on the particular type of business you should start. Yet selecting the specific business suitable for you and your people group is the paramount decision for your life and work overseas. Whatever you decide will ultimately determine your impact on transforming lives for the King. So, what kind of business should you start? Only you will be able to answer that question. To maximize your chances of success, you should consider closely six pointers.

Pointers for Staking Your Tent

1. Choose a Business You Know Intimately
Trying to learn a new industry or skill at the same time that you are getting your business up and running will add a lot of unnecessary stress to your new venture and lower your chances of success. Sure, it might be fun to operate an exercise gym, but if you have spent the last five years in a photo studio and do not have any experience with exercise programs and weight lifting, you might be better off starting your own photo shop, video production business, or teaching photography. That is not to say that you cannot learn a new business—but you should learn how to run a gym before you blow your life's savings on a room full of exercise equipment.

2. Choose Something You Enjoy Doing
It is much more difficult (and a lot less fun) to make a success of a small business that does not interest you. For instance, do not open an auto-parts store when your heart is really in graphic design. Part of our assignment is to be joyful, so laugh often! Take care of your spiritual, family, and

personal well-being. If you are not smiling on a regular basis, recalibrate. There will be rough times, even rough years. So select a business you believe in. Sacrifices will be made in starting out, but there is no need to sacrifice your joy.

In considering the kind of business you should start, you need to factor in the types of work experiences you have done in your life, classes you have taken, and special skills you have developed through a hobby. Starting a business is like having a child—like it or not, you must be all in. The same goes for business. If you do not enjoy the business you are planning to do, you probably will not want to commit to it, and it will likely fail. The first year or two you can expect to work fifty to eighty hours a week. You need to enjoy what you are doing.

3. Consider the Timing

Building a business is neither for the faint of heart nor the speed demon. Climbing Mount Everest is not done in three easy steps. Build systems for the long haul and focus on small, connected steps. Google tells us that it takes 26,364 steps to climb Mount Everest, and that is starting from halfway up at Base Camp. The point is *plan ahead.*

Many people do a thorough study of the culture, marketplace, and people before making decisions based upon the current needs of the land and the people. Then they prepare themselves and train for the next one to four years. But when they finally get to the field the local needs have changed. Instead, it is better to be fast to market than to wait until your offering is perfect. Sun Tzu teaches, *"Whosoever is first to occupy the battlefield to await the enemy will be fresh and at ease."*[76] There are advantages in being the first—that is, being the pioneer. Pioneers often can command the top market shares and, initially, may benefit from premium pricing. However, to be a pioneer means that you must be able to see things before others see them. It requires a sharp mind; if the things were easily seen, others would have taken them up earlier. In addition, it requires boldness.

If you can get in at the beginning of the need for a product or service, you will be able to stay a long time. If you come in too late, you will be the first kicked out of the country. Timing is important both to succeeding in the business and winning government favor. Like seniority in a job, you want to be first—a trendsetter, not a follower.

---

[76] Sun Tzu, *Art of War* (Charleston: BookSurge Classics, 2002).

4. Choose a Business that Will Turn a Profit

The best way to determine your business's potential profitability is to prepare a "break-even analysis," which is a financial projection that will estimate how easy or difficult it will be to turn a profit. Writing up a thorough business plan is part of this process. Do not guess; do your homework. There are too many factors impacting a business to guarantee its success, but a solid business plan should provide probable cause for succeeding at keeping your family out of the poorhouse.

One of the consistent points of failure in starting a BAM business is the thought, *"I like the product, and I think the business will work."* You may like the idea, and your friends at home may like the idea, but verify that the *locals* like the idea too. One former B4Ter opened an exercise gym in a major Muslim city. There were no modern well-equipped gyms, and the B4Ter thought the business would certainly succeed. After two years, and spending over $80,000 of his friends' money, he closed shop and went home. He had never taken the time to study the market to learn if there was a market for such a gym. Do a solid business plan *first* to ensure the business will be profitable.

5. Choose a Vocation

One core question to ask is, *"Where do my gifts, skills, and motivations best fit the needs of the people I am reaching?"* In reality, there are varying needs in different countries and among different cultures. The initial step is to research needs related to any vocations in which you are interested. It may be helpful to take a vocational work profile test to better understand yourself—your interests, task motivations, and abilities. David writes from Central Asia, *"Gaining some experience in a proposed vocation is extremely helpful because many workers end up working in jobs they have never really observed or experienced before."*

Starting a service business requires less capital up front, as opposed to manufacturing. In addition, service industries are more nimble and adaptable. However, they create fewer jobs and are not as welcome by government officials as are factories. You need to prayerfully weigh the pros and cons of each. Remember, whatever business you choose to start, it is important to determine the amount of risk you are comfortable with. You also need to have that *"peace . . . which surpasses all understanding"*[77] that will guide and guard you as you step forward.

---

[77] Philippians 4:7

6. Go There

Solomon teaches us, *"An intelligent man is always open to new ideas; in fact he looks for them."*[78] Jesus said to look on the fields. Looking involves seeing. This includes searching for new ideas. To "see" something, we must be where it is. Go to the land, the city, Jesus has placed on your heart. In the Spirit and in prayer, go and gain His perspective for the place. It's best to do the research yourself. Study the opportunites and types of businesses that might succeed. Learn what living life there might be like, including educational opportunities for your children. Experience has shown us that prayer walking, or doing a short-term project in country is helpful, but more importantly we also need to *see* the ways business works in the country.

One idea that several have done successfully is to organize an advance team that goes with you to survey the land. This team should include experienced businesspeople. Include known nationals too who may help research and investigate specific aspects of the particular business that you have in mind.

Ed in Indonesia writes,

> Before moving to our country my partner and I visited numerous times. By reading the newspapers we learned of the government's plan to educate the people in English and computers. After prayer, these seemed to be good businesses to get into. Having a computer background, my partner opened a software consulting and training business. I learned to teach English and opened a tutorial school.

Never select a business at home thinking it will work overseas. Many people work a job at home and think, *"I enjoy this. I am good at this, and it pays well,"* and then come to the conclusion that they should do this job overseas to reach people. Some jobs are readily transferable to an overseas context, but many are not.

I have said this before, but it is worth repeating: *Do your homework before you go.* Find out who makes the decisions in the community, and learn their rules for doing business. When you know who the key local leaders are, make an appointment to meet and talk over your ideas with them. Unless you have established yourself through a previous contact, often a proper appointment is better made by a local go-between. This is especially true in Asian countries. Invite the local leaders to meet at

---

[78] Proverbs 18:15

the best restaurant in town. Be prepared for your meeting. Be ready to suggest business or job options they want and which will be in their interest to cooperate with you on. Do not tell your opinions, or state your own ideas; simply ask for input and listen. Express your interest by writing down their answers. It should not be too difficult to show them that you are working in the best interest of the community and also their own best interest.

Jack in the Arab world writes, *"Just go! . . . Many people get in by just showing up and seeking a job, even after failed attempts through mission agencies or even business placement agencies. Just arrive as you are, knock on doors, and find jobs."* Fred adds, *"In Asia, relationships built on mutual trust are very, very important. Thus, it is important to go there and meet people who will help you get in."*

Clearly it is the Lord who empowers our successes. Discuss these six practical guidelines with Him as you *look* into setting up your own business.

Starting a Business

There are significant advantages to operating your own business overseas. Business owners are able to stay indefinitely in the country if they are providing something of real value to the community, such as creating jobs, generating wealth, providing training, etc. Business owners have more freedom for witness within their company and community. Work, profitability, and godly values are all huge value add-ons for the local officials. The central nonspiritual need in developing countries is solid and lasting economic development that brings prosperity to the local community. A business's prosperity impacts all corners of a community.

In starting a business, there are also some big hurdles to overcome— taxes, regulations, customs, and cross-cultural work ethics. Legally required taxes can be so high it makes profitability virtually impossible. Bureaucratic regulations can be paralyzing. Dishonesty and fraud may be so common that running a business is unworkable. One helpful step is to find a local to partner with you who can guide you through the government bureaucracy and around the cultural pitfalls.

You do not have to do everything well yourself, but you do need to know how everything works. If you do not know how everything works, the employee who knows how to do what you do not, may hold you or the business captive. So learn every task from the beginning. As the business grows, well-trained employees will be able and willing to take on more responsibility, enabling you to delegate more.

Buying a Business

Before you seriously consider buying an existing business, find out as much as you can about it. Thoroughly review copies of the business's certified financial records; these include cash-flow statements, balance sheets, and accounts payable and receivable. It also means employee files—including benefits and any employee contracts—major contracts and leases, and any past lawsuits or other relevant information. This review (lawyers call it doing "due diligence") will tell you a lot about the company that you are buying and will alert you to any potential problems. For instance, if a major contract does not allow the current owner to assign it to you without the other party's permission, you should enlist the owner to help you obtain the other party's consent.

Do not be shy about asking for information about the business. Here are some other details you should determine before you commit yourself to buying a particular business:

- Who holds the title to company assets?
- Is there any potential or ongoing litigation?
- Have there been any workers' compensation claims or unemployment claims made by company employees?
- Has the business consistently paid its taxes?
- Are there any potential tax liabilities?
- Are there any commercial leases or major contracts that can be assigned to a new owner?
- Has the company given any warranties or guarantees to its customers?
- Does the company own any patents or copyrights?
- Does the company hold any registered trademarks?
- Are the licenses or tax registration certificates of the business transferable?
- Is the business in compliance with local zoning laws?
- If the business is a franchise, what will it take to get the necessary franchisor approval?

This is not an exhaustive list. You should review any business records that will provide you with information to help you decide whether the business is a smart purchase. If the seller refuses to supply any of this information, or if you find any misinformation, this may be a sign that you should look elsewhere for the right business to buy. Be sure to enlist a lawyer to walk through all the local and international issues related to buying the business.

Dan, an OPEN worker, agrees when he adds,

> Don't find yourself scrambling to put important pieces of the business's structure in place after you've opened your doors. Be sure you have a lawyer who walks with you through all the major issues in registering the business, securing a facility and promoting the business locally beforehand.

If you have thoroughly investigated a company and wish to go ahead with a purchase, there are a few more steps you will have to take. First, you and the owner will have to agree on a fair purchase price. A good way to do this is to hire an experienced appraiser who can estimate the company's fair market value. If all goes well, you and the business owner will agree on a fair price as well as other aspects of the purchase, such as which assets you will buy and the terms of payment. Most often, businesses are purchased on an installment plan with a sizable down payment.

After you have outlined the terms on which you and the seller agree, you will need to create a written sales agreement. Again, be sure to have a lawyer review all the paperwork before you sign on the dotted line.

Service Industries Versus Manufacturing

There is an ongoing debate in the B4T world whether it is better to start a manufacturing business or a service-related business. Service-related businesses are simpler and thus easier to manage. They usually require smaller facilities and fewer employees. Being smaller, they often require fewer government permits and approvals.

Most countries welcome manufacturers. This puts you in favor with government officials. Usually factories also create large numbers of jobs. Jobs add value to the local community in more ways than any other service or kind of business. In addition, creating lots of jobs provides influence and input into the employees' lives. With each job you create, another opportunity is available to model and share the gospel. Bill, an owner of a large factory in China, says, *"I work alongside hundreds of people every day. Ministry is right here in my factory."* For impact, manufacturing is a strategic way to bless a community.

On the other hand, factories require a large investment up front. Nathan, also the owner of a large factory in China, needed nearly $500,000 to begin operations. And like any machine, a factory has varied multiple parts. As the owner, you not only need to know how to run the business, but you also need to know how to operate the machinery.

As with any business, the shipping of products is another concern. Caleb had a good product and good reviews, but being located in Central Asia, his shipping costs were prohibitive, finally forcing him to close the business. Shipping and packaging costs need to be included in your initial business plan.

When you build something, it is important to also be aware of the need to protect your intellectual property, which can be very difficult in some parts of the world. Many businesses and one B4T business lost their exclusivity when a local copied their product and then undersold them. Depending upon the country of manufacture, you may need to factor political instability and corruption into your "risk assessment." It is much more difficult to pick up a factory and move than a service business. It is important that you invest time understanding the constraints of manufacturing in your adopted land.

Hiring

Many B4Ters have trouble hiring the right person for the right role. Do not be overconfident about your interviewing skills. Invite Jesus to be a part of every interview, and review each applicant with Him. From the outset establish which traits the job demands beyond experience, training, and enthusiasm.

Before you begin hiring, you need to know what kind of people you need. When you are looking for new employees and team members, ask yourself: Who dreams like you dream? Who do you need, in view of your current and future context? Who fits in? And always hire a *person*, not a skill or a tool.

You should hire for attitude and train for skill. When you hire people and try to convert them to your way of doing things, you create a horrible tension as if training is supposed to "fix" employees. Hire people to be themselves. Train them well in the areas of their interest and they will work hard for you. Too many bosses are looking for people to fill a role. If you use people to accomplish your purposes, they will be quick to pick up on it. In time, your attitude will demotivate the employee and reflect poorly on Jesus too. Hire people whom you want to invest in, people whom you want to help succeed in life.

Whatever your line of work, you must hire the best people regardless of race, religion, or relatives. This is especially true in service industries, as their product is their people. In my own business if we have two people applying for a position and they have equal qualifications, we will always hire the Muslim over the non-Muslim, as we are here to witness to Muslims. However, if the non-Muslim is better qualified, we hire the non-Muslim. Your business is first and foremost a *business,* so you need to hire the best people to ensure it will succeed. Yes, your business is there to minister to people, but if you have unqualified employees, your business will fail. Then, not only will you *not* have a business, you will *not* have a ministry either. David's assistant manager resigned, so the manager wanted her best friend hired to work as her assistant. Despite the advice of his mentor, David hired her best friend. Within four days the manager's best friend was no longer her friend, and the assistant had to be released.

Never hire friends or relatives of employees unless they are absolutely the best person for the job. If there is pressure to do this, make it a written rule in your business. Never hire Christians just because they are Christians. Allow me to repeat myself: whatever your line of work, you must hire the best people regardless of race, religion, or relatives.

How do you hire good people? Obviously there are no guarantees, but asking good questions helps. Here are six questions we use in our office:

1. *What is the biggest misperception that people have of you?* This question clarifies just how self-aware the applicant is, which is important to know. *Leaders and good workers are usually self-aware.* For the same reason, I sometimes ask, *"Why wouldn't I hire you?"*

2. *How do you relax?* Some people are eager to show us that they will work themselves to the bone, put in overtime, etc. Such commitment is appreciated, but that is not good for them or the company. If they get the job and become stressed, their answer enables me to recommend and remind them of ways to refresh or reenergize themselves.

3. *If I gave you $50,000 and told you that you had to spend it all within twenty-four hours or return it to me, what would you do with the money?* I want to find out if they will spend all of the money on stuff for themselves, or whether they will use it to bless others. I want to hire generous people.

4. *Who is your favorite person in history (dead or alive) that you try to pattern your life after?* I want to learn who they emulate. I am looking for people who follow religious leaders or people of higher moral character, because such people are usually more trustworthy and easier to motivate, plus they are often more open to the gospel.

5. *What is most important to you in your work?* I like this question, as it gets to the point of what I want to know, beyond skills and experience. What motivates employees is essential to keeping them happy and productive.

6. *What are your career goals? What do you hope to be doing ten years from now?* Anybody who says working in my business is their life's ambition is either not being honest, or is a low achiever. I want to know where people are headed so I can help them get there.

It is also wise to have people work through some problem solving that relates to the job. Have them do accounting if they are dealing with finances. If they are managing people or involved in marketing, give them a case study or three and ask them what they would do in each situation.

In addition, there are two practical tests you may implement with those applying for key positions.

1. Invite the applicant into a room with many chairs. Soon after he sits down, have another employee come into the room and state, *"We need five of these chairs in another room."* You and the employee pick up two chairs each, then leave. Watch to see if the applicant picks up a chair and follows you. This reveals the servant attitude and work ethic of the applicant.

2. While an applicant is waiting in the lobby, have an employee walk through, shuffle some papers, and drop a five-dollar bill. The employee then exits the room pretending not to see the dropped bill. What does the applicant do? Chase after

the employee? Turn the money over to the receptionist? Pocket the money? Or leave it lying there? Each action reveals a bit of the applicant's character.

Negotiating

B4Ters need to learn the art of negotiation. The Japanese word for "businessman" can be translated "economic warrior." Stripped of perfunctory niceties, business is like war, and every deal is a hostage exchange. In our dealings we need to heed Jesus' exhortation to *"be wise as serpents yet innocent as doves."*[79] Deal as much as possible on a cash basis. Proverbs teaches us to *"never take an IOU from strangers, and whoever refuses to shake hands in a pledge is safe."*[80] Getting your money up front eliminates the risk of not getting paid. This also tests whether the other side is serious about the deal. If people promise you money, wait till that money is in hand before spending it. I have made this mistake twice, once resulting in having to let two workers go. It was one of the hardest dismissals I have ever made as an employer. So if you are relying on outside financing, do not commit to a project or to paying anyone else until you are sure your financier or debtor will step up to the plate. And if you are footing the bill and things begin to go bad, do not hesitate to pull the plug. Savvy buyers won't pay everything when a deal closes. They insist on the right to hold back money to cover against future problems.

You need to learn the art of negotiation. Every country negotiates things differently, so learn the methods of negotiation that are acceptable in your adopted culture. What are the rules for negotiating? What is considered "doing business," and at what point is it offending the other person? There are three basic rules to keep in mind that transcend most cultures when negotiating:

1. Determine the value of the product to yourself before negotiating. Do not waver on that price. If the seller is nowhere near your price, then walk away.
2. Your initial offer should be half of what your real offer is. Our office building was valued at $185,000, and the owner was asking $187,000. When I got him down to $175,000, though this was a bit over our budget, I thought I did well.

---

[79] Matthew 10:16
[80] Proverbs 11:15

My Chinese partner told me to withdraw the offer, then he contacted the seller as a new buyer. When I asked him what his initial offer was going to be, he said $80,000. I thought that was an embarrassing offer! But in the end we bought the building for $142,000.

If a seller states his price and you counter with another price, most sellers believe your real price is halfway between what he stated and you offered. Most Americans simply state their real price up front and then offend the Asian seller when they will not budge on the price. So if the seller's offer is out of your price range, offer him a price that is halfway between what he is offering and what you wish to pay.

3. The seller does the work in negotiations, not the buyer. If you are buying, never tell the seller your price. Make the seller work to find where your limit is. I was in India and showed interest in buying a marble elephant for our home. I set the price in my mind at ten dollars. When the seller's opening offer was sixty dollars, I started walking. With patience, I wound up paying four dollars for that elephant!

Never lie, but when negotiating learn to bluff. This is part of being *wise as serpents*. There is rarely a need to say, *"I do not know."* In business you are always saying to the client that you can do it. True, sometimes at the moment you are not sure how you will do it, but once the agreement is made, you go and figure out how and you get it done. Agreement does not mean that you have already done the job in the past, but it does mean you can and will do it. If you have never done the job before, go and figure it out. That is why it is called work!

"Do not be afraid to bluff. Was it lying in school to guess at the answer?"—An OPEN worker

Selecting a Banker

With the right bank, a small business gets more than a ladle in the money pool. A good banker can also provide advice for growing companies and services that help solve financial problems. In finding a good banker, treat it like you would when hiring a key employee. Ask around to find candidates. If you are in a building, ask other tenants which bank they use. Find out who your competitors use. Develop a short list of prospects, and then grill them with in-person visits. You should question your prospective banker closely about four areas: lending abilities, services, fees, and their areas of expertise.

The primary consideration for choosing a banker is how well he knows your business. Many times, small business owners are turned down for loans by banks because the banks do not understand the business. Usually local banks will not loan money to foreigners unless they have a local partner.

Local Laws and Regulations

Surviving the conundrums created by local laws and business strategies requires a number of tactics. First, keep a record of all local laws and regulations. Monitor any changes, which include knowing how they are applied. Rules can change at the discretion of the mayor. Sometimes the rule of the law can be a person. Globalization is causing more places to move away from this, but one can expect laws and regulations to be applied heavily to those who have less influence. For instance, less influential parties may be punished as an example to others, whereas more connected people are able to avoid such consequences or even continue to act against the law with impunity.

Second, build a network of well-connected powerful friends. Government officials should be your friends. The more powerful people you know, the more doors will open up for you. One official was hassling me over the size of the sign in front of our building. When I pointed out that it was the same size as all the other signs, the official insisted mine was not up to code. When I mentioned that Dr. Doh, the Minister of Education in our state, had seen the sign, the official asked, *"You know Dr. Doh?"* When I replied, *"Yes, he is a friend. In fact we had lunch last month,"* the issue was quickly dropped.

Finally, get a written copy of both the local business laws and practices. If an official grants you special permission, get it in writing and have the official put her personal stamp on it. For example, a senior official granted a B4Ter permission to live in a house in a suburb that was off limits to foreigners. A year later that official was transferred to another job, and the incoming official was a good friend of a business competitor of the foreigner. They revoked the original agreement because there was no proof of permission.

The government notary department can legally notarize contracts. This can save your neck. In some cultures, understanding the contract is just the beginning of the negotiation. So if you want to stand on a point in a contract, then you can only succeed legally if the contract is notarized. One situation involved a ten-year building lease. After two years, someone else bribed the leasing agent in order to kick the B4Ter out. This led to a protracted battle that was only won through prayer and the fact that the contract was notarized. If the contract had not been notarized, the outcome may have been different.

Local laws change all the time. It is very hard to know and track these changes. Sometimes you will be caught unaware. A common problem arises if a new official moves in. Make a point of knowing your officials. If there is a new person, welcome her. Take her out to lunch at the best restaurant and win her friendship. Honor her and ask her to keep you informed of any changes in the laws. Tell her you promise to keep her informed of any significant changes in your business too. In the same way, befriend local police. It helps to be seen in public with the police chief. Take a selfie with him and hang it in your office.

Location Issues

As mentioned earlier, the location of the business is often a make-or-break factor. The location may be just as important as the business concept. Visibility, accessibility, and signage are all critical factors. Be sure the location is accessible to the people you are reaching out to. Nathan established the first Western-run English language center in an untapped neighborhood in a large city in India. Because the rent was cheap, he first set up the business in an office on a side street hidden from traffic. Significant marketing and hanging banners all around the area did little to increase his enrollment. But when he moved the language center to a main road, paying nearly double the rent, his business took off.

Not sure if you are ready for a long-term lease? Test the waters by moving to a small office or warehouse environment. Another option is to do sales solely on the Web. With a physical location, it takes longer to recover your investment than with an online store. However, a physical store or office has many advantages in that it enables you to build credibility in the community, gain new customers, establish local loyalties, and reach those who do not like shopping on the Web.

Norman moved to a small Central Asian city. He imported used clothing from his home country and sold them out of his house for two months until he realized that he had a successful business. One restaurant catered banquets and office parties out of their home for six months in order to get enough cash flow to open their own restaurant. Francis, as you recall, in the beginning baked her cakes at home too.

Be selective about a location, but be realistic about what you can afford. Do not get saddled into lease payments that are too expensive. As a rule of thumb, retail rents should not require more than seven percent of your gross sales. Ensure that the area in which you plan to locate is situated in a growing economic area. Are nearby industries working full time or only part time? Did any industries go out of business in the past several months? Are new industries scheduled to open in the next several months?

Write down your opinion of the area's economic base and your reason for that opinion. Never accept local estimates without validating their truthfulness. Any contractual agreements on renting, leasing, and/ or buying must be carefully checked against local laws. Vet any contracts through a local lawyer for compliance, notarized by a government notary in order to avoid future legal problems. Without going through these processes, one might be able to strike deals that look good or work for a season, but later may lead to painful experiences. Be aware of "mandated" local ceremonies or practices. These can involve excessive opening parties, gifts to locals, etc., that may require extra funding. Get government agreement in the initial contract, as it may prove very difficult to do later on.

Remember, only you can choose the right business that fits your passions and God's assignment for you. Prayerfully put each of these issues before God and seek wise counsel.

DISCUSSION QUESTIONS

1. Which of the six pointers (intimate knowledge, enjoyableness, timing, profitability, vocation, going there) were helpful to your planning and why?
2. List some factors to consider before buying a local business.
3. Do you agree that you should hire the best people regardless of race, religion, or relatives? Explain your answer.
4. State two negotiating strategies you should use in your business.
5. Give several reasons why it is good to befriend government officials.

*"If you want to make God laugh,
tell him about your plans."*

—*WOODY ALLEN*[81]

[81] http://www.brainyquote.com/quotes/quotes/w/woodyallen136686.html.

Chapter 10

THE BUSINESS PLAN

"Commit your way to the Lord, trust also in Him,
and He shall bring it to pass."[82]

God seems to have a delightful way of upsetting the plans we make, specifically when we have not involved Him in making those plans. We get ourselves into circumstances that were not chosen by God, and suddenly we realize that we have been making our plans without Him. We claim to be working for Him. We call Him our Master. Yet often we neglect to commit our work to Him. Understand, the only thing that will keep us from fear and worry is to listen and involve God in all our planning.

In spiritual issues it is customary for us to put God first, but we tend to forget or think that it is inappropriate and unnecessary to put Him first in the practical, everyday issues of our lives. If we have the idea that we have to put on our "spiritual face" before we can come near to God, then we will never come near to Him. We must come as we are. Before *doing* any plan, be sure God is involved in the *making* of the plan. This is doubly important in writing up a business plan. Each section of your plan needs to be saturated with prayer.

Why a Business Plan?

Research is hard work and it takes time. But actually starting and operating a business is *extremely* hard work and takes *years* of time. Bill Rancic, winner on Donald Trump's show *The Apprentice*, says,

> If it really were a no-brainer to make it on your own in business, then there would be millions of no-brained, harebrained, and otherwise dubiously brained individuals quitting their day jobs

---

[82] Psalm 37:5

and hanging out their own shingles. Nobody would be left to round out the workforce and execute the business plan.[83]

Starting a business is work. Starting a business requires time, energy, and knowledge.

Jason, an OPEN worker who owns a business in Central Asia, adds,

Do not think that success will come quickly or easily. There are a lot of myths bound up with the concept of starting a business. Success takes long hours, strategic planning, and a commitment to the work involved. The rewards are great, but the effort is, too.

In this day and age the question is often asked, *"Do I really need a business plan?"* After all, everyone is in a hurry. In a world of 140-character tweets, can you really expect anyone to read a thirty-page business plan? Yet you need a business plan for when you finally get that all-important pitch meeting with investors; they will grill you on every aspect of your business. If you have not researched a thorough business plan, you will not have thought through every area of the business and be prepared to answer their probing questions.

From day one, every business needs a strategy for its future. Strategic development begins with prayerfully visualizing where you sense God wants the business and ministry to be in the future, as well as analyzing competitors, industry suppliers, and customers, while seeking opportunities to leverage all of your assets and strengths through the business. A business plan will quantify the goals and objectives of this vision. A good B4T business plan will clarify what products or services the business can profitably provide; who the targeted customers are; and how marketing, human resources, evangelism, and discipleship will be intertwined and dealt with. The plan should also clarify how your business will actually bring transformation to the community.

Even if you are not looking for outside funding, developing a business plan can still be a critical factor for successfully starting a company. This is because it is the planning—not the plan—that is really important. It is the process of researching the plan that is the biggest benefit. The business plan assists you in examining the critical aspects of the business, researching factors and trends affecting the business's success, while asking

---

[83] Bill Rancic, "Power Thoughts," Work It, Sova (Southern Virginia's Business Communities), January 14, 2014, http://www.newsadvance.com/work_it_sova/power_thoughts/if-it-really-was-a-no-brainer-to-make-it/article_fcc49f1e-7d7d-11e3-bbd8-001a4bcf6878.html.

and answering the tough questions. Bottom line—the most important reason for writing a business plan is that it is a vital tool for you. So first and foremost, doing a business plan is for your own benefit, and secondarily, for the benefit of others. Planning ahead is not an option in business. Remember, it was not raining when Noah built the ark.

Key Reasons to Write a Business Plan

Preparing a business plan benefits a B4Ter in at least six ways.

1. A Map
A business plan is like a map; once it is complete you can follow the directions to your destination. The business plan is a written summary of what you hope to accomplish by being in business and how you intend to organize your resources to meet your goals. It is the road map for operating your business and measuring progress along the way. The business plan identifies the amount of financing or outside investment required and when it is needed.

By committing your plans to paper, your overall ability to manage the business will improve. A plan enables you to concentrate your efforts on deviations from the plan before conditions become critical. A plan also creates room to look ahead so as to anticipate and avoid problems before they occur.

A business plan maps out the future as you believe it should be. The plan lays out your goals and action steps, allowing you to guide your business through turbulent economic seas and into the harbors of your choice. The alternative is drifting into any old port in a storm.

2. Information
A business plan provides information to interested parties, whether they are potential team members, investors, or consultants. The business plan is a tool that communicates your ideas to others. The plan clarifies for others the basic needs and opportunities for the business as the company begins to move forward. The plan serves as an understandable guide to operations and a source of direction that can be modified as the business evolves. The plan can also be used to inform and orient sales personnel, employees, suppliers, and others about your operations and goals.

3. Raise Capital

First impressions are important. A well-organized business plan is essential for a lender or investor to assess your financing proposal and to assess you as a business owner. The plan reveals how well you understand your true financial needs. It conveys the opportunities for profit that can be gained from the market, as well as your own experience and strengths along with the people working with you. A business plan makes it easier for investors to get in on the action. By reading the details of the plan, investors gain clear insight into where you are heading with the business. It provides prospective investors the means to determine whether your company is a wise and suitable investment.

There are thousands of businesspeople who do not want to *donate* to BAM businesses, but they will *invest* if they believe they can receive a return on their investment. One key to unlocking their money is the business plan. When businesspeople learn of an investment opportunity the first thing they ask for is the business plan. While few invest solely based on the business plan, a good plan will get your foot in the door to further discussions with prospective investors. Most investors do not want to talk about ideas. They have seen too many business fakers. They want to work with real businesses that are aligned with measurable, spiritual, and financial objectives.

If you wish to raise money from outside your small circle of family and friends, it is essential to have a business plan.

4. Reality Check

The business plan helps you determine whether or not your business is viable on paper before you encounter mistakes in the "real world" so that you can adjust accordingly. The plan enables you to think through the entire business and reveals the business's potential strengths and weaknesses before investing any time or money. It demonstrates your credibility and your attention to detail and will generate excitement and enthusiasm for the business. Therefore, the business plan must be as realistic and accurate as possible. In addition, it should be concise and easy to read.

Rick Love, the founder of Peace Initiatives says, *"Vision without implementation is hallucination."* A solid business plan will show the world the workableness of the business. It forces you to understand the market—whether or not your product or service will sell. It also frames opportunities in realistic terms before you attempt to recruit others and secure financing. A written business plan is an objective, critical, unemotional evaluation of the B4T business.

Chris, working in India, writes:

> We bring ourselves with us when we go overseas. Do not think crossing an ocean will make you a different person. A business plan helps bring reality to the task of starting a business. Missionaries bring a lot of baggage into B4T—they are used to taking shortcuts. They are used to getting things for free. There are no shortcuts on the road to business success, and every road is a toll road. If you cannot put your thoughts down on paper, you do not really have a plan.

When developing a business plan, it is likely that as you progress, aspects of your business plan will change. Some B4Ters, as a result of developing a business plan, decided that their business concept was not viable and chose not to go into that particular business. That is great! The process of developing a business plan gives you a chance to make your mistakes on paper instead of in real life. This is a lot cheaper and will save you a lot of time.

Charlie, one of our first apprentices, worked eight weeks on a business plan. It was well done and thoroughly researched, only for him to realize that this business was not going to ever be profitable in the country God assigned him. Several times he said to me, *"I wasted two months!"* But I replied, *"No, you saved yourself a hundred thousand dollars and maybe a year of your life; those eight weeks were great investment!"*

5. *Personal Development*

A business plan can help you develop as a manager. It can give you practice in thinking about competitive conditions, promotional opportunities, and ways of working in the real world cross-culturally. The research involved should provide you with a better understanding of the industry, the business, and the community you are moving into.

Learning does not stop when you are handed a degree. As an entrepreneur, part of the job is to keep your eyes and ears open, to adopt other businesses' best practices as your own, and to remain flexible, ever-ready to turn on a dime. A business plan requires two skills every worker needs to master: always listening carefully, and never ceasing to ask questions.

6. *Accountability*

A good business plan provides accountability for you and your investors. The plan lays out a timeline of events and financial milestones against which you can compare your actual results. As the owner/manager you will have to give an answer to investors for whatever unfolds.

The business plan defines the parameters of success for the business. For example, will the success of the business be defined in terms of market share, overall sales, volume, profit, customer satisfaction, saved souls, etc.? A plan helps to identify your customers, your market area, your pricing strategy, and the competitive conditions under which you must operate to succeed. This process often leads to the discovery of a competitive advantage or new opportunity for the business, as well as revealing deficiencies in your plan.

Businesses have to be run for the customer; most churches and missionaries do not understand this. The plan states the priorities and strategies for starting and growing the business. It integrates the secular and sacred objectives of the B4T endeavor. Dan, working in China, points out, *"Listen to what your customers are telling you. Remember, without them you do not have a business. And do not forget to show your appreciation for their business and their referrals—it takes a lot more money to create a new customer than it does to keep a current one."*

Bear in mind that anything you leave out of the picture will create an additional cost, or be a drain on your money when it crops up later. If you leave out or ignore enough items, the business will fail.

It is a sad fact that many new business owners do not see this obvious relationship between planning and success. Many think they can "wing it" and make their plans as they go along. Some feel that a business plan would limit their creativity or spontaneity, or that their business is not large enough or complex enough to warrant a plan. Every business can benefit from a business plan, no matter what size it is. The process of making a plan organizes your thinking and helps you sort out your priorities.

"The important thing is to start laying out a plan and then follow it step-by-step, no matter how small or large each step by itself may seem."
—Charles a B4Ter

Involve Businesspeople at Home

Journeys do not always go as planned. It is about taking one step at a time. Solomon speaks to this when he wrote, *"We can make our plans, but the*

LORD *determines our steps.*[84] Entrepreneurs are often praised as visionaries. But vision alone is not enough to ensure success. Susan Houghton and Mark Simon researched the lives and work of entrepreneurs. They found that in evaluating new opportunities entrepreneurs tend to overestimate demand, underestimate competition, and misjudge the need for more assets to make an opportunity a success. In addition, entrepreneurs assessing opportunities tend to be overconfident about their knowledge, draw big conclusions from small samples, become overly focused on the future, and underestimate risk because they believe they can control events. Entrepreneurs are prone to jump quickly into the market. But this focus on the future, while often praised as the epitome of entrepreneurial risk taking, leads many to neglect managerial lessons from the past.[85]

A business plan will reveal the strengths and weaknesses of establishing a business, as well as *your* personal strengths and weaknesses. We need not worry about our strengths; it is our *weaknesses* we need to pay attention to and be concerned with, because Satan rarely attacks our strengths. So it is our weaknesses that may cause the endeavor to fail. As we discussed in chapter 2, in order to understand what you are doing, you first have to understand yourself. The business plan enables that understanding.

Personally, I graduated with a degree in marketing. Five of the first six businesses I started failed. Four failed financially and one failed spiritually. All six were started without a written business plan. I began to see one of my weak points was my handling of the numbers. My wife graduated with a degree in finance, and she is good with numbers. When I brought her into our businesses, she forced me to write business plans, and she took over the finances. Truly we work together like a hand in a glove, which by God's grace, has led to our four most recent businesses all being mild successes. But many of us do not have a partner who balances our weaknesses. Most of us are not going to be able to work in every area of the business, not to mention work *well* in every area. Therefore, we need to recruit to our weaknesses. That is why it is wise to have consultants or coaches whose strengths balance our weaknesses.

Sometimes OPEN workers say, "*I don't know how to do this section of the business plan.*" That is okay. Leave that section blank and complete the sections that you can. For the blank areas there are places you can go for

---

[84] Proverbs 16:9 (NLT)
[85] Mark Simon and Susan M. Houghton, "The Relationship among Biases, Misperceptions, and the Introduction of Pioneering Products: Examining Differences in Venture Decision Contexts," *Entrepreneurship Theory and Practice* 27, no. 2 (December 2002): 105–24.

help, like NexusB4T,[86] which, for a nominal fee, will link you with B4T consultants who will work with you to fill in the blanks. For example, if you are not creative, then find a consultant who can assist you with advertising. If you struggle with numbers, find a consultant with an accounting background. Each consultant can assist in developing that part of the business plan in which they have greater expertise.

An added bonus of using experienced businesspeople back home as consultants is that if you have problems after you start the business, these same consultants are usually very willing to get involved again. If you share your business plan with businesspeople back home and ask them to be a part of it, they get excited! Often when you need start-up money, these same consultants are willing to loan you the money. This involvement early in the planning helps them to get to know you and it gives them a sense of co-ownership.

When launching a new idea, entrepreneurs will lean toward being risk takers. But "going for it" may not be enough to ensure success. Be realistic, expect competition, and do not pin your hopes on the product or service alone; develop the other assets needed for success. Since many risks associated with a pioneering opportunity are beyond your control, it is important to involve businesspeople back home who can help keep you on the straight and narrow. There are times where we are forced to improvise, *but a wise man plans ahead and surrounds himself with many counselors.*[87] Business success is less a function of grandiose predictions than it is a result of being able to respond wisely and rapidly as changes occur. Each aspect of the business plan needs to be reviewed by someone with knowledge in that area. A marketing person should critique your marketing strategy and an accountant your break-even analysis. The ministry side of things should be reviewed by a missionary familiar with the area. Planning is the difference between being bold and merely rash. Getting input from experienced businesspeople back home adds checks and balances to your planning.

Ministry Plan

Integrating your business plan with your ministry plan is a nonnegotiable. You may write them as one proposal or as two separate plans, but when

---

[86] NexusB4T offers a variety of services that train and equip, coach and mentor B4Ters and the churches who send B4Ters. For more information see *www.NexusB4T.com.*

[87] See Proverbs 11:14; 24:6

presented to Christian investors and churches they need to be seamless. A separate, straightforward business plan may be openly shared with a variety of people, including potential investors, local nonbelieving businesspeople, and government leaders. These people can provide counsel that will help find the economic, social, and cultural errors in your planning. A combined business and ministry plan[88] should incorporate both your ministry and business objectives so that churches and supporters can grasp the whole picture of what the Master is leading you to do. Expect to invest time and effort in explaining to churches that the business is not solely an attempt to get a legal visa, nor is it a scheme to make money while pretending to serve God. The plan should assist mentors and churches in understanding how to hold you accountable to both your business and ministry objectives.

Make plans. My own research shows that the initial business plan changes 75 percent of the time, yet those who do not have a plan fail nearly 80 percent of the time. Lay out your plan in writing, and as you move forward stay flexible, making changes to the plan as circumstances change.

Do not fool yourself into thinking that great spiritual goals will overcome a poor business plan. Remember, *"He who works his land will have abundant food, but he who chases fantasies lacks judgment."*[89] And, *"Good planning and hard work lead to prosperity, but hasty shortcuts lead to poverty."*[90]

If you need ideas on developing a ministry plan, reread chapters 7–12 in my first book, *Tentmaking: The Life and Work of Business as Missions.* If you need help in writing up a Memo of Understanding (MOU) or ministry plan, review appendix C of that book.

Adapt

Flexibility is an essential tool in the B4Ter's toolbox. As you learn the language and culture, your awareness of how to live and work will grow. Business ethics and the pace of work vary from one country to another. Jonathan, a tentmaker in China, told me, *"You can assume that anything new will invariably take twice as long, cost twice as much, and involve twice as much work as you thought!"* Write that on your forehead—it is a

---

[88] Note business *is* ministry. In this paragraph I am separating the terms only for clarity as many people still see business and ministry as two separate functions.

[89] Proverbs 12:11

[90] Proverbs 21:5

valuable warning! Things *do* take twice as long and cost twice as much. Dan in the Middle East adds, *"I am learning it costs much more and takes much longer to set this whole thing up than we anticipated."*

I started thirteen businesses in three countries and began a restaurant in a fourth country. I thought I knew better about planning—but I was wrong! The start-up plan called for two years, three key people, and $250,000 to open the doors. It actually took five years, five key people, and $520,000—learn from Dan's and my mistakes.

Joe had a small business in North Africa importing appliances. He thought of his business as an importer, yet as parts were scarce and because it helped build relationships, he also serviced and repaired anything he sold. As his city prospered, appliance stores emerged and cut heavily into his market. However, there was an increased call for quality repair work. When Joe reconsidered his situation, he decided that he was ultimately in the repair business, not the import business; accordingly he reduced his retail business and focused on repair work.

Even with your great idea, thorough research, and hours of hard work, one rule still applies: nothing is certain in business. No one can unfailingly know if a new product will succeed, how investors will receive a start-up idea, or whether a company will survive past the one-year mark. Get feedback from as many outsiders as possible about your business plan, and keep an open mind.

Adapting your business model means finding new business opportunities while staying flexible with the solutions you develop. Flexibility in the business model is another key to success. When we began our language school, our business plan called for creating a market for foreigners to come study Chinese, Indonesian, and English. We advertised our school in Korea, Japan, Thailand, and Malaysia—but after two years we only had a handful of foreigners and we were losing money. So we began to focus on the local market, training hotel staff and schoolteachers. However, that was not making money either, so after another two years we began focusing on the numerous factories in our city that do business overseas and that could pay more. That was profitable the first year, but then the economic crunch hit and we were back to barely breaking even. By God's grace, there was one Arab studying English in our school, preparing to pass the exams so he could enroll in a local university. We soon learned that there were dozens of Arabs studying at this university. We began promoting the school in the Middle East. As a result, we have been profitable the past ten years. The business plan was correct—the best way to make money was teaching foreigners—but we learned our market was Arabs, not Asians. Our willingness to keep changing the plan led us to profitability, stability, and transformed lives.

Focusing on one business idea during the initial start-up phase is common. But is there a way to plan for any eventual business add-ons and spin-off ideas as you are starting out? Lay a broad foundation so that others who come after you can build upon what you have begun. New product and service development should be part and parcel of your plan. It is always better to be open to the possibilities that the idea you are starting with can breed other ideas. Even when just starting up, you can still begin thinking about possible add-ons, tie-ins, franchises, and sister companies that might be good for growth and the gospel down the line.

When validating information or looking for evidence for or against a new idea, three is the magic number. Find at least three sources for data or information about any new issue or idea. Never base a decision on the input of just one person. Many times people will tell you any thought that comes to their head just to get rid of you, or they will tell you what they think you want to hear so as to please you. Neither is helpful; in fact such information can be harmful. I was traveling with Joe and Connie who, after twenty years in the country, speak excellent Turkish. We were out in the countryside, headed for a restaurant they had not been to for years, when they realized they were lost. There was an older Turkish man standing next to a roadside coffee shop. Joe pulled alongside the man and asked in Turkish, *"Do you know the way to Polonez?"* The man paused, thought for a minute, and replied, *"Yes, turn around, take a right at the corner, and go two or three kilometers. When you come to a light, go right. That will take you there."* The men in the café were listening and, after the elderly man had finished, one of the men in the café called out, *"Or if you want, you could go straight ahead on this road over the hill about one kilometer and that will bring you to Polonez."*

Leonardo da Vinci believed that he would never understand a complex subject without looking at it from at least three angles (what we now call "triangulation"). Always validate any information—three is the magic number.

Business Plan Components

Business plans are not complex; they simply require a good amount of work. There are many free websites with an outline template for writing a business plan, as well as sample business plans. Most of these templates are very similar. Do not fret over which plan to use, just pick a template, work through the plan, and then implement it. The OPEN Network website also has some solid business plan samples and a recommended template. There are many specialized business plans that you may buy. Some include consulting and some are specialized for specific businesses like schools, hotels, or restaurants. Usually these are excellent business plans, but if you are short on funds, here is a list of free websites with helpful business start-up ideas and templates for putting together a business plan:

- www.entrepreneur.com/bizplan
- www.entrepreneur.com/businessplan/index.html
- www.bplans.com/sample_business_plans/index.cfm
- www.allbusinessplans.org
- www.sba.gov

These websites will go into much greater detail, and it would be wise to take some time and explore these sites to find a plan that fits your business idea.

The standard business plan outline or template contains six or seven sections. When completed, most plans are between twenty to thirty pages in length. Unlike high school term papers, length is not usually indicative of quality.

The plan should begin with a cover page that includes the name of the business, the address, and contact numbers (telephone, fax, email, website, etc.). This cover page should also give a two- or three-sentence overview of each section of the business plan.

The following is a brief introduction to the key sections of a business plan. Different plans will have different section headings, and plans will vary in the number of sections. All plans, however, cover the following basic key components. If you choose one plan, then stick with it. There is no need to mix templates.

Business Description

This is one page that describes the company or business—when it was or will be founded, how the product or service originated, why the product or service is worthwhile and viable, and what markets it will serve.

Industry and Market Description

This page should explain who will use your product or service, the size of the market, the types of customers that will buy your product, and how you plan to get your product to the end users.

Management Team (or the People Involved in the Business)

List the key people who will be working with you by title and give a brief description of their work history. Set out the pertinent information of each member of the team. Use the term "confidential candidate" for names you cannot or do not want to divulge. The management plan details the credentials and experience of those in a decision-making role. People are an all-important factor in a business. Many investors bet on the jockey, not on the horse, so describe the team with short biographies highlighting each person's education and experience that is relevant to the business.

Company's Products

Describe the products or services being offered, and highlight the potential they have for penetrating the existing market. Point out the features of the product/services and the benefits of those features. State clearly what is unique about your business and its products/services. Include an overview of who your competition is, and give hard data and an explanation of why you believe you can compete with them. This proprietary information is essential, as it describes what sets your products/services apart from your competition.

Sales and Marketing

Explain how you plan on selling your products/services to customers. Who will do the selling? Will you use direct sales or distributors? The marketing plan provides an overview of the business, its location, and your marketing strategies.

Financial Projections

In this section, give projections on what you expect for revenues (income) the first year in detail and for the next two to three years. For investors, this is the most important section and is often the longest section in a business plan. List your anticipated expenses and forecast a profit or loss.

The financial projections should mirror reality as much as possible. As you are able, use actual numbers for rents, insurance, equipment quotes, prices, etc. Some investors say that if they see too many zeroes or too many blanks, they know the numbers are not reliable. Take note, if you underestimate capital or operational expenses, you may end up overspending in the future and eating into your working capital. When you have to make an educated guess on costs or expenses, guess high. The trick is to use conservative assumptions but still show strong projections. This is wise because investors will compare your projections to industry reports on the average performance of different kinds of businesses.

Break-even Analysis

How can you tell if your business idea will be profitable? The honest answer is that you can't. But this uncertainty should not keep you from researching the financial soundness of your idea. Preparing a break-even analysis is part of your financial projections, and it is *so* important that it warrants special attention. It is a simple tool that can help determine whether or not your business will succeed. Your break-even analysis shows you the amount of income you will need to earn to cover your expenses. If your expected sales revenue exceeds your anticipated expenses, then your business has a good chance of becoming profitable. There is no point in writing a complete business plan if your break-even analysis does not reveal that the projected sales revenue will exceed the costs of operating the business.

Exit Strategy

The final portion of the business plan should lay out your exit strategy. It may seem strange to plan an exit when you are just beginning, but potential investors will want to know your long-term plans. Plus, if you have a partner, it is important to be clear who gets what and when, long before it comes time to split. Too many good friends are no longer on speaking terms because of the way they exited their business.

Money can be a divisive tool. If you sell the business who benefits? If you choose to join a mission, most organizations are happy for you to do business as long as you are not making money. But if you start making serious money, and I hope you do, it is interesting to see how quickly they expect a piece of the action. It is important to clarify ownership and how profits and ultimately the sale of the business will be handled before you open the doors to the business.

Exiting a business involves a variety of strategies. You may *let it run dry* by exhausting its resources and then shutting its doors. If you are a co-owner you may *sell your shares,* but be clear at the outset to whom those shares may be sold. You may also *merge* with another business. If you are in a hurry, you can just *liquidate* the assets, pay off any debt, and stuff the cash in your pocket and run. Or the most common B4T strategy is to *sell* your business outright.

Building a pathway to profit requires diligence. Prepare well so there are no potholes in the path. Work through each of the above steps, following the business plan outline or template you choose to work through. The bottom line is that the business plan is your proof of concept.

Lee Iacocca writes:

> Go home tonight and put your great idea on paper. If you cannot do that, then you have not really thought it out ... Whenever one of my people has an idea, I ask him to lay it out in writing. I do not want anybody to sell me on a plan just by the melodiousness of his voice or force of personality.[91]

Additional Business Issues

In addition to writing up a solid business plan, there are a handful of other issues to take into consideration.

Naming Your Business

The name of your business is one of its most important assets. Select a name that appeals to your target market while stating what you do and represent. Names that are difficult to pronounce or sound foreign often will be easily forgotten by clients, and names that are difficult to spell are not easily found online or via multi-media. Do some digging to find out whether another business is already using a name that is identical or similar to the one you want to use. You must use different search tactics to hunt for both registered and unregistered trademarks. Find a name that has an easy-to-remember domain name. In many countries there will be a website listing the existing names of companies operating within the country, which will help you in eliminating choices.

Accounting—Who Will Keep the Books?

Finance is a weak area for most entrepreneurs. But as Marshall, a NexusB4T coach, is well known for saying, *"No books, no business"*—meaning the numbers run the business. It is the numbers that tell you if the business

---

[91] Lee Iacocca with William Novak, *Iacocca: An Autobiography* (New York: Bantam Books, 1984) 59.

is healthy or not. Strong sales do not guarantee profitability. One OPEN business was doing nearly $800,000 in sales a year, but it went belly up as its expenses exceeded its income. If you are not aware of the numbers, then your business is not really under control. The numbers tell you how to make the most money in the least amount of time and with the least effort. But first you have to earn it, and the numbers can tell you how to do that as efficiently as possible, provided you understand their language. If you are poor at numbers, from the beginning enlist a consultant who can assist you in that area of the business.

The most important hire for any business is an accountant. If your business is small, a good part-time bookkeeper is sufficient. If this is the path you choose, it would be wise to outsource your year-end audits to a qualified accountant to ensure your numbers are accurate. Shop around for a good accounting software program that fits the needs of your business. This is the most efficient way to keep track of all expenses, payroll, accounts receivable and payable, and taxes.

When launching a new business, review your numbers daily. Track monthly sales and gross margins. Break down the expenses and income by product category or service type, as well as by customer. Do the math yourself so you are on top of what is really happening in the company. To be successful, you need a solid sense of the relationships between the various numbers so you can determine which ones are critical and need to be monitored. Yes, your bookkeeper keeps the official records, but allow me to repeat this: the first year or two *you need to know the numbers yourself.*

Scott, another NexusB4T coach, adds, "No area of business is more important than your financial team. That is where the company's money meets the road."

As the business grows, to save money, accounting work such as routine bookkeeping can be done in-house by an employee. If you are starting a business and are not good with numbers, outsource your bookkeeping. Find an accountant you can trust. They will need to know the business inside and out. If they are good and trustworthy, they will tell you where you can and cannot put your money, as well as serve as a consultant in planning and operating the business. If your accountant is not listening or giving you the right advice, find another accountant; otherwise you are going to have a much harder time growing your business.

Customers

Business is not about making money, cash flow, employees, or products. It is about customers.

The customer is king. The customer overrules all product or service decisions. Simply stated, a business is an organization of people using their resources to provide products or services that customers will honor by paying a price greater than their costs.

Relationships are paramount. One-time customers cannot sustain a business. You need repeat customers to build a profitable annual sales volume. People do business with people they *want* to do business with; that is why relationships are so important. As my local business partner puts it, *"You do not negotiate a contract. You negotiate a relationship."* This is also why businesses are good places to model and speak the gospel. Get to know your customers. Learn their names, their interests, and their needs. People do business with those who show an interest in them—people they know. This not only creates an opportunity to make a sale, but also an opportunity to witness.

Before producing a product, ensure that you have customers first, not just a handful of large churches back home to sell to. Your church network can only stretch so far, and once people have your product, then whom will you sell to? Too many BAMers focus on developing a product that will help their local community and create jobs, but they have not found buyers for their product. Before you begin to produce a product, ensure that you are offering something a significant number of people want to buy.

Opening an Office

Do you need an office? Many Western executives today work from home and meet clients in coffee shops or restaurants. That may be true in the West, but it is not true for many of the emerging market countries. One of the first things people ask when they get together is, *"Where do you work?"* Be sure if you are working at home that many others in your culture are doing the same. Otherwise, expect to draw the suspicion of your neighbors and the authorities.

If in the beginning your business is a one- or two-person show, the initial office setup bill may be hefty. In such cases, renting a space at a business center or an executive suite (as they are called in Europe) is often a cost-efficient alternative to renting a larger office. Employees can travel the region knowing that they have secretarial backup in their "virtual office" without having to commit to an expensive and largely empty office.

Business centers offer a wide range of services and office infrastructure, such as conference rooms for client meetings. Companies have the option of either taking office space in a center or simply having their calls answered by a full-time secretary. In countries where style often wins out over substance, it may be important to have a prestigious address and glitzy nameplate on the door. Clearly a home will not provide that, particularly if you have children. On the other hand, an office in a business center is made to look like a real office. Many centers allow clients to display logos and name boards.

Sung, whose business deals mainly with government officials, says,

> I normally meet contacts in the boardroom at the business center. They always think it is my office because they think the receptionist and staff are working for me only. We are a small company; the business center gives me a prestigious address and the backup when I need it.

Cash Flow

Profit is like food, air, and water to a business, and even to a civilization. Without profit, tools are not replaced, new products are not developed, loans are not repaid, investors earn no return, charity dwindles, wages decrease, and the company goes out of business.

Money does not have to be elusive, complicated, or difficult to control. All it really takes is a commitment to two things: an understanding of the relationship between money and your business activities, and creating, and daily implementing straightforward money management tools and strategies. When you understand how money flows in your business and you can control your money systems, you will make informed decisions about prioritization, management, and investments. You do not have to be a finance expert; you just have to understand enough to make the decisions that matter.

When your company begins to turn a good profit that is when you have to be particularly prudent. Do not confuse cash flow with profits— they are two very different things. Many profitable firms go bust because they run out of cash. In the beginning, there is a need to invest in long-term assets and working capital. We failed to understand this and gave away one-third of our first two years' profits. Five years later we still had not recovered from our misguided generosity.

It is important to give and to be generous, but you need to manage your cash on hand wisely. The first two and a half years, concentrate on building up your cash reserves. After two years you will have observed and measured two annual business cycles, enabling you to better estimate what your cash needs will be week by week over the third year. Having a minimum of three months of cash reserves on hand is wise; six months is wiser. Jay, who worked in Morocco, clarifies: *"The worst thing when starting the business is to run out of money five months after you start."*

Motivating Employees

Your employees are the face, hands, and feet of your business. They are the ones your customers interact with. The role of the business owner or boss is to enable people to excel, help them discover their own wisdom, engage themselves entirely in their work, and accept responsibility for work. Train your people well and they will work well. Learn their career aspirations and help them accomplish what they aspire to do. Jesus says, *"Whatever you wish men would do to you, do so to them."*[92] As leaders, we are to serve. Employees who are well trained and held in esteem will return such godly leadership by working hard for you.

Your employees are also the first line of witness to the goodness and reality of the Lord in your life. You need to walk and work in the Spirit every moment that you are at work. The following are some helpful comments from OPEN workers about how they keep their employees motivated and His light shining before all men at work.

- Recognize employees in your staff meeting for work they have done well. Constantly be on the lookout for chances to praise your people's work.
- Try to involve employees in your thinking and making plans related to the business. Not only will they know the local market better, including suppliers and customers, but they will strengthen the marketing of the business's goods and services.
- Learn what the employees really value and provide that. In some locales the workers desire opportunities for personal growth, while in others they want respect, promotions, responsibility, and often more money.
- Give employees a chance to develop new skills that enhance their worth in their current position, and prepare them for future advancement inside or outside the company.

---

[92] Matthew 7:12

- Be relational. It may not be possible to hang out with employees, but celebrate their birthdays and personal holidays; get to know at least the names of their family members. Ask about their lives, their joys, and their struggles. Pray with them.
- Thank people for their efforts. This simple tool is often underused. Reward people with notes or little gifts of encouragement. Make sure the feedback is specific and frequent.
- Maintain a transparent culture in your business. Discuss company information with employees regarding future plans and strategies, new products, and the department's and employees' role in the overall plan. Involve employees in decision making, especially those decisions that affect them.

Technology

One huge advantage most Westerners have over the local competition is their understanding and ability to use up-to-date technology. Ensure that your marketing efforts include an online marketing strategy. There are many good tools for building a website and promoting your firm online. The OPEN Network has several IT businesses who can help. If you are not a tech person, find a coach who can help you in this area. Be sure to secure your website as well. *LastPass.com* and *KeePass.com* are two sites that offer good security systems for free.

DISCUSSION QUESTIONS

1. For whom do you write a business plan? Explain your answer.
2. List six ways that writing a business plan may benefit you.
3. Why is it good to validate all information with three different sources?
4. What are five possible exit strategies for a B4T business? Which one do you favor?
5. What are some lessons you have learned about "cash flow"?

"I couldn't wait for success, so I went ahead without it."

—JONATHAN WINTERS[93]

---

[93] http://www.brainyquote.com/quotes/quotes/j/jonathanwi100484.html.

Chapter 11

PAYING FOR YOUR TENT

Planning

As we select a business, build a business, or exit a business, we need to be aware of the world around us. There are dozens of creative opportunities around us all the time—new communities being built, new laws being enacted, new products and services coming available—but because we have not been trained to look for them, these opportunities are often invisible, despite being right under our noses.

> Sigmund Freud discovered that if he asked someone to look up toward the sky and report what they saw, even though there was a high-flying bird above them the person would not usually see it. But if Freud said, "Look at that bird!" the other person would see it at once—although Freud had not pointed in either case. It seems that in many situations we only see what we are specifically looking for.[94]

I think this may also be true when it comes to seeing important opportunities that might be of God and integral to His plan for our lives. Most of us just don't see significant opportunities.

Plan ahead, for the fruit of the past is the present. The world is changing at an alarming rate. Change is not just a matter of reacting faster; it has to do with solid decision making. When it comes to decision making, we have a hard time keeping up. Each of us has a limit to our ability to cope with change. Thus, we need to prayerfully plan our next steps. If planning were merely a matter of gathering information, then computers might adequately do the job. But planning also involves budgets, goals, means, and interests—all of which may change drastically due to conditions beyond our expectation or control. The world is developing so fast

---

[94] Tom J. Fatio and Keith Miller, *With No Fear of Failure: Recapturing Your Dreams through Creative Enterprise* (Waco Texas: Word Books, 1981).

there's little time to think through the complexities of the decisions we need to make. At such moments, moral standards and choices must be made quickly, and our character becomes a chief factor in our planning.

Hasty decisions are risky decisions. Solomon teaches, *"The plans of the diligent lead to profit as surely as haste leads to poverty."*[95] Author Doug Evelyn contemporizes this with his tweet: *"Long-range planning works best in the short term."*[96] If you do not develop a strategy for your business, you will become reactive to external circumstances. The absence of planning is fine if you do not care where you are going.

Whether you spend two dollars or two million dollars on a business idea, it does not mean you can make the idea work or that you will want to spend the rest of your life doing it. Just as you probably would not get married after the first date, it is wise to date your idea for a period of time while asking the tough getting-to-know-you questions.

One question to ask early in the process is, *"What's the worst thing that can happen?"* Go through various worst-case scenarios to see how long your business idea will last if nobody buys your product or service. An idea needs to be thoroughly prayed over, studied, and assessed. Thinking through, plotting, and daydreaming about your business plan can help you anticipate and even avoid future problems. Remember, an idea is just an idea until it is marketed and sold. After you have your business idea, review the questions in this book, asking yourself and the Lord if both of you are comfortable with the answers. The worst reasons to start a business are because you *"like the idea"* or you *"think that it will work."* Write a solid business plan first to prove you are right. Down the road it may save you much time and a lot of money.

"By failing to prepare, you are preparing to fail."—Benjamin Franklin[97]

Business Questions to Ask Yourself

If you want your business to be successful, you need to understand what is at the core of your business. Yes, Jesus is at the core of your business, but is this really the distinguishing factor to your customers? Many businesses, and hopefully all B4T businesses, will claim Jesus to be core to all that the business does. So understand that all Christian-owned businesses in

---

[95] Proverbs 21:5

[96] http://www.newsadvance.com/work_it_sova/power_thoughts/long-range-planning-works-best-in-the-short-term/article_db7f6720-3a0c-11e4-b38c-0017a43b2370.html.

[97] http://www.brainyquote.com/quotes/quotes/b/benjaminfr138217.html.

the world but one are exactly the same. Your business is different from every other business in the world, including the other Christian-owned businesses, because your business has *you*, and every other business does not. Is it true that the difference between success and failure is

- getting the right financing?
- getting good suppliers?
- getting the right customers—and enough of them?
- finding the right staff?

Maybe. But more likely the difference between success and failure is *you*. The problem with many businesses is that the owners work hard, but the business does not work at all. A primary objective in owning a B4T business is for you, under the Lord, to own the business and not let the business own you. Each of us needs to learn the skills and tools for working *on* the business and not *in* the business. As has been stated several times, if you want to succeed you must know yourself, which includes determining three key points:

1. Determine what your overall objective is.
This is not about setting a profit goal, nor having quality standards, nor even having a nice store or a beautiful office. Rather, prayerfully determine what you expect your business to give to you and the community. A paycheck? A sense of fulfillment? Deep down, why are you starting this business? And when you are done with the business, what to you expect will it have accomplished?

2. Determine what you want your business to do.
If I walked through your door and asked the receptionist or staff, *"What does this business do?"* what would you want them to tell me? If we ask any business owner to tell us what their business does, they usually start with one line, and from there they begin to clarify why their business is different, why it's better, why it's already great but is going to be greater. In explaining, they become interesting and their business becomes interesting. So what do you want your coworkers, suppliers, financiers, and customers to say about your business? The difference between what they say and what you *want* them to say is determined by you. And the solutions to what you determine should be central in your marketing plan.

3. Determine how much your time is worth.
In truth, few B4Ters are paid the amount of money our education and talents deserve. If you *did* get paid for what you are truly worth, how much money would it be? Nearly every failing business has a common theme:

the owner is indispensable. The business cannot do without them. The leader is irreplaceable. Nothing can happen without them and everything happens because of them. And most of these business owners are not paying themselves for their labors.

Understand, we need to get our businesses into a place where it is working for us, and not vice versa. Every penny that your business earns that you were not involved in is free money. The only way to value this free money is to make sure your business and employees are earning it and you are getting to steward it. Ask yourself if you are earning enough. Could your business earn more for you? For the kingdom? The difference between working for your business versus your business working for you is found in your personnel plan and your financial plan. It is the difference your business should be making to your life and calling.

Perhaps the biggest lesson I have learned over the past twenty years while starting and running businesses has been to ask questions. In the early years I was both too timid and too proud to admit that I did not know everything. These days it is different; I know how much I do not know. The old saying is absolutely true: the older I get the less I know—and that is not due to Alzheimer's.

By asking questions over the years, I have discovered that sometimes advice or replies are more on-target than at other times. In the beginning it appeared to be due to the experience of the person being queried. Maybe he did not have the wisdom or innovativeness that I needed. Lately, however, it has become clear that the difference is really the way I ask the questions. The quality of the advice received is directly related to the quality of the questions asked. Ask the wrong question and you will get the wrong answer. Ask a superficial question and you'll get a simple answer. Pose a thoughtful, researched question, and you will likely receive a much deeper and more valuable response.

So before asking questions of a fellow professional, invest time to review what your main objective is in seeking advice. Formulate a question, write it down, and then ask yourself, *"Is this what I really want to learn?"* Be sure to write the question down. Doing this involves more of your senses and often gives you a different perspective compared with only rummaging the thought around in your head. Such effort will take you deeper into the matter. Often, after contemplating and writing down the question, a core issue will pop up that you are trying to solve, one that may have been hidden. In this way, you may uncover some good questions and will invariably get meaningful answers.

For casual business matters you may not want (or need) to do this much soul-searching. But when you are facing some tough issues in your business or any area of your life and you need some wisdom, take time to construct your questions carefully. Doing so lays the groundwork for receiving advice that can have a profound impact.

Funding

There are two areas to pray and seek counsel over when it comes to funding. One is the business, and the other is your personal income. Raising start-up capital is among the more difficult tasks when starting a business. Raising personal financial support for the initial two to three years while you are learning the language and culture is strategic, as well as faith-building. Everyone understands the need of raising start-up capital for a business. Few understand the wisdom of raising support for the first few years of language and culture learning, registering the business and writing a business plan.

Church Funding

Raising support via churches and friends for your initial years enables you to support your family while moving ahead with your B4T venture. Some businesspeople believe that getting money from churches and your business is cheating on the system, and some mission agencies see it as "double dipping." However, that is exactly what Paul did in Corinth; he received some income from churches and some income from his business. At the outset, Aquila and Paul and the team worked together as leather workers or tentmakers. But when Silas and Timothy brought monies from the churches in Macedonia, Aquila and Priscilla kept working while Paul focused on ministering the Word.[98] Learning to mix the two income streams while being accountable for our monies is an important part of getting started.

Business is not about money. Business is about people. The gospel is not about money. The gospel is also about people. All businesspeople would agree that money is essential to the life of a business. However, not all church leaders would agree that money is essential for the gospel—thus the sacred and secular divide. Yet nearly every church leader gets paid for the services they render to their congregation. Every mission agency

---

[98] Acts 18:2—5

and their workers also get paid salaries. Where do these salaries come from? From businesspeople who donate the money. In church we pray for people to give; in business we pray for customers to spend. Both are dependent on God.

Through business God enabled Paul plus his team, and today God similarily enables us to shine forth His light and pay the bills. *Jehovah-jireh*—our Provider[99]—is not concerned about money. God's concern is centered on His glory among all peoples.[100] The gospel is about God and people, not churches and businesses. Churches and businesses are tools intended to bring glory to His name. Money is just a tool. Jesus warns us that whenever we worship a thing, money included, we have created an idol.[101] The primary reason we do anything, whether that be to serve in a church or work in a business, is not to make money, but to glorify Jesus. I do not wish to dwell on the theology of work, as this is a hands-on book. But you need to be comfortable with the fact that work and worship are meant by God to be integrated. If you have questions about business, God, and how they are interrelated, read Wayne Grudem's *Business for the Glory of God.*

Whether in a church or a business, money is a tool for reaching people for God's glory. If we claim to be doing business, we need to be striving for profitability. Subsidizing businesses by using church money over a period of many years is poor stewardship. A business by definition is a profit-making enterprise.[102] "Businesses" that are subsidized by churches are *charities,* not businesses. Yet utilizing funds from family, friends, and even churches to learn the language and culture and launch a business seems wise.

B4T is modeled after Paul's life and work. Paul integrated his business work with his mission work. B4T is a seamless model that intertwines these two disciplines of life. Raising support for the first couple years facilitates your family to get settled and acculturate before jumping into the business. Raising support in this way has several distinct advantages:

1. Family Life

It takes time and energy to move a family overseas and settle in. If you work for a large corporation, housing will be provided; and you will have servants, coworkers, and people who will meet you at the airport who are

---

[99] Genesis 22:14
[100] Matthew 24:14; 28:19,20; Revelation 5:9,10; 7:9
[101] Matthew 6:19—24; see also Exodus 20:4,5
[102] *Dictionary.com,* s.v. "business," http://dictionary.reference.com/browse/business?s=t.

paid to help you settle in. These people will assist you in the adaptation process. Independent entrepreneurs do not have such privileges. A church income enables you to take time and assist your family in the adjustment process, which will reduce tension once the business starts.

2. Language and Culture Learning

My first book covers this topic well, but as a reminder, my research[103] validates that language fluency is the number one factor in the success or failure of B4T workers. It is essential to learn the language well enough to do business with it. If you are studying the language full time for six to eighteen months, you will need an income to support your family. My research also shows that if you do not learn the language well within the first three years, it is unlikely that you will ever learn the language well. In addition, the local culture will greatly impact your family life and your business practices. Time is required to learn the nuances of local life and implement them into your own personal routines and habits. Once you start the business, there is very little time for anything other than the business. Income from churches and friends enables you to take the time necessary to learn the language and culture up front, before starting the business. Learning the language by all accounts is a "ministry expense." So it is both legal and logical to raise funds for this initial period of service overseas.

3. Time and Space

Time is needed to learn the business culture, build relationships with government officials and business leaders, and explore which business is right for the city and you. Some church income will enable you to move forward at your own pace. This should help reduce mistakes and save money for the business, as well as reduce tensions at with your spouse and children. Without these funds from home, you may be rushed into decisions that could lead to greater problems and expenses in the future.

4. Balanced Accountability

Raising support to get a business started overseas forces us to be accountable to the church. To be both "mission centered" and "business centered," we need accountability in both disciplines. A business keeps us accountable, because if it does not make money it fails. Having some church income forces us to be accountable to our home church leaders

---

[103] Patrick Lai, *Tentmaking: The Life and Work of Business as Missions* (Colorado Springs: Authentic Publishing, 2005). 35

as well; ensuring we are doing outreach and discipleship through our jobs. In addition, we have learned within the OPEN Network, "no pay, equals no pray." B4T workers who receive some support from their home church, also receive more prayer, care, and encouragement. Churches, like everyone else, tracks with those they invest in. Once the job begins, it is still wise for workers to get at least a small amount of support from churches to ensure the church is tracking with them.

When raising funds, be aware of and be sensitive to public concerns. Be ready to address the "dangers" of working in a Muslim country and issues related to raising your children in a foreign land. Acknowledge changes in political arenas, and know the business environment and attitudes of the current government. Find local articles to support your case for doing business in your adopted city. Be prepared for friends and relatives who are going to attempt to dissuade you from following the King's commission.

Business Funding

Understand that there are many workers overseas who are operating "platforms" or fake businesses. These businesses are a cover for doing ministry. These workers have little intention of earning a profit or creating jobs for locals. These workers often sound and look like real B4Ters. A few even have a business plan. Because of the plethora of platforms, experienced investors are leery of jumping in feet first to invest in true B4T/BAM businesses. These bad models make garnering funding difficult. In addition, start-ups generally have a bad reputation with investors.

According to Bloomberg, eight out of ten entrepreneurs who start businesses fail within the first eighteen months. That means about 80 percent crash and burn.[104] However, an article in the *Washington Post* reviews three different studies that refute this claim, showing the number of failures to be closer to 50 percent. *"Basically, after four years, 50 percent of the businesses are open. As time goes on, the success rate decreases, but it never gets to a failure rate of 'nine out of ten.' Seven out of ten businesses do not survive ten years."*[105]

[104] Eric T. Wagner, "Five Reasons 8 out of 10 Businesses Fail," *Forbes,* September 12, 2013, http://www.forbes.com/sites/ericwagner/2013/09/12/five-reasons-8-out-of-10-businesses-fail/.

[105] Glenn Kessler, "Do Nine out of 10 New Businesses Fail, as Rand Paul Claims?" *Washington Post,* January 27, 2014, http://www.washingtonpost.com/blogs/fact-checker/wp/2014/01/27/do-9-out-of-10-new-businesses-fail-as-rand-paul-claims/.

Even at a 50 percent failure rate, investing in a start-up business is risky. One venture capitalist reminds me every time I ask him to consider investing in a start-up, *"Only friends, family, and fools invest in start-ups."* Thus, before approaching any investors, you need to do your homework. Be prepared to present your value proposition concisely, accurately assess the market size, know your competition, and show that your management team is well positioned to grow the company. You also need to have a sound business model and good command of your financials. These are the fundamentals, and all must be part of your business plan. It is essential to be prepared to prove to investors that people will buy your product or service because you are selling at a fair price, offering good quality, and can deliver it quickly. In addition, they will also want to see a clear picture of how the business will transform lives.

Many people make giving and investing decisions based upon a relationship. You need to sell your vision, your business, your calling, and especially yourself. Your words and your attitudes are important. Be passionate when presenting your ideas. More and more investors are choosing to invest in a start-up based on the person, not just the business plan. If you are not excited about what God is leading you to do, do not expect others to want to come join you or invest in your business. Be prepared with an encouraging story or three. People also opt to do business with people who look and act like them or have similar experiences. This is the audience to which you should pitch your opportunity.

Remember, business success is about minimizing risks, maximizing rewards, and setting yourself up for the best possible outcomes. That is why establishing credit and making do with minimal capital early on are both so important. The former fosters funding options as you get older, enabling you to ultimately garner better terms, while the latter forces you to prioritize and think outside the box; both are habits that will pay dividends in the long run. You need to know your business well, and you need to know your investors well, too.

Jason, an OPEN worker in Asia, shares,

> We tell potential investors everything we plan to do and how much it will cost. We present our feasibility study and outline our reasons. We do not ask for aid. We ask for loans. When we want to borrow money, we do not ask for money. We have to show that we really need it for specific purposes, and we intend to pay back all that we borrow.

Financing

If Jesus is the Sender, He is also the Provider. Hudson Taylor put it this way: *"God's work, done in God's way, will never lack God's supply."* If our true reliance is upon anything else, we will fail to bring God the honor He deserves. If that provision means your business is a financial success, He will most certainly make it happen.

Most B4Ters use multiple strategies for gathering the funding needed to get started. The seven main sources of capital that B4Ters use to finance their start-up are: personal funding, friends and family, donations, crowdfunding, grants, bank loans, and equity investment.

Bootstrapping

Funding the business yourself is the most common way that B4Ters get started. Investing your personal wealth in the business is a basic expectation for all B4Ters. When starting out, nearly every person uses their own capital, in addition to any other monies they can find. If your plan is to start a business and none of your own capital is in the business, it will be hard to attract investment from others. If someone is going to loan you money or invest in your business, they expect you to have put some of your own money on the line first. In business we call this "having skin in the game." If you are not willing to make financial sacrifices for God's B4T assignment for you, then why should an investor? A business reflects the passion, dreams, energy, and vision of the founder, so be sure you are personally and financially sacrificing to get the business off the ground.

How much should you invest in your own business? If you are young and starting out, do not look for funding unless you have invested approximately 50 percent or more, of your personal wealth in the business. If you own a house back in your homeland, why bother others for funding of only $20,000? Investors expect B4Ters to assume the majority of the risk. No matter what your funding strategy may be, recruiting other donors and investment begins with sacrificially investing in the business yourself.

Loans from Family and Friends

Many B4Ters draw upon family, friends, and church members for funds. Sometimes these monies are donated and sometimes they are no-interest, or low-interest loans. Garnering monies from friends and church members is a great way to get a running start on your funding. Investors rarely wish to be the first one to fund a project, so if you can fund your start-up

30 percent or more with your own funds and those of friends, it creates a pathway for inviting others to join the process.

Before taking a loan from friends or relatives, you need to know what you are getting into. Anxious and exhausted B4Ters yearn for the solace and support usually provided by friends and family back home. Often, when the going gets tough, you will need a sheltered place to lay your weary head. Be aware that relationships with friends usually change whenever money enters the picture. After all, the adjectives traditionally paired with *cash* are "cold" and "hard." If business problems endanger the family treasure, the B4Ter may find his weary head resting on a cold, hard stone.

One worker in North Africa writes, *"Debt erodes healthy relationships. I wish I had gotten a loan from a bank."* The people who love and believe in us are also those whose fortunes we least want to imperil. There is no risk if family or friends wish to donate money, as they get a tax write-off and have no expectations of being repaid; but loans are different. Prayerfully consider before involving family and friends in funding your business.

Donations

Donations are obviously the most popular and sought after way to generate funding for a B4T business. A donation is basically a free gift that comes with few or no strings attached. The donor is willing to help you, and in return receives a tax deduction. Donations are a good way to link business friends in your church with what you are doing. Unfortunately, the donation model is on the decline. This is partly due to the greater number of mission workers doing for-profit businesses and partly due to the giving tendencies of the non–baby boomers. Donors are not as particular about how their money is being used when they donate to a church or a not-for-profit NGO that is providing some humanitarian service. But for businesspeople, business is business. Even though it is a kingdom-minded business seeking to reach the unreached, if you are making money, businesspeople expect a return on their investment.

Crowdfunding

Crowdfunding is a new and successful way of funding B4T businesses. Crowdfunding involves inviting people to donate a defined amount of money to your business or a project related to your business in exchange for various rewards. Crowdfunding has shown itself to be incredibly effective at honing local or online community support into real, tangible, change. I predict that crowdfunding is the future for charities. There is much potential as a means for communities of all kinds, including BAM/B4T, to invest in their own projects and innovations.

Several OPEN businesses have successfully used crowdfunding to jumpstart their funding. NexusB4T[106] offers a crowdfunding service that gives you access to thousands of like-minded Christians. There are four general categories for crowdfunding as it relates to B4T and BAM: equity, donation, service, and debt.

Equity, as crowdfunding, is asking people to donate to your business or business-related project in exchange for equity. In this case, the money is pledged in the form of risk capital.

Donation, as crowdfunding, is asking people to donate to your business start-up in exchange for tangible, nonmonetary rewards such as a video, special insider information, a T-shirt, one of the products you make, or some other attractive but cheap gadget. The bigger the donation, the better the expected reward. The pledge that is made to the business is essentially a gift to fund the business. Of the four, this is the category of crowdfunding favored by OPEN workers.

Service, as crowdfunding, allows high-traffic brands and publishers to leverage their own traffic and crowd fund right on their site.

Debt, as crowdfunding, is asking people to donate to your business or business project in exchange for a financial return and/or interest at a future date.

Crowdfunding enables you to market your business, generate interest, and receive funds. In addition, your crowdfunding backers can provide useful feedback about your project. Crowdfunding is not limited to a certain kind of business or project. It can be fast, efficient, and effective if done right. Plus, there is little risk involved compared to other funding options. The more creativity and fun you have, the more likely you will get funded. There are at least a dozen crowdfunding websites. Be aware that crowdfunding regulations and taxation can be difficult to work with. Here are five sites that other B4Ters have used or recommended:

1. *www.kickstarter.com* Kickstarter is the number one crowdfunding website. The large number of people who browse this website often results in people you do not even know donating to your business.
2. *www.indiegogo.com* Indiegogo is the second largest

---

[106] *www.NexusB4T.com* NexusB4T offers both donation funding and debt funding.

crowdfunding website.
3. *fundrazr.com* FundRazr has a reputation of being flexible.
4. *www.crowdfunder.com* CrowdFunder is business-focused. It is a smaller site and will require you to have a LinkedIn or Facebook account.
5. *www.openfunding.biz* OPENfunding is a BAM/B4T site managed by NexusB4T that offers donation and debt funding and promotes your business opportunity via its vast Christian business network.

Grants

Foundations often make money available to businesses with a purpose. Their grants are usually in the form of a donation requiring a written report once the business opens. Often the initial gifts are small but renewable, and the amount often grows over the years. Relationships are key to getting the attention of a grant committee or a foundation. The process for most foundations is complicated and lengthy, so if you are in hurry, grants are not for you.

Loans

Loans come in all sizes, shapes, and forms, as well as from many directions. Friends, churches, interested businesspeople, and local banks, have all made loans to OPEN Network businesses. The interest rates for loans can vary from no interest to thirty-three percent. Friends may loan you money at no interest, while banks and credit card companies will extract as much interest as possible. In most countries, getting a local bank loan usually requires having a local partner. Though several mission agencies have facilitated loans to their own members, NexusB4T is currently the only North American organization that makes low-interest loans to B4T start-ups.

Venture Capital

Venture capitalists are primarily interested in those that can show them a good return on investment without too much risk. Usually they will want a high percent return on an investment and will expect 25–40 percent equity in the company. These guys do not buy dreams. They normally ask for a solid business plan, plus figures of past performance and projected earnings for the next three years. In other words, start-ups need not apply.

They also are not interested in the long term, so do not expect them to hold on for longer than seven years. But if you have a solid business and need an influx of cash to move to the next level, this could be the path.

Once you determine that your business needs financing, these are four reminders that will improve your chances of collecting the cash:

1. *Determine what type of financing you need.* Review the above list. Predetermine what is negotiable—terms of the loan, length of the loan, and the frequency and amount of payments.

2. *Have a third party review your business proposal.* Before you meet with a donor or investor, have someone who is experienced at evaluating business plans review your ideas.

3. *Character counts.* When evaluating your application, lenders and investors will study your business plan, your financial projections, etc. However, they will also pay attention to your character. Be sure to present yourself and your business well. Be professional, organized, and confident. Bring God and His assignment for you into the discussion, but do not place the crux of your presentation on prayer and faith alone. We have all seen B4Ters led into His work by the Spirit only to return home bankrupt.

4. *Be prepared.* They will want to know how much money will be needed to start the business and for what purpose. How will you get your money, and when will you need it? What will you buy with the money? How much of the money do you have, and what portion will you need to borrow? How do you intend to repay the money you have borrowed? What kind of products do you wish to sell? Who is your market or customers? Do you know your customers' demographics? Do you know what customers buy now and if your product can compete with others in the market already? Finally, who are you and what is your background and experience? What are your social ties and commitments?

Show Me the Money!

"Everyone looking at our ministry plan and business plan is thrilled. But I can't deposit 'thrill.'"—An OPEN worker

Only close friends or fools will donate or invest in ideas. Friends want to be the first to help, but rarely are your close friends wealthy enough to really make a difference.

When raising start-up capital, you need to sell your idea. Do not present your vision as a dream; rather, talk about it as if it is a done deal. When sharing the vision, be visible, credible, and big. Use the Gideon effect—blow a horn, carry a torch, and appear to be more than you are. Your vision needs a goal. Catch people's imagination. Make investors *see* where God is leading you. Ed, an OPEN worker in Central Asia tells us,

> When starting my language school my business plan called for $25,000 to get started. However, no one wanted to be the first to invest. I knew I needed low-interest or interest-free loans, so I went to two rich friends and told them, "No one wants to be the first to invest in my business. Will you be the first to invest five thousand dollars?" It worked! They both invested, and within six weeks I had the rest of the money.

Remember to involve businesspeople in your plans. Many B4T business plans have not gone beyond the write-up stage because the people who could fund the business were not involved in designing the plans. People are much more likely to invest in a strategy wholeheartedly if they play an active role in developing it. Plan ahead. Involve a variety of people while developing your plans. Email them frequently. Listen and candidly respond to their ideas, whether you agree or not. Involving those with the means to move your business forward will build a commitment to achieving the agreed-upon results. In addition, it elicits innovative ideas that can be incorporated in the plan while ensuring the business plan is realistic.

Jake, an OPEN worker in the Middle East wrote,

> Initially our idea was exciting. But friends, it has been hard work, and not easy to implement. We had one problem after another, especially when getting other people involved and excited. While we found most people were interested when they first heard of our plan, their interest did not result in their participation or sharing their resources to a degree that matched their interest. I wonder if I should have gotten people involved earlier so that they owned the idea with me.

Businesspeople back home want to be involved. They do not simply want to write a check. Right from the beginning, select a handful of businesspeople back home, from a variety of disciplines and solicit their input. Ask them what books you should be reading or what training they suggest you get. Involve them in writing up your business plan. Give them emotional ownership. Request their input as you plan. Then have them review the business plan when it is finished. Invite them to coach or partner with you as you move forward. When it comes time to raise money, they will be much more inclined to invest.

People will tell you that you cannot start a business without a lot of money. Lack of capital is one of the prime causes of small-business failure. The amount needed will vary depending on the location and the business. Dubai is going to be more expensive than Mumbai, and manufacturing semiconductors is going to cost more than establishing a consulting firm. Yet capital is not quite the all-determining factor that it is sometimes made out to be. The average B4T worker starting a one-person business often can get underway with $40,000. Businesses that involve teams shoot a little higher, aiming for $70,000 in start-up capital. While that is not peanuts, it flies in the face of the common perception that it takes a great deal of money to start a business. A business's success will not be based on the amount of money you put into it. Rather, the key is being disciplined to find customers and sell them on your product or service.

"*Expect the best. Prepare for the worst. Capitalize on what comes.*"
—Zig Ziglar[107]

107 http://www.forbes.com/sites/kevinkruse/2012/11/28/zig-ziglar-10-quotes-that-can-change-your-life/.

DISCUSSION QUESTIONS

1. What are some advantages for raising support for your first few years overseas?
2. There are a variety of funding strategies; discuss the strengths and weaknesses of each for a new B4T start-up.
3. What are some ways you can get businesspeople back home interested in funding your start-up?

"There are no secrets to success. It is the result of preparation, hard work, and learning from failures."

—COLIN POWELL[108]

[108] http://www.brainyquote.com/quotes/quotes/c/colinpowel121363.html.

Chapter 12

ENSURING YOUR TENT BECOMES A B4T BUSINESS

Aspiring B4Ters are often convinced they have the next big idea for an app or product or service. Do they know anything about building an app? Well, no. But they want to run a business, so they dive in. As has been pointed out in the previous chapters, there more involved in doing B4T than just an idea. This chapter is based on data collected by the leaders of the OPEN Network. Together we have learned that there are four steps and eleven building blocks that need to be a part of every B4Ter's business and ministry plan if they wish to increase their chances of succeeding.

Henry R. Luce reminds us, *"Business . . . is a continual dealing with the future; it is a continual calculation, an instinctive exercise in foresight."*[109] Even with the perfect business plan there is no guarantee of success. When we combine business and evangelism, the challenges multiply. Here is how we suggest you move forward.

Four Steps

The four steps should shape your initial planning. These four steps must be done in order. Mix them up and it is very likely you will fail. The four steps are language and culture, business, integration, and fruitfulness (productivity).

Step One—Language and Culture

Obtaining language fluency needs to be front and center in your planning. You can share the gospel and even do business via a translator, but unless you have the language you cannot disciple people—meaning you cannot plant a church, either. In B4T if you fail at one thing, you fail at the whole thing.

---

[109] http://www.brainyquote.com/quotes/quotes/h/henryrluc120497.html.

There are nearly seven hundred B4T workers in the OPEN Network, and everyone one of them who has succeeded[110] at B4T is fluent in the language. The goal in learning the language is *fluency*, meaning you are able to do business in the local language. Fluency does not mean you are only able to share the gospel or your testimony or do the shopping. It means you are able to operate your business in the language.

Knowing both the language and culture well is key to succeeding in B4T. Jon, in Asia, has over seventy employees, has seen ten people come to faith, and does sales in eight figures. He is known for having the best language skills among expats in the country. He says, *"The reason my business is doing so well is because I know what is going on around me."*

One of the saddest emails I have ever received was written by a man named Drew.

> After nine years here (Central Asia) I am going home. My business is doing well. We have six employees and have made a profit nearly every year. However, because I never learned the language I have not touched one life for Christ. I can model the Gospel, but without words people are not connecting my model with God's message. Learning the language while operating a business is nearly impossible. For me to stop and learn at this point would require me to shut down my business and I don't have the energy to start all over. In a few months my family is packing our bags and going home. I can do business in the USA without all the hassles and maybe make an impact there for Jesus. Please share my story with others.

Many times people will come and say, "If you are here to do business, why are you learning the language? You can just use a translator." The answer that works in every single culture and country is, "Language is power."

In many places you should plan to learn both the heart language and the trade language. The former is necessary for evangelism and church planting, while the latter is needed for doing business. Plus, if you know both languages like the locals do, they can never talk behind your back. Investing four years up front to master two languages will serve you well in the end. One OPEN worker writes,

---

[110] We define success as having started a profitable business which employs 5+ locals and has seen one or more gatherings of new believers come together.

Learning the heart language is a MUST. It is worth everything you have to do to get it, even if that delays considerably the sowing. The trade language or national language, no matter how good we can speak it, just will NOT do. As someone who has learned both the heart language and trade language, one does not know how much more fruitful a heart language approach could have been.

Another worker comments, "How important is language fluency to what we do? Well, how important is talking to what we do?"

Oftentimes two nationals holding a conversation in English with a Westerner may turn to one another and use their own language, right in the middle of the conversation. Why? They spoke in their native language because they did not want the Westerner to understand what they were saying. Everyone who is bilingual has done this—it is one fun thing about knowing another language. Language *is* power.

When locals ask our coworkers why they are learning the language, they answer, "I am learning your language because I know that if I do not understand what is going on around me, people are able to cheat me, lie to me, or fool me. But if I know the language, they won't be able to do that." From Morocco to Indonesia, local people respond to that answer, saying, "You are really smart; now I know why you are learning the language first." When learning the language, you have nothing to hide. Be up front with people about your motives for learning their language.

In my doctoral research I asked 291 questions of 450 workers in the 10/40 Window. Laid out on the bell curve, language fluency proves to be the *most important factor* for people who have a successful business and are leading locals to Christ. Nothing is more important than learning the language well. And the research shows that if you do not learn the language well within the first three years, it is likely you will not learn the language well ever. Do not make Drew's mistake.

Trust and transparency go hand in hand. Trust is not easy to obtain, but transparency helps. Without transparency it is hard to win trust. People can read you and see your life in the context of their world better than you can. Everything needs to make sense. People need to believe you are placing their objectives in life and work (including culture) above your own. You need to show you understand what is happening around you. You are not simply selling a product; you are selling yourself to fulfill a need. Your strategies, tactics, and goals need to reflect the lifestyle and thinking of the people. You cannot learn these things from books or from other expats. You need to dig in to learn the language and culture of your immediate community in order to grasp what is on their hearts and minds. The better your language, the more transparent you can be.

In order to sell your product, your target market is the environment in which everything you do, in order to sell your product or service, must make sense to people. The local people determine your sales strategy, not your background, experiences, or the latest book. You will never succeed in selling your product if you do not understand your local customer. But to understand the world around you, you need good language skills.

Learning the language allows you to be much more effective in doing business and evangelism. While you are learning the language, plan to study full time or forty hours a week. Some languages, like Indonesian, may require you to study full time for about a year. Other languages, like Arabic, may take more than two years. You can determine the time you need to allocate to language learning by talking to those who have already mastered the local tongue. When in doubt allocate more time, not less. Do whatever it takes up front to learn the language well.

While talking with some workers about the value of language, Jon told me,

> Over the years, we realize it is not the methods we learn, it is the love and relationships we build that impact our friends. People know if you love Turks or Turkey. Our language ability has made a huge difference in our relationships with our employees and friends.

Many missiologists urge us to learn the language in the city where we will be working or setting up our business. I disagree. Rather, learn the language in a *nearby* city that has the same or similar dialect. Make your linguistic and cultural mistakes there. People expect students to make mistakes, but not businesspeople. The locals will extend grace to a student but not to a businessperson. What is more, once people perceive you as a student, it is hard for friends to grasp the switch of your identity to that of a businessperson. In addition, it is a big benefit to be able to negotiate your business setup with the government and locals in their language.

In all my years overseas, I have only met one B4Ter who learned the language while working fulltime at his job. He was not a business owner, but an employee of an international firm. This man told me he met with his language tutor for lunch every single workday of the year for seven years. Learning the language takes a great deal of time and effort. Trying to work a job, lead your family, and fulfill all your other obligations makes it almost impossible to do while starting a business. And it is not any easier if you are working for someone else. We need to take time to learn the language at the very beginning of our working overseas.

When you are three to six months from finishing language study, start working on your business plan—doing the research in the local language, talking to the government officials, and exploring business options. This will enable you to grow your business vocabulary while making practical steps towards starting the business.

This first step of learning the language and culture is a period of getting oriented, getting started, and beginning to move forward. As you begin to work on your business plan and wind down your language study, you begin to move into the second step.

Step Two—Business

Language takes one to three years to learn; starting a business takes two to four years to become successful. If you are an employee of a local or international firm, then having learned the language you can slip right into your new job. But if you are starting a business this step is the most demanding step of the four. It is the step when you or your spouse are most likely to want to quit and go home. Whereas you invested forty hours a week in learning the language, now you need to increase the hours to sixty a week, possibly more.

I had just returned from overseas when I saw a former student of mine. When he spotted me, he rushed over and shook my hand saying, *"Patrick, you are the biggest liar."* Taken aback I responded, *"Probably, but why?"* He smiled and went on, *"You taught us that the business step would require sixty hours a week of our time, but I found working eighty to be barely enough!"* The point is that this step takes hard work and long hours. You and your spouse have to be prepared for what is coming, and you have to have counted the cost and be willing to pay it.

If both you and your spouse are not willing to put in the work and the time while counting the cost accurately, then do not start a business. Many couples can attest to this. Nate and Abbi are a couple we trained prior to their moving overseas. They had been into this business step over a year when they emailed me, saying we needed to talk. A day later they called us, with Abbi saying, "I have had it. I'm done. We are going home. I never see him; all he does is work. We are not doing any ministry!" My wife and I got on a plane to fly out to India to meet with them. After we arrived we reminded them, "We told you before you started that this is what it is going to look like; just stick with it. You are a year and half into step two. Stay the course. You are right on track." And they stuck with it! They now have a solid business and a couple of new believers.

For most, this business step lasts three to four years. You know you are turning the corner when your cash flow begins to turn around and you can hire more employees. As you hire people, they can take on more responsibility, enabling you to reduce your hours significantly and allowing you to then enter into a more natural, integrated phase of life and work. After three to four years you should have better control of your time and better metrics in your business, as well as your ministry. You are able to assess things and step back, reducing your business hours to 30 to 40 hours a week, which is much more manageable. At this point you begin to slide into the integration step.

Step Three—Integration

The integration step sneaks up on you. Not only do you find that you are managing your time well and your children remember who you are, but you realize there is an openness to the gospel among your coworkers too. For several years now your employees have been watching you. They have witnessed the miracles God has done in and through your business. They have watched how you dealt with corrupt officials and employees who lied or cheated you. They have seen how you turned to God to run the business in both good and difficult times. They have observed your kindness to the poor and your generosity when they have done good work, and they have heard your prayers for both your needs and their needs.

Employees, suppliers, and clients have all been observing you the past few years, and with this step they start asking questions about what makes you tick. The first few times you responded to evil with good they thought you did not understand the language or culture. The next few times they just thought you were stupid. But over the years as you persisted in letting Jesus flow through you at work, they began to ask, *"Why are you different? Help me to understand. I like what I see and I want to know more."*

The integration step is where the natural witness of your work and the time and effort you have put into the business begins to bear results. Results come in a variety of ways, most notably in the form of making money, creating a valuable service or product for the community, and those around you beginning to ask about your faith.

One new business owner wrote recently,

I was doing a quarterly review with one of our designers and one of the things he said to me was "Lee, you need to be more mean to me, even if it's just a little bit". Curious I asked, "Why?" He went on saying, "there are no other bosses in the country who treat employees the way you do and I'm worried that if I ever left I wouldn't be ready for an obstinate boss." We then proceeded to have an hour long conversation on why because of what God has done in me I could never be a 'mean' boss and how God Himself is a loving, kind, and compassionate God who isn't out to get you but rather looking for relationship.

Integration is an easier step but it also takes time. People are watching. The opportunities to speak will follow as locals *see* your life and in time will glorify Jesus.[111] We are not growing strawberry plants, but rather almond trees. As you begin to integrate your life and your work natural opportunities to share will arise and in time the fruit will appear. It is then that the productivity begins to happen.

Step Four—Fruit and Productivity

Fruitfulness or productivity is obviously the most gratifying step as it is the fruit of all the hard work of the previous three steps. This is where the harvest is achieved for both bottom lines—profitability and transformed lives. The business is providing opportunities to witness to God's goodness and grace, and the income from the business covers the needs of your growing family.

Nearly three-fourths of the businesses in the OPEN Network are just starting out, but of the approximately twenty businesses that have been operating for ten plus years, all have seen lives transformed and a few—hundreds of lives. Many of these businesses are impacting their communities in tremendous ways. Several have helped start orphanages, or schools, and others are providing an education for the children of needy families. Still others are creating jobs for the handicapped and outcasts—employing the unemployable. Men and women living as slaves to Satanic task masters are freed, then educated and/or employed. Each person finds hope and dignity—a new life, including for some, new lives in Jesus. Each business models new hope and new ways of living and working. Corruption is challenged, love is shared, and forgiveness is offered to hundreds of souls who previously had not a hope in the world.

---

[111]   Matthew 5:16.

Another story about Nate and Abbi occurred when they had been in India nearly eight years. They had followed the four steps perfectly. We were visiting when Nate said, *"It is not working; we have been out here seven years and it is not working! You said that by the seventh year we would start seeing fruit, and yet we have nothing; nothing is happening."* Once again my wife and I told them, *"Just keep the course."* We had barely gotten home from our visit when we received an email from Nate that said, *"We have someone studying the Bible with us!"* It was that fast. Today at least three Muslims have come to Christ through their B4T business.

Remember these four steps must be done in order. Mixing them up means the results will be mixed too.

Eleven Building Blocks

There are eleven building blocks that go along with the four steps. These building blocks do not need to be done in order—in fact, if you look at ten successful OPEN Network businesses, you will likely see all eleven blocks, but each business will have achieved them in a different order. Nonetheless, these building blocks should be part of your thinking and planning from the beginning.

In considering these blocks, notice that starting a business to get a visa is not among them. B4T is not about getting a visa, finding an identity, or any other factors that some mission agencies advocate. While B4T does solve these problems, B4T is about operating an excellent for-profit business in Jesus' name that impacts the local community in a measurable way. Implementing these eleven blocks will put you on the path towards a successful B4T business.

1. Deep Relationship with Jesus

Brandon writes, *"Our new 'normal' is that there are new business issues and decisions and actions to make every day. This is our reality. At the same time, we must work hard at listening to the Lord and each other, while walking together in unity."*

B4T workers need to know how to hear God's voice and feed themselves from His word. They need to know how to thrive (not just survive) spiritually. It is essential that each of us knows our spiritual appetite and how to feed it. The Holy Spirit needs to have an active role in every area of our life and work. In chapter 4 of my first book,

Tentmaking—The Life and Work of Business as Missions, I give many ideas on how to do this.

2. Mentoring—Accountability

My wife has been known to say, *"I love ministering. I just wish it didn't involve people."* Every one of us is a sinner. We each have areas of temptation and sin. We need spiritual elders who will walk alongside us to assist us in maximizing God's glory in and through us. In many situations, peer accountability is fine, but my research shows peer accountability is less effective than elder accountability. I think this is because peers leading one another are like the blind leading the blind.

In business, most reporting is done verbally, face-to-face. Bosses meet or communicate with their direct reports daily. We want to both see and hear that the work is being done and being done correctly. In business, people do not write up reports about themselves. Whether we are Christian or not, when we write up reports about ourselves, we are revealing only what we want to tell. And if we are honest, most of us view our work and ourselves better than we really are.

Business uses a proactive model for gathering information and responding to problems. Business strives to solve problems before they happen. Most missions and churches have a reactive model. When problems arise they are quick to deal with them, but my hypothesis is that many of these problems should never have occurred in the first place.

We need a well-rounded perspective that invites another pair of eyes and ears to watch our life and work. People who are personally accountable look at obstacles as a part of the process and rather than give up, they are energized by them. Research shows that workers who have a tendency to blame others or fail to accept personal responsibility for their actions will most likely stall in any entrepreneurial endeavor. Whatever our temperament, we need to be subject to real accountability. We need someone who understands our background and is going to help us integrate all areas of life and work (marriage, family, team, business, God, character, etc.). This must be someone who will hold us accountable to make sure that everything stays in balance. We need someone who will be critical of our results despite the good it does. Just because we are feeding hungry people does not mean we are doing what is best for the people. We need mentors who will ask the hard questions and patiently guide us when we are struggling for answers.

A good mentor is proactive, initiates contact, builds intimacy, and strives to work to keep the mentee on the course God has put him or her. Mentors hold people truthfully accountable for what is going on in their marriage, their family, their team, their employees, their business, their evangelism—every area of their life and work. Mentors do not set goals; mentees do. In this way mentors know where God is leading and help to speed the mentee along God's chosen path. Mentoring is relational and personal accountability. It is not gathering data. It is what Jesus did—life-on-life accountability.

As a footnote, we need to remind ourselves that education and training lead to potential, not performance. If you consult, make recommendations, but without getting involved. Coaches utilize questions to draw out the thinking that is within the individual, helping them to solve their own problems, but no actions are required. Mentors, on the other hand, bring skills that disciple and help the mentee to run on his own. Mentoring that is done well is relationally based. A good mentor is committed to understanding and then guiding the mentee to maximize his experiences and talents to the glory of Jesus. In the OPEN Network and NexusB4T we stress that mentors are to be a cheerleader, confidant, fund raiser, recruiter, coach, consultant, accountability partner—an advocate for the mentee.

3. Learn to Work

Learning to work may seem obvious, but it is surprising how many Christians do not know how to work. In appendix E of my first book, I listed some of the differing attitudes that Christian workers and businesspeople have toward work. Experiencing the value of working forty to fifty hours a week is essential before moving overseas. In Christian circles, we sometimes talk about "working a real job." What does that imply about working for a church or parachurch/mission organization? That it is not real work. So you need to have practical work experience. Whether or not the work is similar to what you will do overseas does not matter. What matters is that you know how to work and are willing to work hard for many hours six days a week.

4. Access to the People

Access to the people seems obvious as well, but many businesses fail at this point. Too often we emphasize getting a visa in selecting a job or business. As a result, we start an IT business only to discover that the people we are reaching are not educated, so they do not use computers. You do not want to work in a business one place and then minister somewhere else. If you do then you have to do the work of two separate jobs. The ministry should be able to happen right inside your workplace. Two mission leaders have asked if we can help them to start businesses that require only five hours per week of work. The implication is that then the missionary will be free to share the gospel with the rest of his time. Allow me to repeat, *sharing must happen in the workplace.* If we are going to model the gospel first, people need to be able to see us every day of the week. Witnessing and work need to be in step, like a dance. One foot is the job and the other foot is witnessing. It is not easy to dance on one leg.

Getting into a country is one thing, but access to a specific people group is quite another. Your business should be built to maximize profit and minimize risk, but it must also be designed to create witnessing opportunities to the people God has assigned you to reach. Access involves more than just getting in; it also involves becoming close to the people. For the integration step to become a reality, you need to spend time with people in relationships where they can witness the love of God and experience His grace in your life. B4Ters who work alongside those they are seeking to reach are much more effective in seeing locals come to Christ.

If your business does not give you frequent access to the people, then it is probably not a good B4T business. For example, there is a team working in Europe that has a common calling of reaching Muslims, who are a minority people group in their city. The team began a business, which proved to be quite successful financially. It is an IT-related business whose clients are mostly in North America. Though profitable, the team is called to reach a poor, uneducated Muslim segment of society. Doing this with an IT business does not work very well. They cannot hire any Muslims, except the janitor, and they do not sell any products to Muslims, so the team has no natural relationships within the Muslim community. Through the business they are in the country legally and though the business is successful financially, that is all it has going for it. The team has been working eight-hour days and going home exhausted, but they still needed to do ministry in the evenings and weekends. After several years of this, they invited an OPEN mentor to work with them. The mentor told this team at the outset,

> I will work with you on one condition: you are going to have to start a new business. You can use your existing business to fund a new businesses start-up, or you can sell it and use those

funds for starting a new business. But this current business is not a good B4T business, as it is not engaging the people you are seeking to reach.

It took several years working alongside the mentor for the team to make the needed changes. They trained qualified nationals from the majority people to run the successful business. Then they used the money from this business to start two new businesses, which engage Muslims. They started a bakery that is located in a Muslim shopping area and a manufacturing business where they are hiring low-skilled Muslim laborers.

If your business does not give you access to the people you are trying to reach, you will be working two full-time jobs. The business must generate natural touch points with your target people via customers, employees, or suppliers to the business. You need those natural and daily touch points so the people can observe your life and work. Your business needs to provide natural access to the local people you are trying to reach.

5. Bless the Community

Your business needs to bless the local community. Blessing cannot be defined or explained from a Western viewpoint, but it must be understood from the local perspective. The business should be adding value to the local community in ways that the locals, and especially the government, appreciate.

B4T businesses are currently blessing their communities in a variety of ways—job creation, starting or funding social services like orphanages, and funding training for the handicapped. Some businesses offer their services or products to the needy or elderly. Other businesses teach English, health care, hygiene, or computer skills pro bono. Still others provide scholarships for worthy and needy students. A few have collected books for local libraries, and a few have taken part in building schools and clinics. Numerous women have been rescued from slave-like sex and work situations and given a real job with a hope for the future. These are just a smattering of ideas currently being implemented by OPEN Network teams to add value and bring blessing to their local communities.

6. Create Jobs

Everyone wants a job. Job creation is a key to building relationships, modeling faith, and winning favor with government officials. People watch us while we work. Most of the things they observe we cannot plan or prepare for. For example, I cannot plan for a customer trying to cheat me or an employee trying to steal from me. But when employees see how I respond with love and grace to these difficult situations, it is a testimony to God's love and grace. This in turn sows the seed for questions they will sooner or later, ask me about. When employees see how we live out our faith in the workplace, they are often intrigued, and sometimes amazed. Real businesses create jobs, which then generate seed-sowing opportunities and deep relationships with local employees.

When you give people a job, you honor them. You tell them that their gifts, skills, and training are of value to you. And if you treat them with respect, they will desire to return that honor back to you. When fundamentalists criticize us, our employees often come to our defense. We have a conservative imam working in our office. After nearly a year of battling us on many spiritual issues, he nowadays tells his friends that Christians are righteous, not like what they see in Hollywood movies, and that they should read the Injil (Gospels) for themselves. Our words did not change his thinking, our lives and work did.

So much of our identity is wrapped up in what we do. When we meet people, among the first questions we ask is, *"What kind of work do you do?"* If you have been unemployed, you know how that feels—its as if nobody wants your skill; nobody needs your education, training, or experience. You feel worthless. When we come into a community and create jobs we are saying, *"I need you. I need your skill. I need your abilities and experiences. You have value."* Creating jobs is honoring to people. A job gives a person respect.

Your business should be designed to create five or more jobs in the local community. Maybe you won't hire all five employees the day your business's doors open, but within two to three years it is important to hire at least five people. When fundamentalists or government officials persecute you or the business, it is usually your employees who will come to your defense. You need at least a handful of employees so that there is enough of a critical mass to convince the officials of the value in allowing you to stay.

The poster child for this is Morocco. A few years ago, roughly 240 Christian workers were kicked out of the country. The government published a list of about 350 people whom they were watching. Eleven OPEN workers were on that list. Two of those on the list were visited by officials and informed, *"You have a few days to pack up and leave. Say goodbye."* In both cases—two different cities—the employees went to the officials and pleaded, *"Why did you just take my job away from me?"*

As a result the officials went back to both businessmen and said, *"Sorry we told you that you must leave. You can stay."* Not one OPEN worker was kicked out of Morocco during this government purge.

I have had the same experience in Southeast Asia. Three times during the first three years, the authorities paraded into my business. They went straight to our Muslim employees and asked, *"Are these people proselytizing you?"* When our employees said yes, I swallowed hard and thought, *"That's it. I'm done."* However, our workers added, *"Yes they are Christians, but here is what we get paid. Here are the benefits we get working here"*—and this is the best part—*"Working here is like working for family. Don't you dare close this business down."* So, chastened, the officials each time simply said, *"Okay, good to know you are happy,"* and left.

Five is not a magic number, but we have seen in several places that when you have five employees it is enough of a critical mass to voice concerns to authorities. Two or three employees are simply not enough. So choose a business that will enable you to hire at least five locals.

7. Example to New Believers

The business needs to create opportunities to model Jesus, both for the local believers (if there are any) and the people you are reaching. Whether the believers are customers or employees, they need to learn how to integrate their faith in the workplace. Too many churches and Christian communities have failed to teach and model the love of Jesus in the marketplace. It is strategic to be a witness to both the believers and nonbelievers, helping the former to discover ways of being bolder in modeling and sharing their faith in the community.

Good business also is a model to believers, in that it helps eliminate dependency. Whereas many NGO and charity types of ministries are not reproducible, business creates jobs that locals can then learn from, teaching them how to build their own models of financial self-support. In 1989 we had the privilege of being a part of planting a church in Indonesia. Not knowing any better, we raised the monies to help one of the leaders get theological training and become the pastor. Twenty-five years later, the pastor is still supported largely by donors from North America. More recently, we saw another local fellowship birthed. Because we provided jobs instead of money, the believers never expected to be supported, and to this day they do not receive any foreign funds.

If we want to avoid building a dependency model by paying local believers to do outreach; we need to remember that as an NGO worker or traditional missionary our modeling is that of a "charity" worker. We model being paid by churches overseas and new believers simply follow our example. The problem is not in their heart, it is in our modeling. Mission workers model dependency. We model love, joy, peace, patience, kindness, self-control, and being paid by the West. So while reproducing our lives in the local believers, these things become the foundation of our discipleship. The locals see how we act and wish to copy us. They see how we are paid and wish to copy us too. Paul modeled and taught, *"Whatever you have learned or received or heard from me, or seen in me—put it into practice."*[112] People follow us as they think we follow Christ. Being an example to believers in how we earn our money lays the foundation for a ministry that is truly reproducible.

8. Funds National and Expat Workers—Financially Sustainable

Drawing a salary builds off of being an example to believers, but it is a central point in and of itself. Our businesses need to be paying the salaries of everyone who works there. Employees know who gets a paycheck and who does not. Government officials know if we are paying income taxes or not. Yes, it is common for B4Ters not to draw a full salary for a year or three as we struggle to bring the business to viability, but we need to strive toward paying ourselves a salary.

The expenses of Westerners are often higher than those of locals. Therefore, we need to be sensitive to individual needs and set budgets accordingly. The salaries our business pays are fixed. Locals and foreigners receive the same base pay. Six team members work in our business. Two live off of the salary we pay them, and the others get additional income via support from churches at home, via a mission agency. Those who receive additional income have additional expenses, like children attending the international school, which our local salary is not enough to cover. It is okay, even encouraged, to receive additional income from friends and churches. Some income from churches helps hold us accountable to our evangelism and church planting objectives in addition to meeting our needs. However, as the business prospers, we need to be receiving some salary from the business too.

---

[112] Philippians 4:9

9. Invest Your Own Money

When you start a business, you need to invest your own money. Starting a business using other people's money makes it too easy to walk away when the going gets tough. There are two reasons you need to invest your own money in the business: if you do not have skin in the game, investors will be very hesitant to invest in your business, and you really will not work as hard as needed to make the business a success. When our business was on the brink of bankruptcy and going down the tubes, my wife and I looked at each other and said, *"We don't have anything else if this goes under."* We were all in, so we worked extra hard to make it a success. We had sunk our retirement money—everything we had—into this business. If it failed, that was going to be it. When you are in such a situation, you dig a little deeper, you fight a little harder, and often that is what makes the difference between success and failure.

When you are "all in," investors have greater confidence that you will work hard to see that their money earns a return. It is essential to have a significant portion of your personal worth invested in the business to prove you are serious about making the business a success.

10. Equip People Well

Paul writes to Timothy, *"And what you have heard from me in the presence of many witnesses entrust to faithful men who will be able to teach others also."*[113] One common mistake we make in business, discipleship, and church planting is not equipping people well. Caleb writes, *"People told us in India not to manufacture because you cannot trust people. I have learned this is wrong. If you equip people well, invest in them, and sacrifice for them, they will return your trust."* If you played an instrument or a sport, you appreciate a good coach or trainer. The same goes for business. People like to perform their jobs well. Well-trained employees not only yield great returns for the company and require less of your time, they also are more trustworthy. In addition, people who know their job well, enjoy their work more. We bless people by providing thorough, excellent training.

There are five simple steps we use in training people:

1. Tell the person what to do, then have him tell it back to you.
2. Show the person what to do, then have him tell you what

---

[113] 2 Timothy 2:2

you did.

3. Show the person what to do, then have him do it while you are watching, correcting any errors, and then have him tell you what he did.
4. Have the person do the task by himself, observe the results, and ask him to tell you what he did.
5. Let him do it himself and evaluate the result.

Note the emphasis on telling. When people see us doing things, we may think they understand what we did if they can replicate the action or task. However, that does not mean they fully grasp what is happening. When employees or disciples repeat the process verbally many times, it reinforces their understanding of the task, as well as the logic behind why the task is done the way we have them do it.

In the beginning, plan to invest a lot of time training people. It may seem troublesome, but down the road if someone is well equipped, she will reproduce herself. That is where much of the first two to three years in starting a business are spent—training people. In the initial years make it a priority to spend a lot of time with your people. Equip them to do the job well, and down the road you won't have to do everything yourself.

11. Respectable Role

The business you choose needs to provide you with a respectable identity and role in the community. Certain types of businesses or jobs are not reputable in different cultures. Though you may have skills or background in such work and though it is not a job of disrepute back home, it is wise to avoid such businesses overseas. In the end, working a disrespectful job will tarnish your witness. Before choosing a business, invite input from locals concerning what is and is not a reputable business. Do not tell them what you want to do up front since they will want to please you (meaning they will nearly always tell you that what you endeavor to do is a good thing). Rather, list several types of jobs or businesses and get input from a variety of people to discover what is and isn't deemed to be a respectable job. For example, manufacturing bikinis in a fundamental Muslim area may be viewed as disrespectful. Any business dealing with waste materials is considered taboo in some cultures. In a few Asian cultures, operating a retail store, or men teaching young children, is considered to be dishonorable.

In selecting a job and role, you must ensure that everyone is clear on what that job/role is. Whatever is not made clear about your life and work will be filled in for you by the locals—meaning they will invent an identity for you that they can understand. Thus, you must have a genuine job, and you must be transparent about what you are doing and why you are doing it.

Contextualization is an issue for many Christian workers overseas. When we have a respectable job or business, our life and work is naturally contextualized to fit in with the local ways of doing things. Jack writes, *"If you do things that are not respectable, it will not help your witness. To manufacture mini-skirts in a Muslim city will not be respectable. It affects your ability to share truth. Don't sell beef hamburgers in a Hindu area either."* This is another reason we learn the language *and* the culture before starting our business; we need to understand from the local's perspective what is and is not respectable.

Summary

Rarely do these building blocks fall into place naturally. In every OPEN Network business there are ups and downs, three steps forward and then two steps (or maybe three steps) back. This is a common tension that B4Ters live with. Some B4Ters describe it as *"doing the B4T tango."* The right leg is evangelism/church planting, and the left leg is doing business. It feels like you are constantly moving in all directions. One leg seems to lead, then suddenly the other leg is leading. You move backwards, forwards, and all around the room.

Understand that the business leg must always take the lead initially. If the ministry is developed before the business, it is likely you will get kicked out of the country. But if the business goes first, then the ministry will flow through the business as intended. Keep in mind that the business validates the ministry, as well as generates it. Ideally, both legs will move in tandem, but in reality it is often out of balance. That is why having a mentor—accountability—is so important. Like a disc jockey, the mentor helps provide guidance so that we know when to speed up the tempo and when to slow down.

Achieving success at two assignments—evangelism/church planting and business—is tough. It requires hard work. Remember, B4T is the integration of evangelism/discipleship with business. The more seamless these two interact, the better. If you can implement these four steps and eleven building blocks, you are likely to succeed at B4T.

DISCUSSION QUESTIONS

1. What are the four steps of B4T? Why must the steps be done in order?
2. List the eleven building blocks. Which ones will be easy for you to integrate into your business? Which ones will be difficult? Why?
3. In doing the B4T tango, in the beginning, why must the business leg go first?

"An intelligent man is open to new ideas,
in fact he looks for them."

—KING SOLOMON[114]

Chapter 13

MOVING FORWARD

God has given B4Ters the assignment of reaching the unreached via business. Whether He has led us to reach others through owning a business or working for someone else, we commit every moment and every task to His glory. Business is done by people, with people, and for people. But people are naturally sinful beings. As we wrap up the issues that impact starting a B4T business, let's remind ourselves of some key points.

The Heart

Jeremiah says, *"The heart is deceitful above all things and beyond cure. Who can understand it?"*[115] Our brains are wired in ways that tend to prevent us from following tried and true biblical principles in life and business. Our sinful nature often moves us toward being greedy, selfish, or lazy. There are five areas to watch over as you move forward in B4T.

1. Overconfidence.
We often overestimate our own abilities. Overconfidence and its sibling, over-optimism, lead companies to take on projects they cannot possibly finish on time, or make up overly rosy forecasts. You cannot temper overconfidence by having a mentor or discussing new projects or new hires with a coach. Add 10 to 25 percent more downside planning scenarios, and be wary of strategies based on a "certainty" that it will work.

2. Pet projects.
This is the tendency to keep product lines or services in place that are no longer profitable. Leaving them alone in the hope that they will turn around when you know they never will, causes you to hang on much longer than you should and misallocate valuable resources. Avoid pet projects by viewing every business, product, or market as fluid, and constantly

---

[115] Jeremiah 17:9

changing. Take note of the risks of doing nothing as well as making changes. As one worker in Indonesia put it, *"Be ruthless in accountability."*

3. Missing the signs.

This often happens when we jump to conclusions without taking the time to listen or understand another's point of view. It is too easy to overestimate how much others share your views. We create this effect by seeking facts and opinions that support our beliefs. Always encourage frank discussion and seek out differing views.

4. Throwing good money after bad.

Avoid the fallacy of sunk costs. Do not keep investing in incomplete projects despite changed conditions that make it unwise to pursue completion. If you have invested $10,000 in the project to date, and it becomes obvious things are not going to work out, do not continue to invest money in the idea. Control costs by evaluating incremental investments as if they were new projects, and be ready to kill experiments quickly.

5. The copycat.

This is the desire to be like everyone else. But if you are like everyone else, then you have no competitive advantage. Be different. Sprint away from the herd by innovating and reinventing your business regularly. If what has been working ceases to work, cut your losses quickly by axing projects and innovations that fail to meet expectations.

Capital and Churches

The changing world scene is moving Christian churches toward assisting their overseas workers in doing business. Yet the tendency of many churches is to shy away from anything that resembles financial profit, in order not to jeopardize their tax-exempt status. There needs to be further review of the laws and perhaps even some testing of the laws in court. If a business is truly winning souls to Jesus and eliminating poverty, is it that different from an NGO, which does the same and is a tax write-off too? We need to separate the true legal difficulties from the perceived ones. Currently, most churches are afraid to touch anything that has profit associated with it—this needs to change.

Fear and greed come from the pit of hell. Fear and greed will torpedo the B4T movement. If our reaction to doing B4T business is fear-driven, then it is probably not Bible-centered. Greed and fear are major factors in leading us away from the straight and narrow. Each B4Ter needs to guard against easy money, easy due diligence, and easy mentoring. We need a quality of rigor. Cheap money is one of the great threats to B4T, as it draws in fake business. Paul makes it clear, *"So I always take pains to have a clear conscience before God and man."*[116] The standard of having a clear conscience requires us to strive for transparency and excellence in whatever we do.

Missions is viewed differently than business because of its history and relationship with the church. Expectations are different and accounting is different. If a mission agency flushes $10,000 down the toilet, nobody knows. If a business flushes $10,000 down the toilet, everyone knows. Being a new strategy in missions, B4Ters must brace themselves to being held to a higher—and sometimes unrealistic—standard. B4Ters need to manage their money as those who will give an account of it. If a mission agency sends out a new worker to Timbuktu and he returns home two years later burnt out and discouraged, the church will claim that the fault lies at the feet of the devil. If a B4Ter goes to Timbuktu, squanders his investment capital, goes broke, and returns home two years later burnt out and discouraged, the church will say the fault lies with the individual and the strategy of using business to reach the unreached. Balance and reality need to be brought into our understanding before pointing fingers.

Many times seminary professors and mission agency leaders have asked me, *"If she goes into business, won't all the money she makes lead her into sin?"* My reply is always, *"No more than the businesspeople you know in your church."* Of the hundreds of B4T workers I know, I cannot think of one who, after making a lot of money, pocketed it and stopped following God. The church should not be sending out people, including B4ters, if they cannot trust them with money. Our focus should not be on profits—which is idolatry[117]—but on enlisting people whose personal maturity and sense of stewardship will ensure an appropriate use of the money the church sends them, as well as the money their business earns. We must keep the focus on God, not on money or anything else.

Jobs

Businesses impact individuals and communities in many ways. When you have to make things with your hands and trade with others in order to

---

[116] Acts 24:16
[117] Luke 16:13

flourish, it inevitably broadens imagination and increases tolerances and trust. Twenty percent of the world's population lives in Muslim countries, but only four percent of world trade comes from these same countries. This should be a huge opportunity for the good news. When countries do not make things anyone else wants to buy, they trade less—and less trade means less exchange of ideas and less openness to the world. The most open and tolerant cities in the Muslim world today are trading centers—Tangier, Bahrain, Beirut, Dubai, Istanbul, Jakarta, and Kuala Lumpur. Thomas Friedman writes,

> If we've learned one thing since 9/11, it's that terrorism is not produced by the poverty of money. It's produced by the poverty of dignity. It is about young middle-class Arabs and Muslims feeling trapped in countries with too few good jobs and too few opportunities to realize their potential or shape their own future—and blaming America for it. We have to break that cycle.[118]

Regarding job creation, do not focus solely on employment but also on building dignity into the hearts and lives of people. For a job to be meaningful and touch people's hearts, it needs to give value and dignity to the employee. This value and dignity must be seen through the local lens of the people and from biblical principles, not according to Western values and standards.

When our workers have a problem at work or at home, it becomes my problem. Betty, my office manager, was divorcing her husband. He was keeping the house, the car, everything. What was Betty going to do? She wanted to own a home, but no bank would give her a loan without some collateral. Aware of her need, I offered her a loan at two percent interest, the same interest I'd have gotten had I put the money in a local bank account. The payments then would be deducted from her monthly paycheck. When her daughter needed help finding a university to study at in America, we also helped. Asian values dictate that "the family" looks after one another. As the leader in the office, I prayerfully assume leadership of the lives of my workers—my family—which is readily understood in our culture and reflects the principles of leadership in Hebrews 13:17.

---

[118] Thomas L. Friedman, *Longitudes and Attitudes* (New York: Farrar Straus Giroux Books, 2002), 270.

In Matthew 20:1–16, the master approaches the workers who are standing in the market hoping for work. These men were already feeling humbled and probably suffering from a poor self-image. Think of what it would be like to spend most of the day standing around in the hot sun at the corner of the market hoping someone would value your skills enough to give you work so that you could feed your family. The master does not say to the workers, *"Here, each of you take a denarius and go buy some food for your families."* He does not make them into charity cases. He refuses to humiliate them further by placing them on relief. Instead, he gives them the one thing they so desperately want—a job. He values them. He honors them. He tells them they have something to contribute to society. Even though there is no promise to pay them anything, still they accompany him to the fields. It seems clear that the workers sensed the master's compassion and were thankful for his willingness to put aside their public humiliation.

Human rights advocate Mohamed Ali says that the key to overcoming terrorism is entrepreneurism—creating jobs. "Entrepreneurs see the possibilities in the midst of poverty. They are change makers. We need to help people find ideas, develop a plan for these ideas, and then bring these ideas into reality." Mohamed Ali understands B4T when he adds, "For me, entrepreneurship is more than starting a business. It is creating social impact. We are not just selling products, we are selling hope."[119]

We *are* purveyors of hope. We need to hold the souls of our employees in our hands. Remember Charles Sheldon's point that *"in His relations with all the persons in His employ He would be the most loving and helpful. Jesus could not help thinking of all of them in the light of souls to be saved. This thought would always be greater than His thought of making money in the business."* Jobs are intended to give more than a salary; a job must also give dignity.

Think Bigger

In addition to jobs, we need to think about job creation. Creating one job is good. Creating ten jobs is better. Starting one hundred new jobs is better still. If we are going to be significant in *transformation*, we need to be significant in job *creation*. Job creation makes "fertile ground" for sowing the seed of the gospel. As servants of the Lord to every person,

---

[119] Mohamed Ali, *The Link between Unemployment and Terrorism*, TED,. September 2013, http://t.co/Vb8CAIwtmC.

we need to be helping B4T businesses grow from five employees to fifty to five hundred.

It is all too common today to believe and accept that *"opening one coffee shop makes me a missionary BAMer."* That mentality is similar to those who think, *"I need a business so that I can stay in the country."* We need to change our thinking to something like, *"I need to start and grow a business that will employ thousands so as to be transformational!"*

When you are envisioning your business and writing your business plan, ask God to do more than you are able. Ask Him for ideas and plans for employing not just a handful of people, but a large building full of people. Think big. If we think small, we will achieve small. Pray and think so big that unless God gets involved, it will be beyond your own abilities to make the B4T business happen. Such faith not only pleases Him[120] but also keeps us dependent on Him. Donald Trump adds, *"If you are going to be thinking anyway, you might as well be thinking big."*[121]

Looking Ahead

In 2001, the leaders of the OPEN Network predicted that BAM would have a major role in the future of missions. The final chapter of my first book is titled, "We Got Next!" Since 2010, nearly every major mission organization has moved to create a BAM department or desk within their structure. There are more changes coming. Will we need ten to fifteen more years to adjust?

In regards to BAM, mission agencies have unfortunately circled the wagons, with many mission organizations reinventing the wheel. Rather than working together with those who already have experience in doing BAM and B4T, they are creating their own departments to deal with the matter. But at the same time, established B4Ters are questioning the need for staying with their mission agency. In addition, young people are quickly realizing that their BAM/B4T heroes are going independent. This is causing many to rightfully ask, *"Does the mission agency have a role in BAM/B4T?"* For years the agencies have been telling us that you cannot mix business and ministry—perhaps they are right—mission agencies and business cannot mix.

My next book will focus on these issues. We need to take the BAM and B4T discussion deeper than the theological and theoretical levels

---

[120] Hebrews 11:6
[121] http://www.brainyquote.com/quotes/quotes/d/donaldtrum153805.html.

that most conferences and organizations are currently discussing. With thousands of BAM/B4T workers currently on the field, practical matters need to be openly discussed and dissected. Meanwhile, souls are being lost and B4Ters are floundering. Certainly there will be varying views and applications on how to do BAM/B4T, and that is good. Just as Christian leaders have put their heads together regarding the practical outworkings of baptism, speaking in tongues, and many other biblical issues, we need to put our heads together to work out how to do BAM/B4T better. Listing best practices as stated in the previous chapter is a helpful start, but we need to go deeper.

Questions to be discussed next are:

- What is the role of the church in sending out BAMers/B4Ters?
- What is the role, if any, for mission agencies in BAM?
- In an age of transparency, how can mission agencies send workers to the Muslim world?
- What structures, if any, are needed to enhance the work of BAMers/B4Ters?
- How do we provide those without a mission agency the services they may request, such as pre-field training, member care, health insurance, pastoral care, coaching, etc.?
- How can independent workers receive the mentoring or supervision and accountability needed in their life and work?
- What, if anything, needs to be done to help non-Western workers develop BAM/B4T strategies?

Last Words

This book has been an attempt to lay out some steps for those starting out in B4T. Like the Cushite whose information was more meaningful to King David because he had fought in the battle,[122] we've outlined steps that have been tried and tested by hundreds of B4Ters in the OPEN Network. Each step needs to be bathed in prayer. Before moving too far ahead, it is strongly suggested you enlist a handful of coaches and a mentor.

Starting a business requires desire, dreams, recognized opportunities, and responsibility. Expect loneliness, fear, and second-guessing. Commit to seriously studying the situation, writing a business plan, and finding adequate capital. Get advice from experienced people, follow through,

---

[122] 2 Samuel 18

keep a positive attitude, and empower others. Laying out the steps is easy. Following through is the hard part.

In my own culture and many others, a person's last words are the most important. So as you are getting started, remember these last words: learn the language up front, utilize coaches, and find a mentor. Though I have said this already, these things are *that* important.

Doing B4T is hard. Very hard! Talking about it is simple. Missionaries with little business experience, but plenty of vision, start businesses and struggle. Even experienced businesspeople start businesses in new countries and struggle. Following the steps laid out in these chapters will not guarantee you success, but if you walk through them with the guidance of His Spirit, you will be on an adventure that will transform your own life and the lives of others—all for Jesus' glory!

DISCUSSION QUESTIONS

1. Of the five areas to watch over as you move forward in B4T, which will you struggle with most? What can you do to overcome this struggle?
2. Why is "job creation" so important to transforming lives?
3. Review the seven questions under "Looking Ahead" with a church leader. Share what you have learned with him or her and discuss your future plans.
4. What are the three last words to remember as you are getting started?

APPENDIX A

QUESTIONS TO ASK WHEN NEGOTIATING AN APPRENTICESHIP OR INTERNSHIP

This list of questions has been adapted from *Tentmaking*, where the questionnaire was originally devised to align the expectations of new employees / team members with those of a B4T team. It has been adapted to look at the specific issues facing apprentices and interns when negotiating with a B4T firm. It is essential that short-termers have realistic expectations of what their conditions will be like and what they will learn and accomplish. I recommend you get these answers from the leader of the B4T business you will be working for, not from someone in a mission agency home office or even a home church. Talk directly with those you will be working with.

1. B4Ter Role:
   - What role or duties will you perform? What will your workday look like?
   - How will the job you perform benefit the company you work with? How essential is this job to the firm?
   - Will you be able to use your _____ (specific prior experience and training in business, ministry, etc.)?
   - Would this job still happen if you did not do it?
   - Will you be able to fail and embarrass yourself? (Most long-term workers fail frequently, as do most businesspeople. To this end, will your experience protect, pamper, or posture your time so that you have a "good" experience or a "real" experience? You want an experience that is as real as possible. The experience should test yourself so that you know if serving overseas is something the Lord would have you do long-term. A real short-term experience

will expose you to working and making an impact as a Christian in the business environment, as well as teach you new things about yourself.)
- Will there be opportunities for starting a branch of the business you work for in another city or country in the future? What would be your ongoing relationship with the business?
- Will you be paid? Will you need to raise support? How much?

2. B4Ter Relationships:
- Will you spend time with long-term workers?
- Will you be able to live with a B4Ter family?
- How much time and what forms of mentoring will you get with the more mature workers?

3. Ministry:
- Will you be exposed to different types of ministry in addition to B4T, or will it just be about B4T? What kinds of ministries will you be exposed to? What other skills, jobs, or ministries can you expect to be exposed to?
- Will you be able to do evangelism? What kind? (The context may also vary considerably. In discerning His will, it is good to be exposed to as many types of mission work, as well as B4T businesses, as reasonably possible. This will help you discern where to find His pleasure working through you.)

4. Training:
- Will you be given on-the-job training?
- Will there be some formal discipleship or teaching times as part of your training?
- What will the training include?
- Will you have a mentor or supervisor? How often will he or she meet with you?
- May you contact the mentor or supervisor before making a commitment? (By contacting them directly via email, you can ensure that you understand his or her expectations for your short-term ministry and vice versa.)

5. Language and Culture:
- Will you be given language assignments that will test your ability to learn the language?

- How much of the language can you expect to learn? (Learning the basics of the language will also enable you to establish relationships with the local people.)
- Will there be opportunities to meet people, eat their food, and wear their clothes?
- Can you live with a local family for a time?

6. Local Friends:
- Will you have opportunities to make local friends outside of work?
- How much of your B4T work and free time will be spent with nationals?
- What will your free time look like? (As for work time, you will need to act professionally with colleagues, which means expecting to *work* professionally at all times, and not by way of eye service.)

7. Debriefing:
- Will there be a complete debrief at the end of your experience to summarize the firm's impression of your work and ministry in the business, as well as outside it? (The intention of this should be to give feedback on what has not already been said about your abilities and aspirations. It is also a time to seek the Lord's leading for your future. This should help you be a better steward of your experience, especially in regard to effectively sharing your experiences and leading.)

8. Expectations:
- What expectations or objectives does the B4T firm have for you during and after your time with them? (Share your expectations to ensure you have a good understanding of one another's goals. Ask the B4Ters for a brief history of their ministry in the firm, and outside of it. As they ask for your testimony, do not hesitate to ask for theirs.)
- What books, articles, or websites should you read in preparation for going?
- What should you wear? What should you bring and not bring? How should you dress for work?

APPENDIX B

TERMINOLOGY

One of the challenges of hanging around cross-cultural workers is recognizing the lingo we use. Here are some terms that are used throughout this book and what is meant by them.

B4T (Business for Transformation): A business strategically placed in an unreached area designed to create jobs and bless the local community in Jesus' name, generally through transformation and specifically through evangelism, discipleship, and church planting.

BAM (Business as Mission): The integration of ministry goals and business goals to make an impact for God's kingdom. As a strategy, BAM generally describes any for-profit business endeavor that seeks to reach communities for the glory of God and is not artificially supported by donor funds. Justin Forman of *businessasmissionnetwork.com* explains BAM this way:

Business as Mission has four core components. First, it involves the creation of a business controlled by Great Commission–minded owners and senior management who seek to glorify God with every aspect of their business operation. This eliminates *tentmaking*, which focuses on individual impact rather than the business impact. Second, it has profit (or at least sustainability) as a goal. This eliminates business "platforms" and other ministries and *NGOs*, which cannot operate without donor funds. Third, it exists primarily to advance the gospel among less reached peoples of the world. This eliminates marketplace ministries, which are typically not cross-cultural in emphasis. Fourth, it is socially responsible; it does not seek profit at any cost. Restricting our definition in this way is not to say that these excluded strategies are not desirable or effective.

Bivocational: Someone who works two jobs, often one for pay and the other as a volunteer worker or supported by donors—not a B4T worker.

Missionary/"M": Someone who is paid or supported by churches and donors to serve God in another culture.

Nongovernmental Organization (NGO): An organization that is not government sponsored, but is a 501(c)(3) charity. Many mission organizations have multiple NGOs that do a variety of services such as providing medical services, education, job training, or giving aid to the poor. Many microenterprise development projects are also registered as NGOs.

Platform: Often refers to a business identity used by a worker/missionary as a means of legitimizing his or her presence and work among people in limited access contexts. In many cases these businesses are paper fronts or do not produce a profit. The worker is heavily dependent on donor funds.

OPEN Network: A network of 700 plus B4T workers doing business mostly in the 10/40 Window. OPEN's passion is to glorify God by inspiring, connecting, and nurturing B4Ters – one person, and one business at a time. See www.OPENNetworkers.net.

10/40 Window: A band across the globe between ten and forty degrees north, encompassing Saharan and North Africa and almost all of Asia (West Asia, Central Asia, South Asia, East Asia, and much of Southeast Asia). Roughly two-thirds of the world's population lives in the 10/40 Window. This Window is populated by people who are predominantly Muslim, Hindu, Buddhist, animist, Jewish, or atheist.

Tentmaker: A believer who intentionally takes a job with a company in another culture, is fully supported by that job, and strives to witness cross-culturally. A tentmaker receives no donor income.

Transformation: Impacting a community in any of four measurable ways: spiritually, economically, socially, and environmentally.

Worker / Cross-cultural Worker: A person who is serving Jesus outside of his or her home culture; often called a "missionary" by American churches.

APPENDIX C

AFTERTHOUGHTS— NOTEWORTHY QUOTES FROM OPEN WORKERS

In writing this book, I received a lot of input from OPEN workers, all of whom are doing B4T among unreached people in the 10/40 Window. Many of their quotes are included in the chapters. In addition, there were a number of gems that did not make the cut, but you will probably enjoy perusing them here. Since no one wished to have their name used, the quotes are listed without reference. Enjoy!

"The biggest mistake B4Ters make is not doing market research."

"Just because you have a great idea does not mean you have a business."

"The Hollywood belief that, 'If you build it, they will come' does not apply here."

"Taking a business idea to an informal focus group of friends and colleagues is a good start."

"Working solo is not working alone. Success depends on developing and using a network of colleagues, friends, mentors and professionals that can provide advice, assistance and direction in tough times."

"It takes a community. OPEN has helped us develop and nurture a network of colleagues, friends, and mentors. They can offer their guidance, wisdom and connections to your growing business. And remember to pace yourself, keeping some energy and resources in reserve for the inevitable tough spots in the road."

"Be patient. Almost everything takes twice as long as you think it will. I'm telling you that now; you'll read this in business. Other people will tell you this, and still you won't listen, but everybody thinks they can go fast—it doesn't work. Plan for things to take a long time. Work at your own pace; don't let it become all-consuming. You can't plan for everything, but it does take a lot of time to get things together."

"It is important that you know what separates you from your competitors. Whether you market a product or operate a service business, it's essential to clearly differentiate through your marketing that what you offer is of unique value. Your point of differentiation may relate to the way your product or service is provided, priced, or even delivered. The most important thing to discover is the principal benefit you offer that is uniquely valuable to customers and gives you a competitive advantage."

"Here's a list of four things I would do differently:
- I would realize it takes much longer than I thought.
- Be smarter about the mindset of people in government towards foreign business; very naturally, and sometimes against their own interest, they take an adversarial role.
- I would make things clearer at every possible turn to government and other businessmen. As I look back on it, I was very naïve to think we had matching motivations.
- I'd come in with a lot more business knowledge, a lot more."

"When seeking advice, beware of experts. Experts are compulsive about being right. They are too conservative in making decisions and they waste time defending old ideas. We want to be God—thus we create experts. Experts talk only to each other. Experts want others to depend on them. Experts generally are not living in reality."

"I understand the idea of sending an advance team of experts to assist the team in gathering information and setting up the business, but I sincerely doubt they can accomplish much, as they are unfamiliar with the culture and people. Most businesses seeking to set up over here send the same people out at least three times to spy out the land before making decisions. Also, I feel it is a major mistake to focus on working with national believers to set up and/or do business. How will this help us reach our target people? By being dependent on the people we are targeting, we win opportunities to share with them as trust relationships are developed quicker. If we do get into trouble security-wise, who would be a better reference before the government—a known friend and Christian, or a Muslim who we have a good business relationship with?"

"Be aware of what you don't know. Know the warts of your business and recruit people who know these things. Look at reality honestly."

"One thing that I've slowly come to realize is that focus is so critically important. Saying 'no' to great ideas is necessary to get to the brilliant ones. At every step of the way you have to cut towards one path. It is such a hard thing to do as an entrepreneur because you don't really have the confidence in where you are going yourself."

"If you're not being told 'no' constantly, you are not pushing hard enough. I think pushing hard is normal and a good thing. When you are trying to do something disruptive and groundbreaking, there are going to be naysayers."

"Potential customers will part with their hard-earned money only if you convince them that they are getting their money's worth."

"Transformational impact does not come via a showy business, but through deep relationships."

"Investors invest money to make money. They are not donors."

"Be careful when hiring. Understand that often non-Christian employees expect to work, while Christian employees expect grace."

"When you hire Christians, tell them you expect them to work harder and longer hours for the same pay, as a model of Jesus to other employees."

"Too many BAM workers talk vision, and not practical ideas."

"The last door open for reaching Central Asia is business. Russia is saying that all NGOs are platforms for USA agents."

"We read all the books on the coffee business in the USA but none of them told us that overseas it is all cash up front, no credit terms. Property rental, supplies—they all require cash."

"Be in prayer in all you do. We want God to anoint our best, and not be busy fixing our failures."

"Never join a team where the team leader cannot articulate what you will do in a day. The Team Leader's duty is to help you fulfill God's work in and through your life."

"If you are not good at motivating yourself, you probably will not get very far in business—especially as an entrepreneur. When you are starting a company and for the first couple of years afterward, there are a lot of long nights and stressful days, and the workload is heavy. You have to be able to give the job everything you have every day, or it will easily get the better of you."

"I repeatedly heard over the years, 'Get a mentor!' and 'Get a mentor!' Now that I have one, I totally regret waiting so long!"

A useful tool for assessing our business acumen can be found online at www.usatoday.com/money/smallbusiness/startup/week2-etype-test. htm?loc=interstitialskip.

APPENDIX D

B4T/BAM SERVICES

There are numerous organizations that are claiming to provide services for B4Ters. The quality varies. The following are service providers who have been endorsed by OPEN Network workers.

Global Opportunities: Global Opportunities has been training people for ministry skills as they serve God through their professions, business, and university studies in closed countries. Together with Tent Norway, they have been running intensive 4.5-day courses that incorporate a two-week curriculum. The focus of their courses is to equip people to integrate work and faith, to start disciple-making movements that lead to the planting of house churches.
Contact: *ari@globalopps.info*
Website: *www.globalopps.org*

IBEC Ventures: IBEC Ventures is a B4T consulting group that provides consulting and educational services to for-profit kingdom businesses committed to creating local value and disciples of Jesus (triple bottom line). Their coaches, mentors, and subject matter experts serve BAM businesses in the most economically impoverished and spiritually unreached areas.
Contact: *info@ibecventures.com*
Website: *www.ibecventures.com*

NexusB4T: NexusB4T works hand in hand with the OPEN Network. They provide B4T training for new workers, churches, and agencies. They work directly with churches to assess new workers and then link the B4Ter with experienced coaches and mentors who work alongside the church in equipping, sending, and monitoring the B4Ter's life and work. They also help current B4T workers to find experienced coaches and mentors via the OPEN Network. They connect B4Ters to start-up funding too.

Contact: *services@NexusB4T.com*
Website: *www.NexusB4T.com*

Service Provider Network: The Service Provider Network offers a wide variety of services. Appropriate providers of health insurance, international and nonprofit accounting, business help, training, counseling, consulting, security, and dozens of other services that may be hard to find. The SPNet was created to highlight where to meet these critical needs. The SPNet can help someone find or advertise services through their secure, structured network.
Contact: *csteele@mrds.org*
Website: *www.ServiceProviderNetwork.org*

TransformationalSME: TransformationalSME has been providing three- to five-year working capital and capital expenditure finance loans combined with mentoring/coaching and strategic recruitment services to qualifying BAM companies since 2001.
Contact: *kjscan@securenym.net*
Website: *www.TransformationalSME.org*

Transformational Ventures: Transformational Ventures pursues gospel impact through enterprise development around the world, especially where poverty is pervasive. They work with experienced businesspeople to assist local and expatriate entrepreneurs as they launch and grow companies, create jobs, and impact communities. They form teams that integrate the business impact with all kinds of kingdom work, such as discipleship, antitrafficking, and establishing churches.
Contact: *info@TransformationalVentures.com*
Website: *www.TransformationalVentures.com*

WikiBAM: WIKIBAMTM is a free online encyclopedia for Business as Mission / Business 4 Transformation, devoted to equipping the BAM/B4T community through practical information and case studies. Anyone can read, create, or edit articles on any topic related to BAM/B4T. Includes hundreds of articles and links to additional online resources.
Website: *www.WIKIBAM.com*

BIBLIOGRAPHY

Ali, Mohamed. *The Link between Unemployment and Terrorism*, TED. September 2013, http://t.co/Vb8CAIwtmC.

Allen, Roland. *Missionary Methods: St. Paul's or Ours?* Michigan: World Dominion Press, 1962.

Befus, David R. *Kingdom Business: The Ministry of Promoting Economic Development*. Miami: Latin America Mission, 2002.

Chambers, Oswald. *My Utmost for His Highest*. Grand Rapids: Discovery House Publishers, 2012.

Danker, William J. *Profit for the Lord: Economic Activities in Moravian Missions and the Basel Mission Trading Company*. Grand Rapids: William B. Eerdmans, 1971.

Fatio, Tom J., and Keith Miller. *With No Fear of Failure: Recapturing Your Dreams through Creative Enterprise*. Waco: Word Books, 1981.

Fox, Leslie, and Bruce Schearer. *Sustaining Civil Society: Strategies for Resource Mobilisation*. Washington, D.C.: CIVICUS, 1997.

Friedman, Thomas L. *Longitudes and Attitudes*. New York: Farrar Straus Giroux Books, 2002.

Gerber, Michael. *The E-Myth Revisited: Why Most Small Businesses Don't Work And What To Do About It*. HarperCollins; Upd Sub edition, October 14, 2004.

Gibson, Dan. *Avoiding the Tentmaker Trap*. Fort Washington: WEC International, 1997.

Godin, Seth, "How to Make a Purple Cow." Google ebook: Penguin, 2004.

———. "When to Start." *Seth's Blog*, November 15, 2006. http://sethgodin.typepad.com/seths_blog/2006/11/page/3/.

———. *Seth's Blog*. http://sethgodin.typepad.com/seths_blog/.

Henricks, Mark. "Have These 5 Myths Been Holding You Back from Starting a Business? Time for a Reality Check." *Entrepreneur's Startups Magazine* (March 2006).

Iacocca, Lee with William Novak. *Iacocca: An Autobiography*. New York: Bantam Books, 1984.

Kay, Andrea. "Learn to Think If You Want to Get Hired," *USA Today*, June 8, 2012. http://www.usatoday.com/money/jobcenter/workplace/kay/story/2012-06-09/learn-to-think-listen-interact/55467614/1.

Kessler, Glenn. "Do Nine out of 10 New Businesses Fail, as Rand Paul Claims?" *Washington Post,* January 27, 2014. http://www. washingtonpost.com/blogs/fact-checker/wp/2014/01/27/do-9-out-of-10-new-businesses-fail-as-rand-paul-claims/.

Kriegl, Robert, and Louis Palter. *If It Ain't Broke...BREAK IT!* New York: Warner Books, 1991.

Lai, Patrick. *Problems and Solutions for Enhancing the Productivity of Tentmakers Doing Church Planting in the 10/40 Window.* Dept. of Intercultural Studies, Asian Graduate School of Theology, Manila: Philipines, 2003.

————. *Tentmaking: The Life and Work of Business as Missions.* Colorado Springs: Authentic Publishing, 2005.

Lausanne Committee for World Evangelization. "Business as Mission." Lausanne Occasional Paper No. 59, 2005. http://www.lausanne. org/docs/2004forum/LOP59_IG30.pdf.OPEN Network, http://www .opennetworkers.net.

O'Reilly, Brian. "What It Takes to Start a Start Up." *Fortune,* June 7, 1999.

Rancic, Bill. "Power Thoughts." *Work It, Sova* (Southern Virginia's Business Communities), January 14, 2014, http://www.newsadvance.com/ work_it_sova/power_thoughts/if-it-really-was-a-no-brainer-to-make-it/article_fcc49f1e-7d7d-11e3-bbd8-001a4bcf6878.html.

Sheldon, Charles. *In His Steps.* Grand Rapids: MI. Zondervan, 1967.

Simon, Mark, and Susan M. Houghton. "The Relationship among Biases, Misperceptions, and the Introduction of Pioneering Products: Examining Differences in Venture Decision Contexts," *Entrepreneurship Theory and Practice* 27, no. 2 (December 2002), 105–24.

Spurgeon, C. H. *Morning by Morning.* Peabody: Hendrickson Publishers, 2006.

Taylor, Ros. *Work/Life: Develop Confidence.* Google eBook: Penguin, 2006.

Tunehag, Mats. http://www.matstunehag.com/wp-content/uploads/ 2011/04/The-Mission-of-Business-CSR+1.pdf.

Tzu, Sun. *Art of War.* Charleston: BookSurge Classics, 2002.

Wagner, Eric T. "Five Reasons 8 out of 10 Businesses Fail." *Forbes,* September 12, 2013. http://www.forbes.com/sites/ericwagner/2013/09/12/five -reasons-8-out-of-10-businesses-fail/.

Walck, Brian. "9 Missiological Insights into Business as Mission." Work as Worship Network, February 23, 2009, http://www. workasworshipnetwork.org/9-missiological-insights-into-business -as-mission-brian-walck/.

INDEX